CAMBRIDGE IBERIAN AND
LATIN AMERICAN STUDIES

GENERAL EDITOR
P. E. RUSSELL F.B.A.
*Emeritus Professor of Spanish Studies
University of Oxford*

ASSOCIATE EDITORS
E. PUPO-WALKER
*Director, Center for Latin American and Iberian Studies
Vanderbilt University*
A. R. D. PAGDEN
*Lecturer in History, University of Cambridge*

The architecture of conquest

*The architecture of conquest* deals with the practice and ideology of colonial architecture in Latin America, referring particularly to the Viceroyalty of Peru during the period 1535–1635. Colonial building has generally been regarded as being merely a provincial reflection of mainstream European art, but Valerie Fraser argues that, on the contrary, it had its own distinct identity, and that architectural projects were a powerful tool in the subjugation of the native people of South America by the Spaniards. Although the majority of labourers and craftsmen responsible for the churches, towns and cities of the Spaniards were natives, very little evidence of their own traditions of craftsmanship can be found in this colonial architecture.

Thus, while the architectural forms employed by the early *conquistadores* are clearly derived from the European tradition, their purpose and meaning are completely different, being defined by the colonial context. The deliberate display of architectural motifs, the organization of building practice and labour are all shown to have served the ends of political, religious and economic conquest.

CAMBRIDGE IBERIAN AND LATIN AMERICAN STUDIES

HISTORY AND SOCIAL THEORY

ROBERT I. BURNS: *Muslims, Christians, and Jews in the Crusader Kingdom of Valencia*
MICHAEL P. COSTELOE: *Response to Revolution: Imperial Spain and the Spanish American Revolutions, 1810–1840*
HEATH DILLARD: *Daughters of the Reconquest: Women in Castilian Town Society, 1100–1300*
ANDREW DOBSON: *An Introduction to the Politics and Philosophy of José Ortega y Gasset*
JOHN EDWARDS: *Christian Córdoba: The City and its Regions in the Late Middle Ages*
LEONARD FOLGARAIT: *So far From Heaven: David Alfaro Siqueiros' 'The March of Humanity' and Mexican Revolutionary Politics*
VALERIE FRASER: *The Architecture of Conquest: Building in the Viceroyalty of Peru, 1535–1635*
DAVID GIES: *Theatre and Politics in Nineteenth-Century Spain: Juan de Grimaldi as Impresario and Government Agent*
JUAN LÓPEZ-MORILLAS: *The Krausist Movement and Ideological Change in Spain, 1854–1874*
MARVIN LUNENFELD: *Keepers of the City: The Corregidores of Isabella I of Castile (1474–1504)*
LINDA MARTZ: *Poverty and Welfare in Habsburg Spain: The Example of Toledo*
ANTHONY H. PAGDEN: *The Fall of Natural Man: The American Indian and the Origins of Comparative Ethnology*
EVELYN S. PROCTER: *Curia and Cortes in León and Castile, 1072–1295*
A. C. DE C. M. SAUNDERS: *A Social History of Black Slaves and Freedmen in Portugal, 1441–1555*
DAVID E. VASSBERG: *Land and Society in Golden Age Castile*
KENNETH B. WOLF: *Christian Martyrs in Muslim Spain*

LITERATURE AND LITERARY THEORY

STEVEN BOLDY: *The Novels of Julio Cortázar*
ANTHONY CASCARDI: *The Limits of Illusion: A Critical Study of Calderón*
LOUISE FOTHERGILL-PAYNE: *Seneca and 'Celestina'*
MAURICE HEMINGWAY: *Emilia Pardo Bazán: The Making of a Novelist*
B. W. IFE: *Reading and Fiction in Golden-Age Spain: A Platonist Critique and Some Picaresque Replies*
JOHN KING: *Sur: A Study of the Argentine Literary Journal and its Role in the Development of a Culture, 1931–1970*
JOHN LYON: *The Theatre of Valle-Inclán*
BERNARD MCGUIRK & RICHARD CARDWELL (eds.): *Gabriel García Márquez: New Readings*
JULIAN OLIVARES: *The Love Poetry of Francisco de Quevedo: An Aesthetic and Existential Study*
FRANCISCO RICO: *The Spanish Picaresque Novel and the Point of View*
DOROTHY SHERMAN SEVERIN: *Tragicomedy and Novelistic Discourse in 'Celestina'*
HENRY W. SULLIVAN: *Calderón in the German Lands and the Low Countries: His Reception and Influence, 1654–1980*
COLIN P. THOMPSON: *The Strife of Tongues: Fray Luis de León and the Golden Age of Spain*
DIANE F. UREY: *Galdós and the Irony of Language*
MARGARITA ZAMORA: *Language, Authority and Indigenous History in the 'Comentarios reales de los incas'*

*Frontispiece* Chincheros, near Cuzco. View of the sixteenth-century church above a niched Inca wall which serves to divide the church atrium from the village square below.

# The Architecture of Conquest

Building in the Viceroyalty of Peru
1535–1635

VALERIE FRASER
*Department of Art History and Theory, University of Essex*

CAMBRIDGE UNIVERSITY PRESS

CAMBRIDGE
NEW YORK   PORT CHESTER
MELBOURNE   SYDNEY

Published by the Press Syndicate of the University of Cambridge
The Pitt Building, Trumpington Street, Cambridge CB2 1RP
40 West 20th Street, New York NY 10011, USA
10 Stamford Road, Oakleigh, Melbourne 3166, Australia

© Cambridge University Press 1990

First published 1990

Printed in Great Britain at
the University Press, Cambridge

*British Library cataloguing in publication data*
Fraser, Valerie
The architecture of conquest: building in
the Viceroyalty of Peru, 1535–1635 –
(Cambridge Iberian and Latin American
studies).
1. Peru. Buildings. Architectural features,
1535–1635
1. Title
720.985

*Library of Congress cataloguing in publication data*
Fraser, Valerie.
The architecture of conquest: building in the viceroyalty of
Peru, 1535–1635/Valerie Fraser.
p.   cm. – (Cambridge Iberian and Latin American studies)
Bibliography.
Includes index.
ISBN 0-521-34316-X
1. Architecture – Peru.   2. Architecture, Colonial – Peru.
3. Church architecture – Peru.   I. Title.   II. Series.
Arch. NA913.F73 1989 90
720'.985–dc19   88-36548   CIP

ISBN 0 521 34316 X

SE

To my parents,
HUGH AND MARJORIE FRASER,
with love and gratitude,
and
to the memory of
AIMÉE TOROK

# Contents

| | |
|---|---|
| *List of illustrations* | *page* xi |
| *Acknowledgements* | xiii |
| Introduction | 1 |
| 1 The idea of architecture | 21 |
| 2 First foundations | 51 |
| 3 The builders | 82 |
| 4 Questions of style | 108 |
| Conclusions | 154 |
| *Notes* | 168 |
| *Select bibliography* | 188 |
| *Index* | 201 |

# Illustrations

## Maps

| | |
|---|---|
| 1 South America: modern political boundaries. | page 2 |
| 2 The Viceroyalty of Peru: main colonial towns and cities. | 3 |
| 3 The province of Chucuito. | 12 |

## Plates

*Frontispiece* Chincheros, near Cuzco. Sixteenth-century church on Inca foundations.

| | |
|---|---|
| 1 Sacsahuaman. Inca ritual site above the city of Cuzco, *c*.1500. | 9 |
| 2 Chucuito, Santo Domingo; early 1550s. | 13 |
| 3 Chucuito, La Asunción; *c*.1595. | 14 |
| 4 Ilave, San Miguel, lateral portal; *c*.1565. | 16 |
| 5 Acora, San Pedro, end portal; *c*.1600. | 17 |
| 6 Juli, view of the town (photo: Tim Butler). | 18 |
| 7 Acora, view of San Juan. | 19 |
| 8 Plan of Cuzco, from George Squier, *Peru. Incidents of Travel and Exploration in the Land of the Incas*, London, 1877. | 28 |
| 9 Pisac, near Cuzco. Inca architecture; *c*.1500. | 30 |
| 10 Ollantaytambo, near Cuzco. Inca architecture; *c*.1500. | 31 |
| 11 Plan of Riobamba, from Guaman Poma, *Nueva Corónica*, p. 995. | 54 |
| 12 Lima, Plaza de Armas. View of the Cathedral, the Sagrario and the Archbishop's Palace. | 56 |
| 13 Chucuito, Plaza de Armas. The *picota* or *rollo*, now converted into a sundial; 1567. | 58 |
| 14 Plan of Mendoza, Argentina, 1562, AGI Mapas y Planos, Buenos Aires, 10 (by kind permission of the Archivo General de Indias, Seville). | 60 |

## ILLUSTRATIONS

| | | |
|---|---|---|
| 15 | Quito, San Francisco; late sixteenth century. | 65 |
| 16 | Cuzco, Santo Domingo. | 66 |
| 17 | Jauja; remains of a small sixteenth-century chapel on Inca foundations. From Torres Saldamando [Lima Cabildo], *Libro primero*, II, Appendices, 2nd series, plate 183 (by kind permission of the British Library). | 67 |
| 18 | Quito, San Francisco. Detail of the *alfarje* ceiling at the crossing. | 102 |
| 19 | Portovelo, Panama. Elevations of the interior of a church; 1626. AGI, Mapas y Planos, Panama, 43v (by kind permission of the Archivo General de Indias, Seville). | 105 |
| 20 | Andahuaylillas, near Cuzco; later sixteenth century. | 112 |
| 21 | Cuzco, Calle Zetas, no. 400. Inca-style colonial doorway, mid-sixteenth century. | 118 |
| 22 | Cuzco, Plaza de Armas, SW colonnade. Detail of bracket capital; mid-sixteenth century. | 120 |
| 23 | Cartagena cathedral, lateral portal; 1602–12. | 122 |
| 24 | Urcos, near Cuzco. Rural chapels; early seventeenth century. | 124 |
| 25 | Huaro, near Cuzco. Main portal; early seventeenth century. | 125 |
| 26 | San Agustín, Potosí. Façade; early seventeenth century. | 126 |
| 27 | Acora, San Pedro, lateral portal; *c*.1600. | 127 |
| 28 | Tunja cathedral façade. Bartolomé Carrión, 1598. | 128 |
| 29 | Potosí, Santo Domingo. Main portal; 1606–9. | 129 |
| 30 | Tunja, San Francisco. Main portal; *c*.1610. | 131 |
| 31 | Ayacucho, San Francisco. Main portal; late sixteenth century. | 132 |
| 32 | Ilave, San Miguel, interior. Entrance to a side chapel, *c*.1565. | 134 |
| 33 | Cuzco, Casa de los Cuatro Bustos; late sixteenth century. | 135 |
| 34 | Tunja, Casa Mujica y Guevara, 1592. | 137 |
| 35 | Lima, Casa Pilatos; late sixteenth century. | 138 |
| 36 | Tunja, Plaza de Armas. Casa Suárez Rendón; mid-sixteenth century. | 140 |
| 37 | Tunja, house at Carrera 10, 21–04; late sixteenth century. | 141 |
| 38 | Bogotá, San Ignacio. Giovanni Baptista Coluccini; 1610. | 143 |
| 39 | Ayacucho, Plaza de Armas; late seventeenth-century *portales*. | 144 |
| 40 | Juli, San Juan. Lateral portal; eighteenth century. | 148 |
| 41 | Arequipa, Santo Domingo. Lateral portal; 1677–80. | 150 |
| 42 | Quito, La Merced. Lateral portal; 1596. | 151 |
| 43 | Juli, La Asunción; between 1602 and 1620. | 163 |
| 44 | Juli, view of the roofs of San Juan from the atrium of Santa Cruz. | 164 |
| 45 | Juli, San Juan. Brick portal, west end; 1590. | 165 |

# Acknowledgements

This book has a long history and the debts I have incurred during its production are many and various. Most important of these is that I owe to the intellectual traditions of two institutions, the School of Comparative Studies at the University of Essex, and the Warburg Institute of the University of London. From the interdisciplinary approach which both espouse I like to think that I have learnt how to ask interesting questions, as well as where to seek some answers. Among the many individuals who have been important in this respect, at the Warburg I must single out Sir Ernst Gombrich and Michael Baxandall, and at Essex, Dawn Ades and Gordon Brotherston. J.B. Trapp at the Warburg has been unfailingly supportive as have Michael Podro and Thomas Puttfarken at Essex both of whom have read the book in draft and have helped to clarify both the text and the argument; Jules Lubbock and all my other colleagues in the Department of Art History and Theory have been important in different ways, not least in managing to retain a sense of collective purpose and enjoyment in both teaching and research in the face of persistent attacks on the value of higher education. My thanks, too, to erstwhile fellow students at the Warburg, Alice Friedman, Katharine Park and Nigel Llewellyn; to Helen Carr and Peter Hulme; to Anthony Pagden, with whom I have regularly taught on the M.Phil course at the Warburg Institute, and who has been so encouraging; and to the many students, both at the Warburg and at Essex, on whom I have tried out my ideas.

The initial field work for this study was carried out in Colombia, Ecuador, Bolivia and especially Peru during 1976–7; on this and on other occasions I have received financial help from the Research Endowment Fund of the University of Essex. A two-year Sotheby's Junior Research Fellowship at the Warburg Institute from 1977 to 1979 was vital in affording me the time to make some sense of the heterogeneous material I had gathered in South America before embarking on a very full-time teaching career at Essex. I acknowledge with gratitude a grant from the Erasmus Prize Fund of the Warburg Institute towards the cost of the illustrations.

I am grateful to the staffs of numerous libraries, museums and archives, both in Europe and Latin America, especially the Archivo General de Indias in Seville, the Biblioteca Nacional in Lima, and the British Library in London. The range of Latin American material held by the library at the University of Essex continues to astonish me: my thanks to all the staff here, especially Chris Anderton; also Terry Tostevin, for his efforts in pursuing obscure articles for me through the invaluable inter-library loan service.

The maps were drawn by Barry Woodcock who has also been helpful with photographic problems, and generous with the loan of his darkroom. Unless otherwise indicated the photographs are my own, taken during trips to South America in 1976–7, 1979 and 1986. I can offer no more than a general acknowledgement to the many, many people who gave me access to places and permission to take photographs, who gave unsolicited help and advice, and who shared their knowledge of their country, their town or their village with me. In Lima during 1976 the late Emilio Harth-terré was exceptionally kind in encouraging me to make use of his own library and archive, and in providing me with photographs, plans and off-prints. I am very grateful to Katharina Brett and Margaret Jull Costa of Cambridge University Press for their help with the final stages of preparing this book for publication.

Finally it gives me great pleasure to thank my good friend Cristina Escajadillo, from whose warmth and hospitality I have so often benefited whilst in Lima, and above all I thank Tim Butler, *compañero querido*, for his faith and his continued enthusiasm for a subject so far from his own.

# Introduction

The architecture of conquest: this is a book about the towns, the houses and churches the Spaniards built during the first century of their domination of South America. And, since architectural metaphor is inherent in the vocabulary of imperialism, it is also about the construction of an empire in a more general sense. Within a hundred years of Cortés' conquest of Mexico most of Central and South America was dotted with new towns and new buildings in an unmistakably European style. From these colonial centres handfuls of Spaniards exerted control over hundreds of thousands of non-European peoples whose large towns and often highly sophisticated and ancient cultures seemed to disappear from view. An empire had been built and the foundations were proving firm, literally and metaphorically. In the American context the architectural metaphors also have another equally forceful application. The Bible and the history of Christianity are permeated with imagery of God the father as the great architect, of Christ as the sure foundation, the cornerstone, of Peter as the rock upon which the edifice of Christianity was to be erected and of the Church as both institution and architecture. Las Casas' reference to the Catholic Kings, the first architects of the gigantic evangelization programme, as the *apóstoles arquitectónicos* of the Indies is both perceptive and appropriate.[1] Nowhere has this sort of vocabulary carried such resonance as in Spanish America; nowhere have Christian churches been erected in such numbers and at such speed.

The architecture in question is that of the Spanish Viceroyalty of Peru with special emphasis on the territories of modern Peru and Bolivia which had previously been under Inca control, although many of my conclusions hold good for the whole of Spanish America[2] (Maps 1 & 2). The time span is roughly a hundred years from the foundation of Lima as Viceregal capital in 1535 until 1635. By this date Spanish hegemony is well established, and new buildings are erected in a different atmosphere and as a result of different

Map 1 South America: modern political boundaries. The geographical limits were not precise but in the sixteenth century, in principle, the Viceroyalty of Peru comprised the whole continent with the exception of the Portuguese territories of Brazil.

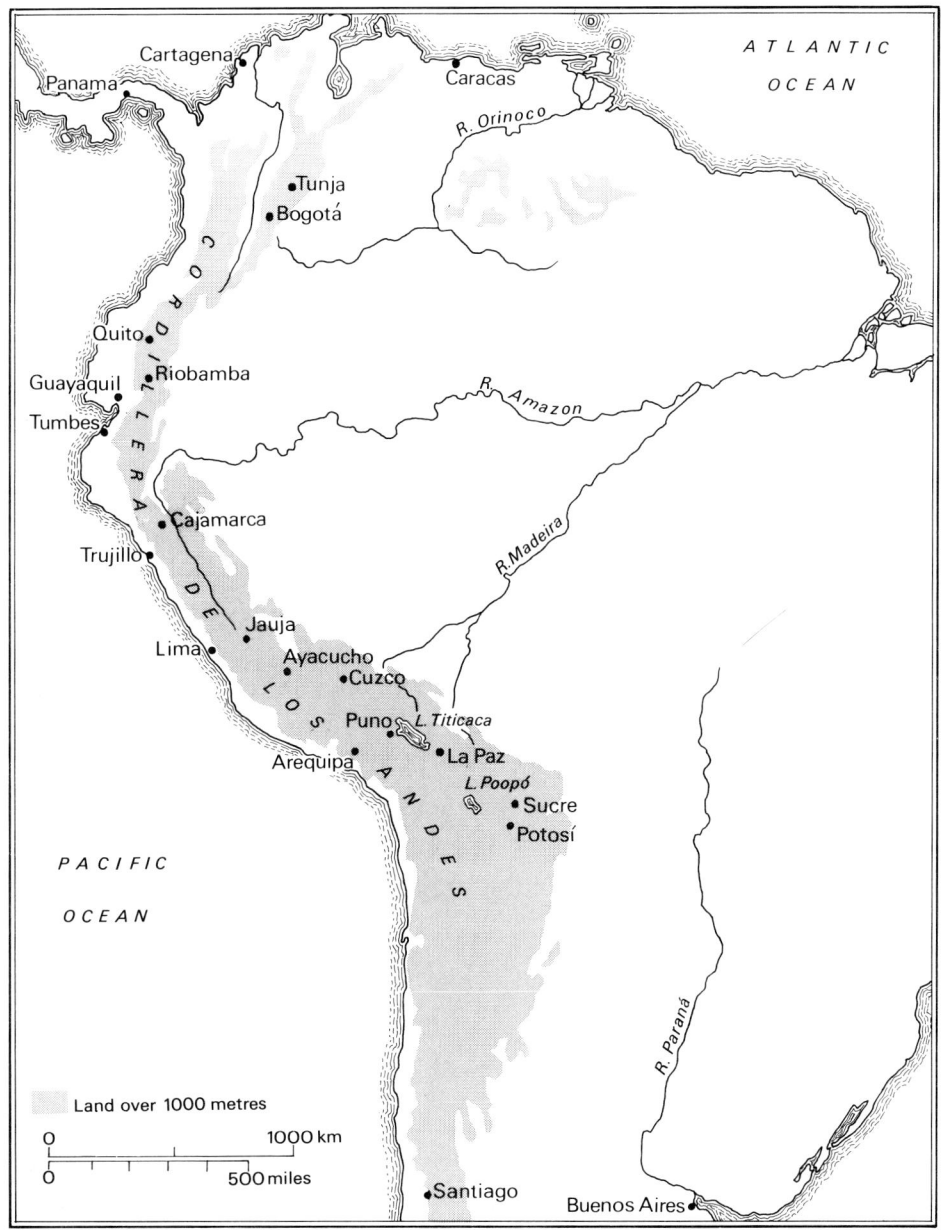

Map 2 The Viceroyalty of Peru: main colonial towns and cities

preconceptions from those which predominated during the first century of colonization.

My argument centres on the nature of a *colonial* architecture and in so doing raises questions of definition and of art-historical method. Colonial architecture is necessarily closely related to the architecture of the metropolitan country, but is it simply imitative or derivative? Is it, in other words, a distant but essentially provincial style, or can we identify specifically colonial features, features which can be seen to suggest that this architecture is but one aspect of a system of domination of one culture by another? This question might be thought to be answered by isolating alien details introduced by Indian craftsmen into the sculptural decoration on the buildings of their Spanish masters, the survivals or revivals of indigenous iconographic, stylistic or technical traditions, or by pointing to evidence of native misunderstanding and reinterpretation of the forms they were required to imitate. In South America especially, this approach tends to produce a distorted picture of colonial architecture because the cases where the hand of the indigenous craftsman can be identified with confidence are relatively rare, and do not suffice to distinguish the colonial from the metropolitan style.

To view early colonial architecture as a series of imitations of or variations on European stylistic themes with perhaps the occasional exotic intrusion to represent the hand of the native craftsman is really to avoid the colonial question. Colonial architecture cannot be value-free: its very existence presupposes the suppression of native culture and the exploitation of native labour. The tone was set before the discovery of America with the opening words of the Papal Bull *Ineffabilis et Summi* in which the King of Portugal was entrusted with the conquest of Africa. They are taken from Jeremiah 1:10 and the distinction between what is and what is not metaphor is blurred:

See, I have this day set thee over the nations and over the kingdoms, to root out, and to pull down, and to destroy and to throw down, to build and to plant.[3]

This is an inescapable element of Spanish American colonialism: the domination of the native populations, the destruction of their cities and temples, and the suppression of their culture and beliefs. All this goes hand in hand with the achievements of the conquerors. The Indians sustained the Spaniards, they tilled their fields and worked in their mines, and they also built their towns, their houses and their churches. This central Indian involvement in the construction of the Empire is no less true for being all but invisible in those very towns, houses and churches. They did the work but they had no say in the appearance of the product; yet that very product, while implicitly – and in some ways explicitly – denying their own cultural values, at the same time served to reaffirm those of their conquerors.

Assumptions about stylistic change in colonial architecture cannot be made in the way that they can in European architecture. The relationship between the culture of early colonial Spanish America and that of Spain is not like that between Spain and Italy, nor is it like that between Estremadura and Castile, or Arezzo and Florence in the same period. During the initial phases of the conquest and colonization of America the conditions under which towns were founded and houses and churches erected were quite unlike those which obtained in Europe at the time. Take the case of churches. A new parish church in Tuscany would take its place in a long line of Tuscan parish churches, and within the long-established framework of Christian society. Most of those built in Europe during the sixteenth century were in any case replacements or renovations of older churches and in comparison with Peru or Ecuador, a church in such a context seems almost a luxury. Even in Spain, where the previous centuries of the *reconquista* had lent a much greater urgency to the construction of churches, it was still a *re*-conquest: Christians and Moors alike knew what a church was and what it represented. It would have been seen and understood by all concerned, by builders, clergy and parishioners, in relation to other Christian churches, local, national, perhaps even European; its purpose would have been self-evident.

In sixteenth-century Spanish America, however, the primary concern was not – except in a few instances – the erection of buildings which could be seen in terms of other similar buildings, as variations on a well-known theme, in which considerations of fashion and style, of visual cross-reference, or of innovation, play their part. In America a parish church in the first years of Spanish colonization was a basic and urgent necessity, perhaps the only one of its kind in a whole province. It was built by and largely for people totally ignorant of the traditions of Christian architecture and of Christian religion. This is not to say that an isolated parish church in Spanish America was not part of a tradition: it still belonged, of course, to a Christian, European world familiar to the colonizers themselves, but a world which was not physically, visibly present. Such a church therefore had to represent, to *recreate* that absent reality within an alien environment, amongst cultures with very different traditions of both religion and architecture, and it had to point up those differences if it was to succeed on its own terms. Much of mainstream art in Europe since at least the time of the Greeks has been profoundly self-conscious and self-referential, addressed to inward and often backward-looking audiences, audiences who are familiar with the traditions within which such art operates. This is indeed one of the basic assumptions of much art-historical research, as it is of literary and musical criticism. In the case of the architecture of early colonial Spanish America such an assumption is almost always inappropriate.

The problem of identifying the colonial in the appearance of the buildings themselves is not easily resolved. Despite the occasional intrusive stylistic or iconographic detail revealing the presence of the Native American craftsman early colonial architecture looks unmistakably European in origin. It is classical – classical in a general sense – which is why I use the term *European* rather than Spanish or even Italianate. I mean that this is an architecture which employs the classical vocabulary of columns, capitals, entablatures and pediments, but which cannot be easily linked with any particular school, region or country. This is especially true of the Viceroyalty of Peru where not only is visual evidence of Native American involvement in the architecture extremely rare – much rarer than in Mexico – but the use of classical detail is very rigorous. Architectural decoration is almost entirely restricted to framing doors and windows, to marking the entrances to buildings. The various architectural members are clearly defined, properly used and well proportioned; even the orders, notably the Doric, are usually handled with assurance. Evidence of any licence, of any imaginative flourish or inventive decorative detail, whether at the hand of native or European craftsmen is extremely rare especially on the façades of churches. This would seem to be an architecture where the rules are unequivocally respected, the bare bones of the classical architectural system explicit. This is all the more extraordinary in that throughout the sixteenth century evidence for the use of architectural treatises and manuals, and for the presence of European craftsmen in America is negligible.

The same general points can be made about town planning. Throughout Spanish America regular grid-plan towns were founded, chequer-boards of streets with a central square formed from a single block of the grid. The cathedral or main church (the *iglesia mayor*), was sited on this square as were the other buildings important to the colonial administration, and other parish or monastic churches were placed further out but always in accordance with the plan, each with a large open space in front. Like the orthodox classicism of architectural detail, this is the realization of an ideal type; it is what the Spanish conquistadors thought towns ought to be like, even though in Europe they were not. But the case is not as clear cut as it is with the favoured architectural style. A number of specific sources for the ubiquitous Spanish American grid plan have been suggested, and the question will be dealt with at greater length below.

The emergence in early colonial Spanish America of a uniform town plan and of a style of architecture which seems unhesitatingly to extract the fundamental elements of the classical architectural vocabulary: these require explanation. Surely some clearly argued treatise or some firm guiding hand must lie behind such startlingly orthodox homogeneity of style? There is, however, no evidence for any such thing nor, on reflection, should this surprise us. America was a New World. No amount of education or of practical experience of the countries and cultures of the Old World could prepare the Spanish colonists and missionaries for what they would find or for what they had to do. The instructions and directives issued by the Spanish Crown and the officials in Spain could not possibly be expected to meet all the unforeseen and largely unimaginable contingencies of the discovery, conquest, colonization and evangelization of America. Still further removed from the practical urgencies of establishing colonies were the architectural theorists who in the earlier sixteenth century seem barely to be aware of America at all. Throughout the century it is those who cross the Atlantic for themselves that matter most. It is they who have to assess the native cultures, it is they who have to find ways of manipulating and controlling the Indians, and of converting them to Christianity, and it is they who shape the new empire, the new towns and cities, the new churches and cathedrals, the new squares, town halls and market places. But, as I say, the visual evidence points clearly to the fact that they did not respond with arbitrary empiricism to the demands of the situation but rather with an astonishing unity of purpose. It is as if the Spanish colonists were drawing on some sort of cultural memory, an inherited, almost instinctive knowledge. Under the special circumstances of America the sense of what was right and proper in architecture and town planning comes to the surface to be transformed into physical reality.

An understanding of architecture so deep as to be at the level of unconscious assumption rather than conscious thought is, of course, difficult to prove. Had the Spanish colonists and missionaries articulated their ideas about architecture clearly, had they written them down and discussed them, then the terms of my argument would be very different. Literary evidence there is, but it is largely fragmentary; it has to be confirmed and can often be clarified by reference to the visual remains of colonial architecture.[4] The most obvious sources – the official instructions about how to found towns and what to build in America – are on the whole the least helpful, although even in these certain recurrent words or phrases can help to build up a picture. After all, if my argument is valid, it must be the case that those who compiled the official instructions were also the possessors of this same set of deep-rooted cultural assumptions but that in Spain these remain shadowy and ill-articulated. It is only the practical necessities of America that render them visible.

An infinitely richer source has proved to be the various histories and chronicles of the conquest and colonization, and in particular those sections dealing with the native peoples and cultures of America. The impact of the discovery of the New World on the Old has been the subject of much interest in recent years.[5] Scholars have studied the ways in which the various mental sets which Europeans brought to bear on the new territories, the unfamiliar flora and fauna, the inhabitants and their social, political and cultural orders conditioned what they saw and how they interpreted it. The prime concern of the chroniclers was not to examine the 'otherness' of America, but on the contrary, to identify the similarities, to measure the achievements of indigenous American culture up against those of the European and to find ways of assimilating the new into their own, old familiar world.[6] In so doing the writers reveal their own underlying preconceptions more clearly than in descriptions of their own culture, where so much is taken for granted.

The literary evidence implies or partially articulates a number of mental sets that can only be confirmed by close cross-reference with the visual material. The choice of area, the Viceroyalty of Peru with particular emphasis on the territories previously under Inca domination, has proved fruitful in unexpected ways. To sixteenth-century Spanish observers the Inca were closer to a European idea of a great imperial power than any of the other major Native American states (although they would not have put it quite like this). The Incas controlled numerous different peoples, imposing their own language – Quechua – on them all, exacting carefully calculated tributes to support the bureaucracy, the state religion, the standing army and the Inca aristocracy, as well as the people themselves in times of need. They maintained regular contact between the capital Cuzco and the provincial seats of government, using an impressive network of well-kept paved roads. Everything suggested that this was an extremely efficient, orderly and prosperous regime: public warehouses full of foodstuffs and cloth; huge flocks of llama and alpaca in the highlands; sophisticated irrigation systems; state-financed inns along the roads to meet the needs of travellers and messengers;

Plate 1 Sacsahuaman. Inca ritual site above the city of Cuzco; c.1500.

gangs of tribute labourers building roads, bridges, temples and palaces at the Inca's behest. The architecture in particular was (and is) awe-inspiring in its scale and grandeur, and in the extraordinarily high quality of its masonry. It served as a dramatic manifestation of the Inca ability to organize and control thousands of tribute labourers (Plate 1). Many early commentators were very impressed by the achievements of the Incas, and between the caveats and disclaimers it is easy to identify attitudes of astonishment and respect. Cieza de León expatiates on the main north–south roadway:

I do not believe . . . there has ever been such a road as this, running through deep valleys and over high peaks, through snow-covered mountains, across quagmires, over bare rock and beside turbulent rivers . . . it cut through the rock, it was walled alongside the rivers, and above the snow-line there were steps and rests; everywhere it was kept clean and swept and free from rubbish, with numerous lodging houses, storehouses of riches, temples to the sun and staging posts all along the way. Oh! can such an achievement be claimed of Alexander, or of any of the powerful Kings who ruled the world that they built such a road, or could provide the supplies to be found on this? Neither the road which the Romans built in Spain nor any other of which we read can compare with it.[7]

Such enthusiasm is not untypical. The Inca state offered a more profound and more wide-ranging series of challenges to European values than did that of the

Aztec in Mexico or the Chibcha in Colombia. And in architectural terms it evoked the most rigorous response. Early colonial architecture in the territories of the Inca is much more strictly classicizing than that being produced in Mexico at the same date. It is as if everyone had tacitly agreed to pull all the stops out and make the clearest possible statement of what they believed to be the fundamentals of European architecture. Although architecture is only one aspect of a culture it is nevertheless an important and very public aspect, and so to some extent it must also stand for all that culture's less visible, more ideological values.

This brings us back to the question of the visibility of the colonial in Spanish American architecture. The classical architectural detail may be strictly orthodox, more so than most of that being produced in Spain at the time, but at the same time colonial architecture is highly innovative: a clear visual distinction is always made between secular and religious buildings by means of the shape of the entrance. In the sixteenth century throughout Spanish America churches have arched doorways, secular buildings do not.[8] The combination of the classical architectural frame and the round arched portal is the rule for church façades, whereas even the most important secular buildings are entered under a lintel. This sets the church, both the individual buildings and the institution, apart from everything else. It sets it apart from secular colonial buildings and also, and more importantly, from indigenous traditions of architecture, where the use of the arch was unknown. In Peru, where so much magnificent architecture survives from the pre-conquest period, the contrast between the arched church portals and the lintelled Incaic buildings is especially striking, but even in areas where little or no indigenous architecture survives the neat visual distinction between ecclesiastical and secular architecture remains constant. This is a remarkable innovation for which there is no obvious European source either in theory or in practice, and as such it is a key identifying feature of colonial architecture. Other aspects of colonial architecture which at first sight appear thoroughly orthodox are also in some senses innovative, as is the universal application of generally held precepts about the ideal town plan, or the use of elevated podia and great open squares and atria to emphasize and enhance the importance of the churches. These have their roots in European theory, but nowhere in Europe was the ideal realized on the scale it was in America. Even the most ambitious of utopian dreams failed to imagine the towns and cities, the churches and squares of a whole continent organized along the same grandiose lines.

The visual evidence to support such contentions needs to be drawn from as wide a range as possible. My examples are drawn from the whole of the vast Viceroyalty of Peru and occasionally from Mexico as well, but particular emphasis has been given to Lima, the Viceregal capital and the most metropolitan of the colonial cities of South America on the one hand, and to the distant province of the Collao in the southern Andean highlands on the other. In other words, the detail is drawn from the centre and the periphery. For an argument such as this it is not sufficient or appropriate to concentrate only on a few large and prestigious buildings because for these special conditions usually apply. It is among the smaller, less assuming buildings, especially those outside the main colonial centres, that we must look for evidence of what was considered essential and what dispensable in architecture. A consideration of some of the architecture of the province of the Collao in the sixteenth century will serve as an introduction to some specific – and typical – visual examples and to the sorts of question which they raise.

In the area known in the sixteenth century as the province of Chucuito, or more generally the Collao, the seven main towns along the southeast shores of Lake Titicaca were the focus of an energetic building programme from the 1550s onwards[9] (Map 3). In the sixteenth century the province was designated Crown land which meant that no Spaniards were permitted to reside there other than missionaries. Initially it was assigned to the Dominicans but after 1572 these were replaced by secular clergy in most of the province and by a Jesuit college in Juli in 1576. Fifteen churches still stand in the region whose foundations can be dated reasonably securely to the first sixty or so years of Spanish rule, and there are records and local memories of at least half a dozen more. Some of these original churches have been rebuilt or heavily restored, but more than half are unmistakably sixteenth century in origin, and there are a number of useful contemporary documentary sources including a contract of 1590 drawn up on behalf of the Crown in which sixteen churches were commissioned for the province. This region, therefore, is unusual in that it combines good visual and documentary evidence.

Even to the casual visitor the surviving churches still astonish by their enormous size, their solidity, their imposing positions and the often surprisingly elegant proportions of their brick or stone portals. The earliest surviving church in the region and almost certainly in the whole of South America is that of Santo Domingo in the town of Chucuito, the provincial capital. The Dominican missionaries arrived in the wake of the conquerors and based themselves here in the early 1540s. In little over ten years they had

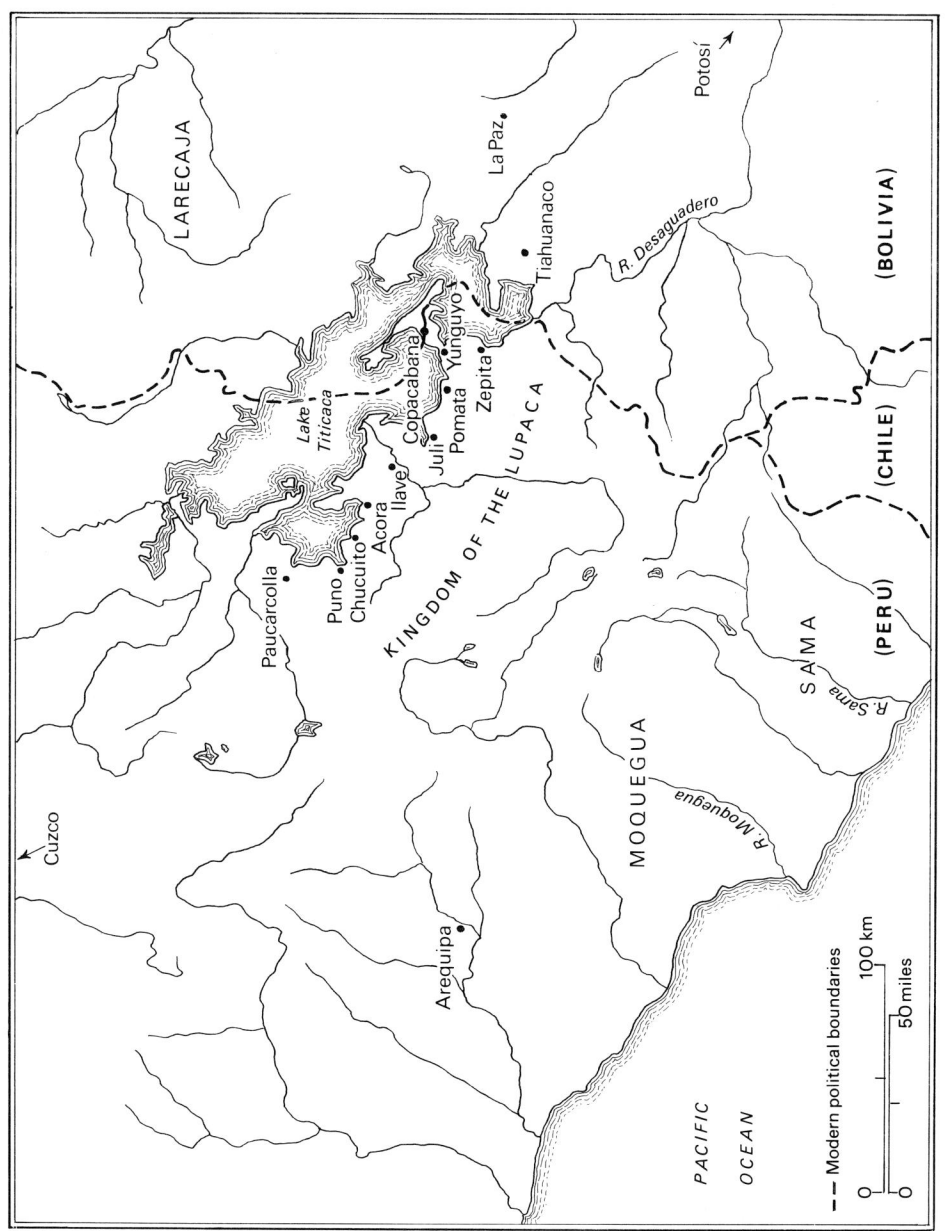

Map 3 The province of Chucuito

Plate 2 Chucuito, Santo Domingo, with the arcaded walls of the atrium and cemetery on either side; early 1550s.

built themselves a huge church and a monastery in the town, as well as churches in other towns in the area, at least two of which were on the same scale as Santo Domingo. By 1555 they had founded monastic houses as well as churches in all seven towns: no mean feat for a few friars in a bleak and treeless region far from a Spanish colonial town.[10]

Santo Domingo can illustrate all the main features of provincial churches in the early colonial period (Plate 2). It is spectacularly situated, high above the lake with extensive arcaded walls on either side enclosing the cemetery to the north and an atrium to the south. It stands amongst the ruins of the large ritual centre dating from the Inca period, some of the masonry from which appears to have been utilized in the base of the bell-tower. The plan of the

Plate 3 Chucuito, view of La Asunción from the main square, through the arches of the atrium wall; c.1595.

church is simple: a massively long nave with a square-ended apse and two large chapel-cum-transepts. The walls are of a mixture of stone and *adobe* (sun-dried bricks), the roofing of a timber framework that would originally have been thatched but is now covered with corrugated iron. The main portal at the end of the church, opposite the high altar, is set back between the projecting side walls and beneath deep eaves. It is damaged by time and perhaps by restoration but the basic elements of the classical architectural vocabulary are still visible: a round-arched entrance framed by pilasters and entablature, and topped by a fragmentary pediment and niche. A lateral portal, opening on to the cemetery, is even simpler in design consisting of an arched doorway decorated with little more than impost mouldings which, if not particularly sophisticated in execution, nevertheless represent a sort of architectural understatement. It is not just any old classical detail that is included: it is those mouldings which mark the crucial juncture between the supporting jambs and the springing of the arch above.

The other church which survives in Chucuito is that of La Asunción, a few streets away (Plate 3). This runs laterally across the whole of the upper side of the main square in the centre of town and is aligned at right angles to Santo Domingo, so that it marks the other axis of the pre-conquest grid plan of the town. The two churches seem to confront one another across the intervening streets and houses. La Asunción is built on a similarly massive scale and is again emphasized by ranges of arches enclosing the atrium in front of it and by the raised platform on which it stands. The arched entrance to the atrium frames and echoes the main portal, a round-arched door with in this case a slightly more elaborate version of the classical surround than those on Santo Domingo: paired pilasters supporting entablature and pediment, with niches between the pilasters, roundels in the spandrels and, a little eccentrically, coffering on the outer faces of the voussoirs. The end portal, opening into the cemetery, is a simpler variant, with clean lines and pleasing proportions.

La Asunción was probably built as a result of the 1590 commission but the site had previously been occupied by a parish church of San Pedro. San Pedro had been built in the early 1550s, at the same time as the Dominicans were building their church, during a brief period when there were secular clergy in the town, but after their departure the parish church was abandoned, to be pillaged by the friars for building materials. Such in-fighting between Europeans is not unusual in Spanish America. Colonial history is full of tensions between the different groups, between the Church and the State, or, within civil government, between the officials and administrators sent out from Spain and those born and bred in America, or, within the Church, between the monastic orders and the episcopal church, and so on. In Chucuito both the secular and the diocesan authorities were highly suspicious of the wealth and autonomy of the Dominicans, but although San Pedro's successor dominates the town by virtue of its position, there is nothing else in its appearance to indicate that the parish and monastic churches were, in the sixteenth century, bitter rivals. On the contrary, they are stylistically very similar.

The other sixteenth-century churches in the province all follow the same pattern: gigantic in scale, imposingly situated, and simple in plan. All have arched portals in brick or stone which prominently display the essential elements of classical architecture. It is always the street façade that matters; this is where the unequivocal statement of the rules is to be found. In Ilave, for example, the lateral portal of the church of San Miguel, dating perhaps from the mid 1560s, follows the basic triumphal arch pattern and is as severe and as grand as one could wish (Plate 4); in the interior, on the other hand, the

Plate 4 Ilave, San Miguel, lateral portal; *c.*1565

Plate 5 Acora, San Pedro, end portal; *c*.1600.

Plate 6 Juli, view of the town from the atrium of La Asunción, with the façade of San Pedro to the left and roofs of San Juan, extreme right.

chapel entrances are defined by a series of elegant, almost light-hearted ogival arches. In Acora the end portal of the upper church of San Pedro faces out over the town, and in the sunshine the shadows from its deep brick mouldings make the design clearly legible from far down the road (Plate 5). In several of these towns but in Juli in particular, the churches still play a crucial part in defining the spatial order of the whole town (Plates 6 & 7). They mark the positions of the main squares, their principal façades facing towards the town centre and often across it to their opposite number on the other side of the town. Aligned as they are along one or other of the axes of the standard grid plan, their long roofs tower above the surrounding buildings suggesting the overall urban order of which they are a part.

These churches pose a number of rather pressing questions. Why so many and so large? At the time of the Spanish conquest the province of Chucuito was certainly densely populated, but can the population of Juli, for example, ever really have justified the need for four such gigantic churches all within a few hundred yards of one another? Who built them? There was no local centre of Spanish population nor anything like, for example, a temporarily resident standing army to coerce the Lupaca Indians of the region into erecting such huge and manifestly alien structures. Throughout the period during which these churches were built there were probably no more than fifteen or twenty resident clerics at any one time. How, therefore, did so few achieve so much?

Then there are the questions of style and technique. Despite their size – they are often 200 feet or more in length – the overall structure of these churches is not complicated; they are in effect little more than gigantic barns with walls of adobe or stone or a mixture of both and with timber-framed roofs that would originally have been thatched, none of which is very far removed from native traditions. But the bell-towers and more especially the decorated portals in brick or stone are unmistakably European in style, the latter with arched entrances and at least a suggestion of classical architectural vocabulary in the form of pilasters and mouldings. These stylistic details are self-evidently European imports, as are the techniques of constructing regular semicircular arches in stone, and of making bricks and tiles out of fired clay. European craftsmen were few and far between at this time, even in the main towns; some may have passed through on their way to La Paz or Chuquisaca or Potosí, and perhaps stayed to work for a few days or even weeks, but it is difficult to imagine there would have been much incentive to hang around these lakeside towns, inhabited as they were only by Indians and penny-pinching friars. It hardly seems possible that all these classicizing details can be attributed to the occasional itinerant mason.

Plate 7 Acora, view of San Juan from the front of the church of San Pedro. Note the length of the nave.

It has previously been assumed that the majority of these churches were constructed as a result of the contract of 1590, that in other words they all date from the years around the turn of the century.[11] If this were the case then it would be reasonable to argue that they were built as a result of the consolidation of colonial rule, but further documentary evidence makes it clear that there was more or less continuous building activity on a very substantial scale in the area from at least the 1550s, of which the 1590 contract represents only a part. This means that the construction of these churches must be seen not as a result but as an integral part of the conquest. For the Indians of this as of many other areas throughout Spanish America the missionaries were their main, almost their only point of contact with the new foreign power, and building the local church and receiving instruction in the new faith, were therefore the first important areas of interaction between the two cultures, at the material and at the spiritual level. The church was usually the first major, visible aspect of Spanish culture which the Indians would have encountered, and yet those same Indians were centrally involved in its creation. In other words, the churches in the Province of Chucuito and, I would argue, elsewhere are not so much a reflection of Spanish achievements but rather an important constituent of the very process of colonization.

# I
# The idea of architecture

Bernabé Cobo, writing in 1653 after having spent nearly sixty years as a Jesuit missionary in America, believed that Spanish culture was by then so well established that it would be impossible to eradicate. There were so many solid and indestructible features,

> so many towns built to our design, so many rich buildings of stone and mortar, so many stones worked with the skill and art of Europe, in the shape of columns, bases and all manner of carvings and mouldings

> tantos pueblos edificados a nuestra traza, . . . tantos edificios suntuosos de cal y canto, . . . muchas piedras labradas con el primor y arte que se labran en Europa en forma de columnas, basas y todo género de labores y molduras[1]

that he could see no reason why these things should not last as long as time itself.

What exactly does Cobo mean when he talks of towns built to *nuestra traza*, our design? Towns in Europe were and still are notoriously heterogeneous in plan. What is the particular skill and art, *primor y arte*, of European stone masonry to which he refers, and why is it associated with columns, bases and mouldings? The classical architectural style implied in Cobo's reference to columns and bases was not the norm in Europe during the early period of the conquest and colonization of America except in Italy. In Spain in particular, architects were building in a variety of styles throughout the sixteenth century. But the towns and the architecture of Spanish America are indeed a testament to the success of the colonizing enterprise, and they are also remarkable for the degree of uniformity between them. Whatever Cobo's precise meaning they are all unmistakably European in origin. This chapter considers the ideas behind Cobo's categories – 'towns built to our design', 'rich buildings of stone', and 'the skill and art of Europe' and explores some of the possible sources for the uniformity he implies; subsequent chapters will consider how this was achieved, and why it was so successful.

In order to build up a picture of the sorts of assumptions held by sixteenth-century Spaniards about the nature of architecture and the rôle which it could play in civilized society we need to consider evidence from a wide range of sources: official decrees issued by the Spanish Crown concerning the founding of towns and the erection of public buildings, letters and reports sent back from the colonies, the council minutes of newly-founded towns, legislation concerning the erection of monasteries and churches, and the numerous chronicles of the discovery, conquest and settlement of America. All these have been useful, and the chronicles especially so. Whether written by priests or soldiers or official historians, they are more descriptive and more discursive than the bureaucratic documents; they often attempt to set the events of the conquest, the exploits of the conquistadors and missionaries, within a broader historical context and as a part of God's plan. They usually include a section on the geography, climate, flora and fauna of the New World, followed by a section on the native inhabitants, their culture, customs and pre-conquest history, together with an assessment of their relative civility (used in this study in the strong sixteenth-century sense of 'the state of being civilized' [*OED*]).

The first Europeans found much in Native American culture to evoke strong reactions – astonishment, admiration, fear and disgust – and many writers exclaim in despair of ever being able to describe the strange things they have seen. For my present purposes the sections dealing with native society and native art and architecture are invaluable because Europe was, not surprisingly, always either explicitly or implicitly the yard-stick by which the cultures of non-Europeans were judged. In trying to describe indigenous American culture, in groping for some vocabulary or for some appropriate category, or in suggesting an approximate European comparison or contrast, the writers tend to expose the deep-seated attitudes which underlie their perceptions. They try and explain things which if they were describing an aspect of European history or culture would need no explanation, just as Cobo does not feel the need to explain the idea of towns built to 'our design' because he does not doubt that the reader will understand.

The earliest accounts of the discovery of Inca Peru are those contained in letters and reports, and were written by the participants; by, for example Pizarro's secretaries Francisco Xerez and Pedro Sancho, by his cousin Hernando Pizarro, and by Miguel de Estete and Diego de Trujillo, soldiers present at the capture of the Inca Atahualpa.[2] These writers are principally interested in the towns and buildings of Native America in so far as they suggest the existence of substantial Indian populations which in turn might indicate the outlying settlements of a large state or empire such as that which

Cortés had discovered in Mexico. Grand architecture and well-organized towns would indicate a large, settled Indian population, as well as land that was fertile and suitable for habitation; this in turn would suggest a well-organized, hierarchical central government which, again on the model of Mexico, it might be possible to manipulate from the very top by capturing or controlling the ruler in some way. And last but not least, all these things might also imply that there were other, more immediately obvious benefits: gold, silver and precious stones were always uppermost in the minds of the first explorers. One of the earliest descriptions of Peru is that contained in the so-called Relación Sámano-Xerez, according to which Pizarro and his men, exploring down the Pacific coast from Panama in 1525,

found some small pueblos beside the sea, and made peace with some of them; eventually they understood that . . . inland, behind a large mountain range, there were a great many pueblos, where there was a great deal of gold.[3]

The same source describes how on a later exploratory voyage the Spaniards capture three Indians who tell them more about the unknown territory:

There are four towns together all under one Lord . . . where there were many sheep and pigs and cats and dogs and other animals, and geese and doves, and where they make cloth (*mantas*) . . . of wool and cotton . . . and objects of silver and gold, and by all appearances they are a people of great *policía*, and they have many tools of copper and other metals with which they till their land and mine gold and they keep all sorts of stores, and these towns have very well laid out streets, and they have all sorts of fortresses and they enjoy great order and justice amongst themselves.[4]

The breathless excitement of this passage is revealing. The author sees all these different things as interrelated: the Indians' various skills and crafts; their well-planned towns; their *policía*, a crucial word meaning a civil society with a just form of government, and implying a broad range of attributes of civilized life such as politeness, cleanliness and rationality; and their order and justice, *orden y justicia*, another important recurring phrase, often, as here, found in conjunction with *policía*. These are all signs of a prosperous and civilized people, a people well worth conquering.

The same ideas are evident in the various early accounts of the rise to power of the Incas: pre-Inca history is usually characterized as a period of barbarism, when the Indians lived in trees, caves and faraway places. One of the Incas' greatest achievements, according to these chroniclers, was to bring the population together into well-ordered urban settlements, the sort of settlements which so impressed Pizarro's men when they first arrived in Peru.

Juan de Betanzos' account, dating from 1551, is typical of many: before the rise of the Incas, he says, the town of Cuzco was 'a small village of about thirty mean little straw houses' set in the middle of a marsh.[5] There was a gradual improvement under the early Incas, but it was the great Inca Pachacuti who really took things in hand. He inspected the whole area and found everything in a poor state of repair and lacking in *arte*, 'and the houses of the inhabitants were of straw, small and poorly constructed'.[6] Betanzos credits Pachacuti with draining the whole area and rebuilding the town from scratch. He drew up and laid out the plan and he designed the buildings, modelling them in clay. This for Betanzos is the mark of a great and powerful ruler, to found and establish a city from the first to the last detail. Agustín de Zárate, writing at about the same time, holds similar assumptions although he attributes much of this civilizing work to the later Inca Huayna Capac. In Zárate's view it was Huayna Capac who was responsible for reorganizing the whole population into a civil and cultured state. The phrases he uses are telling: Huayna Capac was possessed of 'justicia y razón'; these people, 'bárbara y sin letras', came to comport themselves in a most harmonious and orderly fashion, 'contanto concierto y orden', because he *reduced* them to polity and culture, 'la reduxo a policía y cultura'. *Reducir*, to reduce, is another key word in the conquerors' vocabulary. It means to resettle people previously living in a number of villages or hamlets into one bigger, orderly township, a *reducción*.[7]

This general view of Inca history is developed by numerous later writers. Fray Martín de Morúa, writing towards the end of the century, is typical of many. He believes that before the Incas the peoples of Peru had lived scattered about the countryside, 'without organized villages or *policía*', and the Incas 'as peoples of such great worth and understanding organized and domesticated them, ordering the way they were to live, and planning and defining boundaries'.[8] Following Juan de Betanzos, he credits the Inca Pachacuti with the major part of this 'domesticating' effort: it was he who collected the Indians together and reduced them into towns when previously they had lived in caves amongst the hills.[9]

He put his Kingdom into such good order, and with such prudence, that even if he had read the Politics of Aristotle and all that moral philosophy can teach, he could scarcely have improved it.[10]

A number of interlocking ideas can be identified in these passages. Clearly urban life is seen as a prerequisite for civilization and that one of the duties of a ruler is to move people from their scattered farms and hamlets into townships before any progress can be made towards a state of *policía*. Bound up with this is the importance of order. The people have to be ordered. The towns have to be ordered. People cannot live in *policía* unless they live in orderly towns. It is not clear from these various texts exactly what form this order should take, but the Europeans recognized it in what they saw in Peru and in what they understood of the past history of the Inca dynasty, and it must be assumed that their readers would understand what was meant.

Another basic assumption which soon emerges from the accounts of native art and architecture is that concerning the relative value of different materials and different technical skills. In Europe from the times of Herodotus, and of Pliny and Vitruvius, a simple linear hierarchy of value has been attributed to different types of material, a value that is apparently determined primarily by economics. According to this scheme rarer, more precious materials – gold, marble, porphyry, crystal – are more valuable but they are also better in some general sense than cheaper, more accessible ones such as clay, wood or straw. Thus, at least until the twentieth century, it was considered only fitting that a prestigious building should be constructed in stone, preferably marble, or in the case of mythically fabulous buildings, in porphyry or crystal. This hierarchy of materials is linked to a hierarchy of technique: the technical difficulty of producing, say, a bronze sculpture is much greater than (or regarded as much greater than) that of producing a wooden sculpture, and technical difficulty contributes its own value to the artefact, not only because a complex technical achievement will be more expensive than a simple one, but also because technical achievements are, in Western eyes, highly valued as evidence of human wit, as marks of cultural progress. In other words, these hierarchies correspond to a view of history within which there is a natural tendency for a culture to ascend the hierarchical ladder: as soon as a technique has been mastered it is assumed that, finances permitting, people will choose the new techniques and the more valuable materials wherever possible.[11]

The first Spaniards to discover and explore the New World all viewed the art and architecture they encountered there through eyes conditioned by these attitudes. They used these related hierarchies of materials and techniques as another guide to the relative level of civility attained by the indigenous peoples. The pre-conquest cultures of what is now Colombia, for example, impressed the first Spaniards for a variety of reasons: it was a densely populated region, and the people lived in orderly townships linked by good wide roads. More immediately impressive, however, was their extensive use of high quality materials, emeralds and finely-worked gold, to decorate both their persons and their houses. All these things suggested a relatively advanced culture. Their architecture, however, was another matter: many writers sound apologetic or slightly confused by the fact that even the houses of the great leaders such as the Chibcha chief Sugamuxi were built of straw and not of stone.[12] This upsets the expected pattern within which it is assumed that a level of technical skill in one material will be matched by an equivalent level of skill in another. These Western ideas about cultural progress and the hierarchy of materials are very persistent and some modern commentators still feel there to be an uncomfortable discrepancy between the Chibcha expertise in working gold, and their apparently 'primitive' houses. It was recently written of the Chibcha that,

the Indians who made up the basic population – excepting in the sphere of goldsmithing – did not demonstrate a capacity for great artistic achievement ... The large temple of Sugamuxi was nothing but a shack of mud and straw, even though its walls were hung with sheets of gold.[13]

The concept of an important building constructed in mud and straw was to Spanish eyes a contradiction in terms, and it is not surprising to find that there is no word for such a building in Spanish. From an early date a word was introduced from Carib to meet the need. Pedro Simón explains that during the conquest of the Caribbean islands the Spaniards kept hearing the Indians talk about *bohíos*, and gradually they came to realize that they used the word with reference to their houses,

and so it has remained throughout the Indies, that houses of straw, whether of Indians or Spaniards, are called *bohíos*.[14]

It is the material, not the shape or size, which is the identifying feature of a *bohío*, and it is not surprising that the word quickly comes to have disparaging overtones. It is a poor sort of building, and it is the mark of a poor sort of culture. Thus, wherever the indigenous Americans lacked either a material or a technique which was commonly used in Europe the Spaniards saw this as a sign of the general backwardness of the people concerned. The lack of fired clay as a building material, for example, is regularly remarked upon. Adobe and thatch seemed, and to many still seem, the primitive forerunners of brick and tile, just as lashing timbers together with ropes or leather thongs seems to pre-date the Western techniques of carpentry.

The interlinked hierarchies of materials and techniques are therefore an important aspect of a generally evolutionary view of history which is based on the European model. The neat archaeological categories introduced in the nineteenth century of Stone, Iron and Bronze Ages are derived from the same sets of assumptions which shaped the responses of the sixteenth-century Spaniards: these categories were seen as universal, that the various stages are normal, even natural, that (wars, plagues or other major upheavals apart) there will be steady progress in all branches of culture more or less simultaneously and that the sequence will repeat itself elsewhere in the same form. This model is the one most of us were brought up with, and the strength of the model is such that it is not always easy to recognize alternatives. It is not uncommon, for example, to hear the Incas described as 'essentially a Stone Age people'. This is true in so far as the Incas did not use iron or steel, but of course the associated ideas of simplicity, backwardness, brutishness and so on are entirely inappropriate.[15]

It was the hierarchy of materials which was primarily responsible for conditioning the first Spanish reactions to the Inca culture. In Peru they found a land which, like Colombia, had numerous well-planned towns and cities, with good wide roads and so on, but also they found the architecture to be of exquisitely finished stone. They found huge temples, palaces, storehouses, raised platforms and walled enclosures all built of stone, as well as tiers of stone-faced terraces climbing steeply up the hillsides and miles of irrigation channels often made from tightly fitting stone blocks or even cut from the solid rock. European attitudes concerning the relative value of different materials, combined with ideas of orderliness and urban living predisposed the Spaniards to admire the Inca state. They were duly impressed and it evoked some of the most glowing of the early European responses to any indigenous American culture. Comparisons are often made with the achievements of antiquity, and it is significant that the word 'empire' crops up in relation to the Inca at a relatively early date.[16]

The first detailed description of Cuzco, the capital city and heart of the Andean kingdom, was written by one of Pizarro's secretaries, Pedro Sancho, who was among the triumphant band of soldiers who rode into the city in November 1533.

> The city of Cuzco . . . is so beautiful and has so many buildings that it would be worthy of admiration even in Spain, and it is made up entirely of the houses of Lords, because no poor people live here, and each Lord builds his own house . . . The majority of these houses are of stone . . . and they are well-ordered, the streets are set at right angles to one another, all quite straight, and all are paved, and down the middle of each runs a stone-lined water conduit.[17]

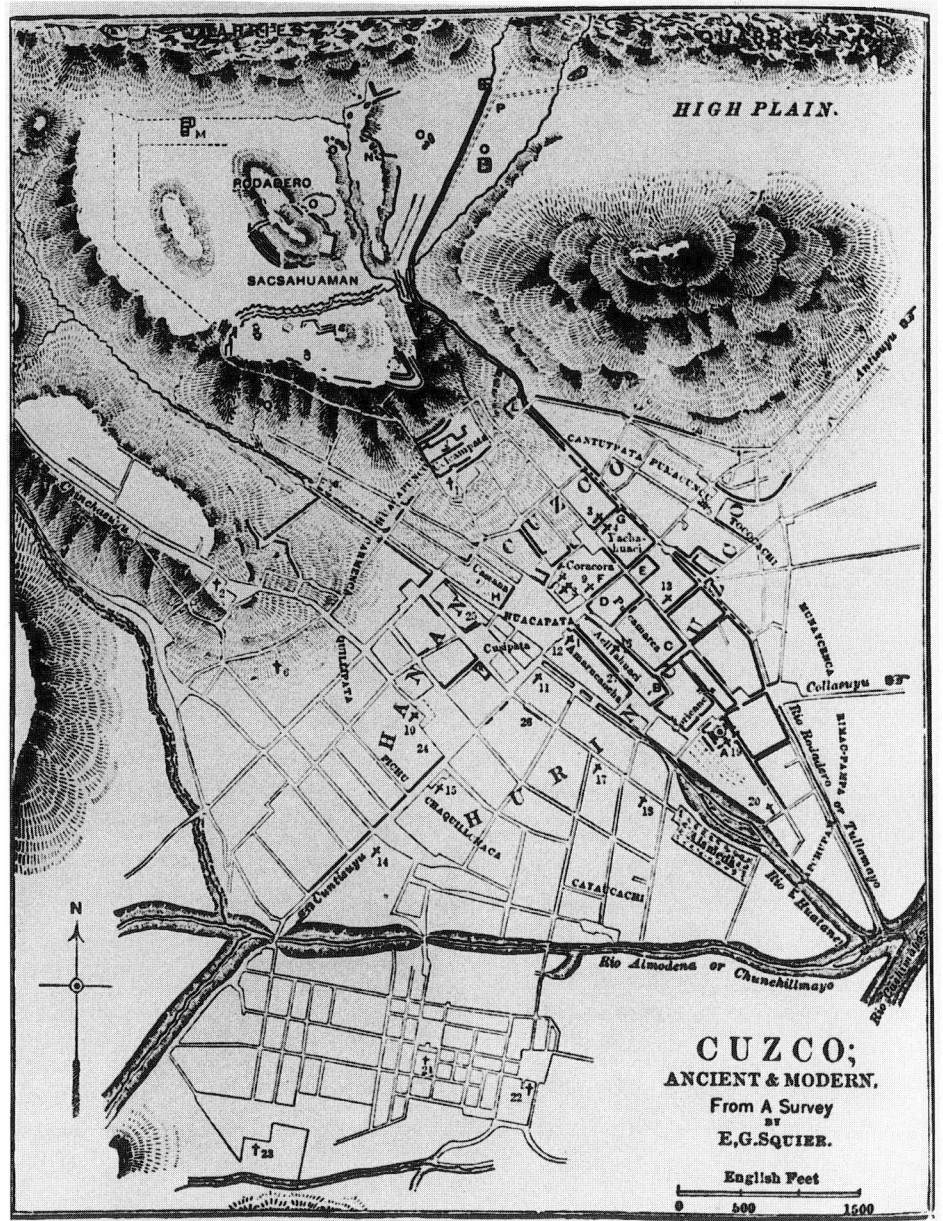

Plate 8 Plan of Cuzco, from George Squier, *Peru. Incidents of Travel and Exploration in the Land of the Incas*, London 1877.

Sancho mentions almost all the features of the city which were to impress other observers: the wealth and social distinction of its inhabitants, the large stone houses, the drainage, the straight paved streets, and the regular grid plan, all of which are evidence of the *policía* of the Incas (Plate 8). The general concept of urban orderliness, which the Spaniards associated with civilized life, is here unmistakably related to a town or city laid out on a grid-plan basis and built of solid materials. Another early impression of Cuzco is that of Pedro Cieza de León, who makes an explicit connection between the admirable organization of the city and the sophistication of its creators:

> In no other part of this Kingdom of Peru has been found a city laid out with such noble design as was this city of Cuzco . . . Cuzco had great method and distinction, and must have been founded by people of great ability.[18]

It is easy to see how later commentators would use such descriptions as the basis for comparisons between Cuzco and Rome and the Incas and the Romans.

To sixteenth-century and modern travellers alike, one of the most striking features of Inca architecture is the extraordinary quality of the stone masonry. It is almost always described in the same terms: with praise for its precision and finish, which were considered the equal to anything in Europe, and with wonder at such an achievement from a culture which lacked both the wheel and iron tools, elements which on the basis of Old World history have traditionally been regarded as fundamental to cultural development. José de Acosta, writing in the late sixteenth century, says of Inca walls that

> the work is strange and wonderful; they did not use mortar, nor did they have iron or steel with which to cut and work the stones, nor machines or instruments to carry them, but despite all this they are so finely worked that in many places one can scarcely see the joints between them.[19]

This description is typical of many.

There are in fact various types of Inca masonry, which can be divided into two main categories: one where the ashlars are regular rectangles and are laid in straight courses, and one where the blocks although equally tightly fitting are unequal, often polygonal in shape, and there is no apparent order to the overall pattern on the surface of the wall (Plates 9 & 10). The first of these styles did not present a problem for early commentators:

> the stones are so smooth they look like polished slabs with the joints in regular order after the usage in Spain

Plate 9 Pisac, near Cuzco. Inca architecture: trapezoidal doorway and niche with masonry in regular courses; c.1500.

Plate 10 Ollantaytambo, near Cuzco. Inca architecture: retaining wall of tightly-fitting polygonal blocks; c.1500.

says Pedro Sancho.[20] The second category is more of a problem because while regular ashlars, straight lines and rectangles were regarded as indicative of quality and sophistication, none could deny the extraordinary virtuosity of the irregular masonry. Bernabé Cobo is unusual in that he really confronts this problem, and recognizes that the Spanish language does not in fact fit the case in hand. He distinguishes the two styles, calling the regular ashlar style *sillería* and the irregular style *mampostería*, which means random rubble or field-stone masonry. Of this latter he says that,

> although these look the most coarse, it seems to me they were more difficult to make than those of ashlar because apart from the face, which they cut as smooth as those of the ashlars, they are not cut regularly, and as they are set so perfectly against each other one cannot imagine what it must have cost them to fit them as we see them now; because shaped as they are, some large and some small, and all different in shape and size, they are nevertheless set with the same skilful joints as those of the ashlars.[21]

The problem is that the vocabulary of the European styles of masonry is inadequate: in *mampostería* or random rubble masonry the stones are not fitted together; they do not have to fit because they are set in plenty of mortar. This implies a more primitive form of masonry than that of *sillería* because it requires less technical skill, less finishing and polishing, and less specialized tools. What Cobo is calling *mampostería* is irregular, disorderly, but he is in no doubt about the skill required to produce it.

There are other ways in which the various European preconceptions and hierarchies under discussion did not always fit neatly with the visual evidence. Some writers, for example, are led to make judgements about the relative age of indigenous architecture based on the materials from which it is made; others make similar judgements, but based on the style and scale of the architecture. Bernabé Cobo is in the former category. Of the ceremonial centre of Pachacamac on the Peruvian coast, built almost entirely of adobes, he writes:

> This great temple was not built by the Inca Kings, but is very much older as the Indians tell, and as one can see from the form and quality of construction, which is different from that of the Incas which were almost all of worked stone; and if this one was, then it could compete with the most magnificent buildings in the world.[22]

Cobo is in fact wrong in this assumption of the relative antiquity of Pachacamac – parts of the centre are indeed very much older, but the main temple is of Inca date – but his mistake is the result of an adherence to the European notion that there will be a natural tendency to ascend the hierarchy of materials as soon as technically possible. The Incas were masters of stone, and for Cobo it was therefore inconceivable that they should ever choose to construct a prestigious building in anything else.

Interestingly, the consideration of Inca architecture reveals in some observers a contradiction within the European categories. As has been seen the simple linear sequence of primitive to civilized, low to high grade materials, simple to sophisticated technology and so on, is usually related to historical progress. As time passes societies tend to move up the scale. But to the sixteenth-century observer Europe's own internal history does not fit this pattern; the classical past was still generally regarded as the peak of achievement, the Middle Ages as a period of decline, and the sixteenth-century present as a Renaissance, as a new period of progress but one in which few felt that antiquity had yet been equalled.

Some writers, struck by the massive overall scale of much of Inca architecture as well as by the size of the individual blocks, draw comparisons with classical Roman architecture. Pedro Sancho compares the fortress of Sacsahuaman favourably with the aqueduct at Segovia and with the Roman remains at Tarragona.[23] Cieza de León goes a step further, and sees these similarities as evidence of the great age of the buildings of Cuzco:

the houses are made of pure stone, with such beautiful joints that they demonstrate the antiquity of the buildings since they were such large and well-placed stones.[24]

This again simply demonstrates that the preconceptions which the Spaniards held about architecture and town planning and about historical progress were not based on personal experience nor empirical data but were generalized ideals.

But it is usually the stone-work which reminds people of the buildings of Roman antiquity rather than the design or lay-out of Inca buildings. Polo de Ondegardo, comparing Inca with Roman architecture, is quick to point out that the similarities are limited:

I say as far as the stone-work is concerned, because in everything else their buildings are without order or proportion, and low and even with little foundation.[25]

Polo does not identify in Inca architecture a particular cause for the lack of height, nor for those crucially important categories, order and proportion; others do. While no-one doubted that Inca (or pre-Inca) methods of cutting and facing and fitting stone – a relatively high quality material – were extremely sophisticated, observers constantly point out that they did not develop the technique of constructing a true arch, which in European terms was a fundamental step towards civilized, high quality architecture. Modern commentators too have expressed puzzlement that a people so evidently skilled in stone-work should have 'failed to discover' the principle of the arch, and so of vaulted interior spaces, but continued instead to use timber and thatch for roofing even their most important buildings, despite the fact that they did sometimes use a corbelled vaulting system for small constructions.[26]

José de Acosta, who was full of praise for their skilful masonry, had little respect for the overall form of Inca buildings:

> Although they were large, these buildings were generally badly divided and utilized, and more like mosques or the buildings of barbarians. They did not know how to construct arches for their buildings, nor had they discovered the necessary mortar.[27]

It is particularly in relation to the use of the arch that we can identify in early commentators on indigenous American architecture an important distinction between 'skill' and 'art': these authors do not doubt that many of the Indians can cut stone skilfully, and can even build good buildings after their own fashion, but they have not grasped the Art of Architecture. Martín de Morúa believed that

> It is absolutely indubitable that had the Inca arrived at an understanding of the form and *arte* with which one builds and erects the arches for stone bridges, they would have done it most excellently.[28]

An anonymous description of Peru dating from the early seventeenth century makes this point even more clearly:

> If the Indians had reached an understanding of the *arte* of architecture and the *arte* of building bridges and buildings, then they would have outshone all the nations of the world.[29]

The important word in both these examples is *arte*; in both it is connected with the principle of the arch, and in both it is seen as something fundamental and immutable, which the Incas failed to attain (*alcanzar*). As with town plans and with building materials, the clear implication here is of a hierarchy of architectural techniques, a fixed ladder up which one climbs towards *arte*.

One of the chroniclers who puts this most clearly is again Bernabé Cobo. Like many other writers he has a section in his *Historia del Nuevo Mundo* about the possible origins of the American Indians, but he argues against any Old World contact, either by means of a son of Noah, or the Lost Tribe, or, most particularly, Solomon's ships trading with Ophir. He believes that, had there been any such contact, then there would be some traces of its influence in America. Early chroniclers not surprisingly tended to search for similarities between the Indians and the Jews, the Indians and the Romans, the Indians and the Welsh, and so on. Cobo looks carefully for such similarities, but sees none. The areas where he particularly expects to find such evidence are in writing and in architecture:

> not one single stone carved in the European way have we found amongst the many ruins of ancient buildings which we have seen. I myself on many occasions and with considerable diligence have seen and studied the ruins of the most sumptuous and ancient buildings of this Kingdom of Peru . . . to see if in any of the blocks and strange stones which are found there, there is any evidence of letters, of characters, or of any carving similar to those of our buildings, and nowhere have I found such a thing, neither stones cut for arches, nor with the shape of bases, capitals, columns, nor other designs which belong to the art of architecture.[30]

As far as Cobo is concerned this is proof that such civilized peoples as the subjects of Solomon had never reached America. He does not doubt that having learnt the arts of writing and of architecture, then these things would never have been completely forgotten. The implication is that they are so obviously, so naturally a step forward towards civilization that it is inconceivable that a culture would not embrace them from the outset. It is clear that for Cobo there is only one true architecture, and that is the classical; in America they could construct buildings, but they did not know of, they had not yet managed to achieve the Art of Architecture.

So far, then, we have identified perhaps three main sets of assumptions. First, that urban life is unquestionably a Good Thing, and that it is essentially bound up with ideas of civility; there is an implication that orderliness in town planning is a prerequisite for social orderliness, or perhaps that the two are interdependent rather than sequential. Second, that certain materials are better than others, as are the techniques required to work them, and in particular that stone architecture is better than architecture of mud, canes, reeds, or wood. From this is derived the idea that the principle of the arch is a sign of technological and cultural progress, but this is also related to a third set of assumptions, that there is a clear distinction between skill and art, and that in architecture there is only one art, or rather, only one style. This is the classical, and involves columns, capitals and so on, but also arches. This style is in part defined by the terms 'order' and 'proportion', although it does not have the monopoly on them as it does for, say, Vasari when he is comparing the classical style of architecture with the Gothic.

## The colonial grid-plan town

Much has been written about the origin of the grid-plan town in Spanish America, and a number of sources has been suggested: actual examples, such as the mediaeval *bastides* in France or the new towns built in Spain during the Reconquest in the fourteenth and fifteenth centuries, or written sources, particularly contemporary theorists of the ideal city such as Filarete or Serlio, earlier writers such as Augustine or the Spanish Eximinic, or earlier still, such as Vitruvius or Plato, as well as the existing Native American towns themselves.[31] The questions raised by this last are different from those of the other possible sources, and will be dealt with at greater length in due course. Whatever the source or sources there was initially very little discussion amongst those directly involved on either side of the Atlantic of what was desirable or what practicable, and yet the grid-plan town became the established norm for Spanish settlements in America from the very earliest years of the conquest. There was certainly no lack of information about the newly discovered territories, and numerous reports were sent back to Spain concerning the various conquests and the potential for Spanish colonization, but there is little evidence that this was used to help formulate a policy on how to establish new towns, the procedure to be followed or the form they ought to take. On the contrary, the initiative seems always to be with those in America while guidance from Spain, certainly before the later sixteenth century, is vague and non-specific.

The earliest of the royal directives to deal with the general question of founding new towns and establishing colonial rule in any detail are those of 1513 addressed to Pedrarias Dávila concerning the foundation of Spanish settlements in the region around Panama known then as the province of Castilla del Oro.[32] In these the King, Ferdinand I, informs Pedrarias Dávila that one of his principal tasks is to choose suitable sites for settlement, sites which have good access for navigation (particularly if they are near mines), which have a healthy climate, a good clean water supply and 'buenos ayres', and which are well provided with woods and arable land in the immediate vicinity. When a good site had been selected, building plots (no shape or size is given) should be distributed according to the 'quality' of the prospective settlers. Presumably the better and/or wealthier prospective citizens should be nearer the centre, although this is not spelled out.[33] As we might expect, given the early responses to Inca towns and social organization, these 1513 instructions go on to stress the importance of *order* in the new towns: the houses, the place chosen for the church, the plaza and the streets should all be arranged from the outset in an orderly fashion because it would be impossible to impose order at a later stage. Of what this general 'orderliness' is to consist is not clearly stated, although blocks, *solares*, are mentioned. Again it is obvious that the concept of order and imposed orderliness is fundamental to colonial thinking.

Brief directions similar to those issued to Pedrarias Dávila are repeated to different colonial governors for the next fifty years or so. In 1529 for example, governors were instructed to found settlements of at least twenty-five stone houses, which were to be completed within five years.[34] In 1556 Charles V sent some rather more extensive instructions to the Marqués de Cañete, Viceroy of Peru, urging the foundation of new settlements but they are even less explicit about the form these should take or the type of housing they should contain, beyond the fact that they should be 'orderly'.[35] What is abundantly clear from all these instructions is that neither singly nor collectively do they constitute a sufficient source to explain the prevalence of the grid-plan form of town in Latin America. Even the references to orderliness and to blocks do not necessarily imply this: Italian Renaissance architectural theorists offer a number of possible plans with square or quadrangular blocks which are unquestionably orderly but which are nothing like the simple grid plan of Spanish American practice. These instructions could only possibly imply such a lay-out to someone who was already prepared to find such an implication contained within them, for whom such an implication was the norm. It cannot be, for example, that Cortés, to whom the 1513 instructions to Pedrarias Dávila were reissued almost word for word in 1523, proceeded to lay out colonial Mexico City on a grid plan solely as a result of such directions; he must have understood that to arrange the church, plaza and streets in an orderly fashion was synonymous with arranging them on a grid plan.[36] He and others like him must already have had the grid-plan pattern in mind.

## The 1573 Ordinances

In 1573 Philip II issued his extensive instructions on the conquest and colonization of new territories, the *Ordenanzas sobre descubrimiento nuevo y población*.[37] These in some ways exemplify the problem of the origins of ideas concerning colonial architecture and town planning. They do not constitute a straightforward source for the use of the grid-plan town throughout Spanish America – the date is too late for that – and most of what they have to say is very conventional, but they reinforce the overall picture. They draw heavily on the earlier instructions, such as those to Pedrarias Dávila, but they are altogether more self-conscious: it is clear from the outset that the author or authors saw themselves as in a direct line of descent from the classical past. The section of founding new settlements is closely based on Vitruvius, beginning with the choice of site and proceeding to the layout of the town and location of important buildings.[38] The site should be somewhere where the existing inhabitants are healthy and live to a ripe old age, where the stars are propitious, where the sky is clear and the air pure, where it is neither too hot nor too cold, and where there are no evil or poisonous creatures (§ XXXIV). The soil should be fertile, with plenty of wood and water readily available (§ XXXV) and there should be Indians around to convert (§ XXXVI). The winds must be taken into consideration, and a site must be chosen where there is good fresh air from the north and south, ideally neither too high and cold, nor too low and damp (§ XL).

The instructions then proceed to deal with the form the new town should take. It should be laid out on a grid plan pattern – this is now explicit for the first time – with a large central plaza surrounded by a series of streets running at right angles to each other. Everything should be laid out by measure and rule, 'a cordel y regla' (§ CXI) and in 'buena proporción' (§ CXIX). As far as possible, the buildings should all be of the same design to enhance the appearance of the town (§ CXXV). The main church should be away from the main square, and isolated from other buildings, and to give it greater authority it should be raised up above the surrounding street level so that it has to be approached up some steps (§ CXXV).

These *Ordenanzas* then are almost entirely non-specific. The sections on the choice of site, derived from standard sources and especially from Vitruvius, have nothing apart from the occasional reference to Indians to suggest that they have been formulated with the particular needs or conditions, the vastly varied climate or geography of America in mind. Not only eighty years' worth of empirical information about America, but also fifteen hundred years or more of evidence from Europe itself often blatantly contradicted these general precepts – the healthiness or otherwise of particular winds, for example, had been recognized since classical times not to be a universally applicable principle.[39] The directions for the lay-out of towns too have their roots firmly in the general Vitruvian/Albertian tradition, combining on the one hand a concern for regularity and symmetry as being conducive to beauty with on the other a desire to give the church some physical pre-eminence to match its spiritual importance. The choice of the grid as the only recommended plan for a new town must, however, be derived principally from American practice rather than a particular European source. The only room for any significant variation in the plan is in the positioning of the main square which in the case of coastal sites may be offset rather than central so that it opens to the sea. This variation is found in Vitruvius, but it no doubt also accorded with contemporary Spanish perceptions. Writing from the vantage point of Spain, seaports were of great importance: Spanish America was no doubt envisaged by those who had not been there – insofar as it was envisaged at all – as little more than a number of seaports from which the produce flowed to Spain, so perhaps it is not surprising to find that the authors of the *Ordenanzas* should wish to visualize these towns as looking seawards, away from the interior.

Not only are the *Ordenanzas* very general but they are in practical terms all but redundant. By this date – 1573 – the general grid-plan scheme if not quite the rule was already the established norm throughout Spanish America, and most of the major colonial centres had long since been laid out along these lines: Mexico from about 1524, Quito from 1534, Lima in 1535, Bogotá in 1538, to name but a few. The *Ordenanzas* are therefore a *post facto* rationalization and confirmation of Spanish American practice. Both the theory and the practice, the one consciously, the other less so, have their roots in the same classicizing cultural ideal.

### The rôle of the expert in 'our design'

The new grid-plan towns of colonial Spanish America were not the product of directives from an expert or panel of experts in Spain. The degree to which contemporary architectural theorists were unaware or unconcerned about developments in America can be illustrated by an extreme case, that of Lázaro de Velasco. In the introduction to his translation of Vitruvius, written in the mid-sixteenth century when colonization was well under way, he stresses the importance of the profession for society as a whole, in much the same way as Vitruvius had done. Architects, says Velasco, are responsible for

> temples, where the holy name of God is invoked, and they ennoble cities with sumptuous buildings... they construct the walls with which towns are defended, they design the houses where people can live and find protection from the ravages of the weather.[40]

Few architects in Europe in the mid-sixteenth century ever had a chance of putting such visions into practice, of designing and building such a variety of constructions, of shaping a whole urban environment. A reference to America would have greatly strengthened Velasco's argument here, but he seems quite unaware of it. At a later point, enlarging on the advantages of having a Spanish edition of Vitruvius, he argues that architecture is as necessary for Christians now as it had been for Romans in the past:

> You will see how much benefit can accrue to the Christian Republic if there are men of ability, of sound judgement and of great prudence and experience, prepared to come here to construct the essential buildings such as churches, proper temples, where the holy name of God can be invoked, monasteries, hospitals and the buildings necessary for the creation of orderly, well-governed cities. And if at some time God should be so honoured that you conquer the lands of infidels, you will know who to be guided by in the building of temples and churches.[41]

'If at some time?' Such myopia seems almost perverse. By the time Velasco was writing dozens of new towns and thousands of churches had been founded throughout the continent. The slowness with which America penetrated the consciousness of anyone other than those directly involved in its conquest, colonization and evangelization has been remarked upon by others, although not specifically in relation to architecture.[42] Such complete lack of awareness from a profession which manifestly had so much to offer, so much to gain, seems extraordinary. Men like Velasco would no doubt have been involved in drawing up the 1573 *Ordenanzas* but their very bookishness precluded the inclusion of fresh empirical information. The American experience *ipso facto* lacked the necessary authority to form the basis of new legislation.

The case of Velasco highlights even more clearly than does a consideration of the official instructions that those in authority in America were on their own. They had to rely on what they already knew, because the authorities in Europe could offer little help beyond some very general guidelines. They had to deal with each new situation as it arose and make decisions on the spot; they had, as with other essentially practical tasks, to rely on something closer to instinct than on something consciously learned.

### The civic, the civil and the Christian: Indian towns to 'our design'

Behind this unanimity about the grid-plan layout for new towns lies the assumption that civility is conditional upon an urban lifestyle. In the case of Spanish America this comes to mean not *any* town, but specifically the grid-plan type and the orderliness of the grid-plan layout is a metaphor for the orderliness and civility of the people who live within it. Spaniards in America should therefore live in orderly towns as a demonstration both to themselves and to the Indians of their inherent civility. But this idea is also extended and modified to apply to the Indians. It was considered at least as important that the Indians too should live in orderly towns but in this case the purpose of such orderliness was not a demonstration of civility but an encouragement towards it. Indian civility is dependent upon orderly urbanization and it is also closely bound up with Christianization: the civic, the civil and the Christian are essentially interdependent. No-one seems to have doubted that the Indians must be reorganized into orderly townships before conversion could get underway and as early as 1503 a royal decree argued that the salvation of the souls of the Indians was dependent upon their being united into *pueblos*.[43] Not surprisingly therefore it is initially the Church which is seen as having responsibility for resettling the Indians as a prerequisite for converting them. The term used in relation to this practice is the same as that used in accounts of the civilizing efforts of the Inca: *reducir*. The Indians are to be reduced into *reducciones* or new orderly towns. Again, it is not at first clear what is implied by the idea of orderliness but from later sources it is obvious that in relation to the layout of towns it means a grid plan. The word *policía* also occurs repeatedly in this context as one of the chief benefits which the Indians will derive from the resettlement schemes.

These ideas are apparent in the earliest documentation concerning the Indians, documentation which in other ways parallels and can sometimes elucidate the instructions from Spain concerning Spanish settlement. In 1516 a set of instructions issued by the Crown to the Hieronymite missionaries covered a wide range of aspects of the conversion of the native inhabitants, including collecting them together into new towns.[44] As with the slightly earlier instructions to Pedrarias Dávila (1513) concerning the founding of Spanish towns, those to the Hieronymites stress that the site must be chosen with care, in a place where there are suitable agricultural lands and rivers for fishing. The Indians are to grouped together into settlements of about three hundred families. In areas where there are mines the towns must be positioned nearby so that the Indians will not have to travel far to work. Houses should be built in the local style. There is no mention of the materials or the overall layout, except simply that there must be a plaza and streets and as good a church as possible, and that the house of the *cacique* or chief must be near the square, and bigger or better than the houses of the rest of the inhabitants. A Spanish administrator should be appointed who should not live in one of these Indian settlements, but somewhere nearby, in a house built of stone. Together with the priest this administrator was responsible for seeing to it that the Indians lived in *policía*, that, for example, they wore clothes, that they slept in beds, that each had only one wife, and that they did not eat off the floor but, presumably, off tables.[45] Although there is no specific mention of order, it is implied at the level of both social class and individual morality.

The instructions to Viceroy Cañete of 1556 mentioned earlier are both for new Spanish settlements and for Indian *reducciones*.[46] There are general references to the need for *reducciones*, for order and *policía*, and for instruction in the faith. There are details about administration, about the redirection of traditional tributes, and about the need for lazy Indians to be suitably occupied (industry being another essential aspect of *policía*), but there is no indication of the form either the *reducciones* or the buildings within them are to take.

On the whole, the instructions about Indian *reducciones* show a slightly greater awareness of America than do those which deal with new towns for Spaniards – they do at least refer to Indians – but there is barely a hint that they were formulated by anyone with access to information about Amerindian cultures, by anyone who had considered the letters and reports that were regularly arriving from across the Atlantic.[47] In the context of recommendations for *reducciones*, the assumptions concerning the Indians are always more or less negative, the assumptions concerning the benefits of *reducción*, of course, positive. These instructions take it for granted that the Indians have little or no religion and little or no civility: they therefore need to be reduced and so civilized, they need converting to Christianity, and they need to work. With the exception of the references to Christianity these instructions could almost be taken from texts describing the very similar efforts of the Romans in respect of the colonization of Europe.[48]

As with the 1573 *Ordenanzas* concerning the founding of new towns, many of the underlying implications of the theory of *reducciones* only became explicit at a relatively late date. One of the clearest and most detailed accounts of how to resettle the Indians and of the form the new settlements should take was written in 1567 by Juan de Matienzo. Matienzo held the post of *oidor* or judge in the province of the Charcas in the south of the Peruvian Viceroyalty. In other words he had a great deal of personal experience of America and of the Indians and he includes many more practical details than does any document emanating from Spain. His tract concerns the government of Peru, how it had been organized under the Incas (whom he considers to have been tyrants), how it is at present organized by the Spaniards, and how the situation can be improved, 'in order to preserve the land, and so that the Indians can be *aprovechados* [here with the sense of both 'improved' and 'made use of'] both in the spiritual and the temporal'.[49] He includes a long section on the need for *reducciones* and the way these could be organized because, he argues,

> no-one is unaware of the disadvantages to having the Indians living scattered about, hidden in caves and ravines, both as regards their *policía* and their conversion, because they can neither be proselytized nor be true men unless they are gathered together in pueblos; and on this matter there is no need for further explanations beyond those known to everyone.[50]

'Known to everyone.' He does not feel it necessary to justify the need for *reducciones*. To him and to his presumed readership the relationship between living in towns, becoming Christians and even becoming *true men* is quite clear. He advised that a Spanish inspector, the *visitador*, be responsible for choosing a suitable site, and that he should reckon on around five hundred Indians per settlement. The settlement should be laid out in squares or blocks, with wide streets and with a plaza in the middle and Matienzo is unusual in that he includes a plan of the ideal lay-out. The blocks are divided into plots or *solares*, usually four plots to one block. The church should overlook the plaza, preferably on the side which is best protected from the winds. The other blocks opening on to the square should be reserved for a lodging house for travelling Spaniards, for the council offices which should have a corral for stray animals behind them, and for a hospital with an adjoining orchard as well as for houses for the resident Spanish official, the *corregidor*, and for the priest, and it is clear from the plan, although not from the text, that the prison should also occupy a *solar* on the square. The remaining plots overlooking the square including, probably, those at the corners, should be for the houses of any other Spaniards who wished to live amongst the Indians. The traditional local chief was to be given either a whole block or two *solares* depending on the size of the population; presumably the more people in the town the more important he was, and therefore the larger the plot he deserved. All the important buildings, the church, the council offices and the houses for Spaniards should have tiled roofs. Matienzo's stated reason for this is that tile is more secure against fire than the traditional thatch, but no doubt he would also have felt it indecorous to roof important buildings in an inferior material, and tile would have an added advantage in that the centres of colonial control, both ecclesiastical and secular, positioned at the heart of the new settlement around the central square, would have been visually distinguishable from the surrounding Indian housing.

As with the instructions to the Hieronymites fifty years earlier, Matienzo is not concerned solely with the overall lay-out of the new settlement, but also with familial arrangements. His plan would imply houses with a square or rectangular plan and he specifies that changes should be made to the internal organization of the Indians' houses. These should have two or three separate rooms so that parents may sleep away from their children – Matienzo and others regarded this as an essential precondition for a civilized existence, contemporary European practice notwithstanding – and the front door of each house should open on to the street so that their activities could be monitored. As with earlier instructions, the *visitador* is required to see to it that the Indians do not sleep on the floor, but on beds.[51]

The appearance of such detailed instructions for Indian *reducciones* at this date and from such a source may, like Philip II's *Ordenanzas* in 1573, represent the general strengthening of Royal authority in colonial matters. Matienzo was a secular government official and it seems likely that he was anxious to stake out a claim and an authority for the Crown in the matter of reductions, to counteract the power of the Church. With the consolidation of colonial rule there was increasing unease amongst secular authorities about the strength and autonomy of the religious institutions especially with regard to the organization and control of Indian populations, and Matienzo's instructions are for *reducciones* effected by secular authorities. Although the earlier instructions from the Crown, such as those to the Hieronymites in 1516, make it clear that *reducciones* should be under the supervision of both a secular and an ecclesiastical authority, in practice the Church was often the sole European representative in rural areas. Matienzo stresses that the resident secular authority is to have a responsibility for overseeing the behaviour of the Indians equal to that of the priest. Matienzo was later to accompany Viceroy Toledo on his extensive tour of the Viceroyalty during the early 1570s and must have helped to shape Toledo's famous instructions concerning *reducciones* which were issued, appropriately enough, in 1573, the year in which Philip's *Ordenanzas* appeared.[52] Toledo was the champion of royal authority in Peru, of secular government over the Church and, where necessary, of the Diocesan church over the regular orders and I shall return to the practical results of his instructions in the following chapter.

Within the Church itself, while the increasing power of the Crown was seen as a potential threat, the internal rivalries became more pronounced as the century progressed. The Diocesan church was beginning to get nervous about the power of the regular orders in outlying communities. The initial conversion of Indians, of which reduction was considered a preliminary, was undertaken largely by the mendicant orders who were not answerable to the local Bishop. Matienzo's instructions for *reducciones* are closely paralleled by some directives issued by the Diocesan church's Third Ecclesiastical Council of Lima in 1583. These instruct that local parish priests must do all they can to ensure that the Indians, having left off

> their barbarous and savage customs, should be made to live in an orderly fashion, with civilized habits such as not going to church dirty and dishevelled, but washed and smart and clean, and the women covering their heads . . . and having in their houses tables to eat at and beds to sleep in, and having their houses resemble in their orderliness, cleanliness, good repair, etc. the dwellings of men not sheep pens.[53]

It is surely not coincidental that at the same time these sentiments can be found amongst those supporting the missionary orders. A Franciscan friar who worked at the task of reducing Indians in Mexico as a preliminary to his work of conversion is described in a chronicle of about 1571 in these same terms. He

> persuaded them to leave the wild and mountainous regions where they lived, and to transfer themselves lower down where the terrain was less hilly, more fertile and fresh. Here he founded orderly cities, and *thus made their inhabitants worthy of being called men*, while they were not so where they had been living before, scattered far from one another.[54]

Whether the motivating force is the Crown or the Church the issues are by now very clear. The *reducción* is above all a method of control and the rivalry between the different power groups is about who is going to exert such control, not about the means or the end product. About this there is complete agreement. The later sixteenth-century instructions concerning *reducciones* are an amplification of earlier ones: the benefits to the Indians come to include not only civility and Christianity, but also *humanity*. Only when reduced will they be worthy of being called *true men*. This may be implied in the earlier instructions, but only with the consolidation of colonial rule and the concomitant decline in power and status of the Indian groups does this become explicit.

The contexts in which Matienzo's instructions for Indian *reducciones* and Philip II's *Ordenanzas* for Spanish towns appeared would seem ostensibly to be very different. Matienzo's advice is based on his personal experience of America and of the Indians, the *Ordenanzas* are based on Vitruvius and classical architectural theory, but the overall results are very similar. They are both, ultimately, derived from the same sets of basic assumptions with which Spaniards on both sides of the Atlantic were working. All the various instructions, whether for Spanish or for Indian towns, and regardless of the rivalry between the different colonial factions, all use the same vocabulary, the same basic concepts. By the later sixteenth century the general assumptions about the benefits of an orderly urban existence are becoming more clearly articulated, and are perhaps also more clearly formulated in the minds of the colonists. The result, as far as questions of town planning are concerned, is that by 1573 there is no doubt that the grid plan was the desirable form for the towns of both Spaniards and Indians because it was the visible manifestation of ordered Christian society.

These general attitudes can be confirmed and further amplified from a variety of other sources. As we have seen, visitors to America considered the pre-hispanic towns and buildings in terms of how far they did or did not conform to European ideals, and not surprisingly, they described the new colonial towns from the same point of view. The subsequent chapters involve a more detailed discussion of what was built and of how far it conformed to these ideals, but a few examples of the sorts of responses which colonial architecture and town planning evoked are appropriate to the present discussion. In 1526 Oviedo described the town of Santo Domingo on Española, which had been founded in 1502, as 'far ahead of all the towns I have seen': many of the houses were of stone, and

the streets are so much smoother and so straight. Because it was founded in our time ... it was laid out with rule and compass, with all the streets of the same size in which regard they are far ahead of other towns I have seen.[55]

For Oviedo this makes Santo Domingo a town unmistakably 'founded in our time', and yet at the same time 'far ahead of other towns I have seen'. This apparent paradox arises from the conflation of the ideal and the real. Santo Domingo corresponds to Oviedo's *idea* of an orderly town rather than to the realities of towns he knows, but as with Cobo, he assumes that the reader will understand his meaning: the idea has been realized in Santo Domingo. It is worth adding that the things which Oviedo admires – the houses of stone, streets that are smooth and straight, a regular plan – these are the same features which Pedro Sancho admires in Inca Cuzco, but neither he nor any of the other commentators could have perceived or described it in these terms.

Cervantes de Salazar's famous description of 1554 of the new colonial Mexico City is much more detailed than Oviedo on Santo Domingo, and more scholarly – it is presented in the form of a Latin dialogue and refers explicitly to Vitruvius – but the categories are by now familiar. Tacuba Street, we are told, arouses the imagination of the European visitor, the wide-eyed enquirer in Salazar's dialogue:

how long it is, how wide! How straight, how level it is! And the whole street is paved with stones to prevent its becoming muddy and filthy in the rainy season.[56]

In this case it is not just the streets and the lay-out which impress the visitor but also the style of the architecture. The houses are especially praised for their uniformity, and for their grand stone portals. Various buildings are singled out for particular attention because of their splendour, their good proportions, and their use of columns and classical mouldings. 'See how artistically the architraves have been made', says one of the guides of the royal palace, disingenuously.[57] The cathedral, on the other hand, is deplored for its humble and unadorned appearance, for its *lack* of all the right qualities; it is considered a quite inappropriate building for the most important church in so rich a city.[58]

Commentators always have such standards in mind. A document of 1585 appealing for funds for the monastery of Santo Domingo in Tunja, Colombia, described part of it as still without a vaulted roof and without mouldings, *sin bóveda y sin molduras*, a situation which must have been considered appallingly indecorous because the combination of these two elements, vaulting and classical mouldings, was felt to be fundamental to civilized architecture.[59] On the other hand, the hospital of San Andrés in Lima received fulsome praise in 1563 precisely because of the richness of its mouldings. The main portal of the hospital church, for example, was

beautifully worked in brick, and made up entirely of mouldings *al romano* [in the classical style] with four columns set against four pilasters, beautifully marbled, and within the niches between them were painted the four Cardinal Virtues.[60]

Towns are judged by the degree to which they conform to these standards of overall orderliness, straight streets, spacious plazas and substantial brick and stone houses with proper portals. Towns without order were scarcely considered towns, churches of straw and mud not really churches at all. I shall return to some of these points in the next chapter.

## Summary

All the various sources, the chronicles of Inca history, the descriptions of indigenous and of colonial art and architecture, the official decrees and reports, all use the same vocabulary. The same words and phrases recur over and again: the presence or absence of *arte*, of splendour, order, good proportions, of columns and arches and architectural mouldings, of a proper *traza* either of a town or a substantial building, laid out *a cordel y regla*, and so on. In Spanish towns these are signs of civility, of *policía*; in an Indian town they are desirable because they are the means by which civility is to be achieved.

This powerful desire for conformity to a particular pattern must at least in part account for what would otherwise appear a deeply contradictory aspect of the contemporary accounts of the Spanish colonization of America. Despite the detailed descriptions of indigenous American cultures, and despite the degree of civility even in European terms to which many of them had attained, in the official legislation concerning the foundation of towns in America these achievements seem to have been almost entirely ignored. Las Casas, like many others with first-hand experience of the New World, believed that:

One does not require witnesses from heaven to demonstrate that these were political peoples, with towns, inhabited places of large size, villas, cities and communities.[61]

But from reading the official correspondence and royal mandates, the impression one gets is that America was if not quite virgin territory, at least only populated by wild and disorganized natives. This sharp divide between the theoretical and the actual state of affairs is exemplified in the case of Mexico City. In 1520 Cortés himself had informed the Crown in detail of the size and splendour of the Aztec capital and of the political organization of the inhabitants. In 1522 he reversed his earlier decision to found a capital elsewhere and began rebuilding the city, 'because it was so renowned and so important'. The Crown's response was to reissue the simple directions originally sent to Pedrarias Dávila in 1513 which I discussed earlier; there is no mention of the Aztec city and the implication is that Cortés was starting from scratch, in an empty landscape. The first reports from the New World concerned the relatively simple, non-urbanized peoples of the Caribbean, and therefore, given the European ideas on cities and civility it is understandable that at this stage Europeans should have stressed the importance of founding orderly towns. The extent and complexity of the Aztec Empire and in particular of its capital city posed problems of a different order, but problems which from this point of view the Spanish Crown ignored, or simply did not recognize.

The tenor of the legislation dealing with the settlement of America and the organization of the native populations remained predominantly patronizing in tone throughout the sixteenth century, despite the efforts of some officials with considerable practical experience and knowledge of the indigenous peoples to push for a reintroduction of a degree of autonomy and self-determination in Indian affairs.[62] It was much easier, from an official point of view, to see the Indians as a unified body, all equally uncivilized and in need of careful, disciplined socialization, like children.[63] The need to organize the Indians into towns as a prerequisite for educating them into a civil state, and the need to oversee all aspects of their lives are constantly stressed, regardless of their existing social or political structures or the size and complexity of the settlements within which they lived. To admit that they often already lived in towns and in highly ordered societies would be to undermine this comfortable, self-satisfied stance, a stance which becomes clearer and more pronounced as the century proceeds.

The general ideas about civility, urbanism and the Art of Architecture with which this chapter has been concerned certainly have their roots in the classical tradition but only in some cases is the connection direct. The important point is that they were not held exclusively by a handful of scholars and intellectuals who helped, for example, to shape the King's instructions to would-be colonists, or who guided the eye and the pen of writers such as Cieza de León. Some writers referred directly to Vitruvius or Aristotle to give weight to their accounts, to demonstrate their learning, to re-emphasize the essentially European-ness of their values and opinions, and so on; but the general attitudes were those of society as a whole, and were not based on particular theories nor on specific existing patterns. The first permanent foundations of European culture were laid in America by a heterogeneous group of people, unified perhaps above all in their comparative lack of a classical education, but a group which nevertheless had clear ideas about what for them constituted culture, their culture, and, when the crunch came, about its superiority to all others.

The 1573 *Ordenanzas* contain a ruling which suggests the almost magical powers which it was believed the right sort of architecture and the right sort of town would have over the indigenous population.

While the new settlement is being completed, the settlers should as far as possible try to avoid communication and trade with the Indians, and should not go to their villages, nor should they amuse themselves nor disperse themselves about the country, nor should they let the Indians into the confines of the settlement until it is completed and fortified, and the houses built, so that when the Indians do see it they are amazed, and they understand that the Spaniards are settling there permanently and not temporarily, and they will fear them and will not dare offend them, and they will respect them and wish to have their friendship.[64]

This can never have been intended as a serious, practicable recommendation: the Spanish settlers would not have considered building their houses and defences themselves when there was Indian labour available; neither, in fact, would the Crown have expected them to do so. What this passage shows, however, is the strength of the idea, and the extent to which it was believed that towns and buildings (and the implication, of course, is European-style towns and buildings) were capable of playing an active part in the ideological conquest of the Indians: it is assumed that Spanish towns will be so obviously superior and imposing that, almost despite themselves, the Indians will be awed into submission. In the quotation from Bernabé Cobo with which I opened this chapter we can recognize this same supreme confidence in these apparently absolute values, the values of *nuestra traza* and of classical architecture. Cobo does not doubt that his readers will know exactly what he means, and that the Indians will recognize the superiority of these values when they see them.

# 2
# First foundations

To have an ideal vision of what the new colonies should be was one thing; to live up to it was another. To build the towns, houses and churches that were considered generally desirable was in practice neither easy nor straightforward – not even the most detailed of the theories extended to cover the practicalities – but there was never any doubt but that the Spanish settlers were going to found towns. The Crown and the Council of the Indies urge it as a duty, while the conquistadors and colonists reiterate that it is their desire, and regularly describe their progress towards that end. Prospective colonists, whether or not they came from urban environments in Spain, saw America as their chance to live out an ideal of civic orderliness.[1] This ideal has always been especially strong in Spain unlike, say, England or France or Italy, where at least semi-permanent country life is often a deliberate choice even amongst the rich and powerful. In America this Spanish taste for city life was exaggerated (even though, from an economic point of view, it was largely inappropriate)[2] and founding towns was always a first priority – towns, that is, for Spaniards not for Indians. It is a measure of their success that the peasantry in Latin America remains predominantly of non-European blood.[3]

## The Act of Foundation

If prescriptive sources concerning the practicalities of establishing a new Spanish town are brief and vague there is nevertheless approximate agreement between descriptive sources about the events which went to make up a *Foundation*. In this the foundation of towns in Spanish America provides an interesting and not untypical example of the interplay between the generally-held concepts discussed in the previous chapter and the means by and extent to which such ideas were realized. Only those with Royal authorization could found towns – Francisco Pizarro in Peru, Belalcázar and

Gonzalo Jiménez de Quesada in the New Kingdom of Granada – although in practice they sometimes authorized others to do so in their names.[4] There were usually several stages.[5] The formal inspection and choice of site was followed by a ritual Act of Possession (there was never any question but that it was appropriated, that the land had belonged to someone else) after which the squares, streets and blocks were laid out and construction could begin. The new residents usually seem to have moved in whenever convenient, so that the settlement was often populated before there was a formal Act of Foundation. This ritual Act of Foundation itself involved a dedicatory mass in a newly erected church or at least on its proposed site, and also a secular ceremony, which usually involved the symbolic instigation of secular justice together with the actual formation of the first town council or *cabildo* by the appointment of the necessary officials. Neither the sequence nor the various accompanying rituals are the same in every case; the moment at which the town is actually planned and laid out is often unclear, and the word *fundar* is used to mean both the general process and the official inauguration.

Take the case of Bogotá. I am not concerned here with archaeology or with precise historical realities, which in this case are very complicated, but with the way the events were perceived and described.[6] According to Pedro Simón the site of the future city of Santa Fé de Bogotá was determined by Gonzalo Jiménez de Quesada in 1538. He chose a place where the land appeared fertile, and where there were abundant supplies of water, wood, stone and '*buenos aires*', all of which accords with the general instructions that had been issued from the earliest years of the discovery. Simón then relates that Quesada

> dismounted from his horse, pulled up some grass and strode about, saying that he took possession of the site and land in the name of the invincible Emperor Charles V, his Lord, to found there a city in his name; and then mounting his horse, he drew his sword, demanding that anyone who would contradict this foundation should step forward, because he intended to found it with his arms and horse. When no-one opposed him he sheathed his sword.[7]

The ceremony was then recorded by the scribe and signed by witnesses although the document itself does not survive. This procedure may sound a little haphazard but Simón does not suggest that it was anything other than a formal and solemn occasion.[8] The origins of possession rituals are unclear – few conquerors could have had much experience of founding towns before their arrival in America, and there is certainly no guidance in the various official instructions concerning the foundation of towns, but nevertheless there appears to have been a general consensus about what was involved. In Buenos Aires in 1580, for example, the formal Act of Possession only took place after the town plan had been drawn up, but the ceremony was similar. In sign of possession the founder Juan de Garay unsheathed his sword, brandished it about and cut some grass, requiring that anyone who opposed the possession should step forward.[9] Simón's version of the sequence of events after the Act of Possession of Bogotá is that the Spaniards immediately marked out plots for twelve *bohíos de paja*, houses of straw in the local style. The ceremony may have been imposing but the founding fathers could not afford to be architecturally ambitious at this stage and straw houses were better than nothing. A prime plot was designated for the church, which was constructed of straw like the houses, and then, when all the buildings were complete, the first mass was said in the new church on 6 August 1538, the day of the Transfiguration.[10] There was no separate foundation ceremony in Bogotá at this time; the town was probably formally founded the following year.[11]

A few years earlier Francisco Pizarro had formally taken possession of the Inca capital of Cuzco and had founded the Spanish town with another ceremony in which possession and foundation were elided.

To mark the foundation I am making and possession I am taking, today, Monday, 23 March 1534, on this *picota* which I ordered to be built a few days ago in the middle of this square, on its stone steps which are not yet finished, using this dagger which I carry in my belt, I carve a knot from the wood of the *picota* so that all of you present may see. I also perform all the other required acts of possession and rites of foundation of this city ... giving as name to this town I have founded, the most noble and great city of Cuzco.[12]

To symbolize possession by grabbing a handful of grass in the central square of Cuzco would have been inappropriate (even if there were any grass around which is doubtful) so Pizarro demonstrates his rights over the place by cutting pieces from a new, central monument – the *picota* – to which I shall return shortly. As with the possession of the sites of Bogotá and Buenos Aires the ceremony sounds in some ways an *ad hoc* sort of affair, but the basic ritual function is clear.

The records of foundation ceremonies, where they are distinct from possession, make them sound less theatrical presumably because foundation was essentially a legal rather than a ritual act. Foundation was intended to signify the instigation of both ecclesiastical and secular power and although

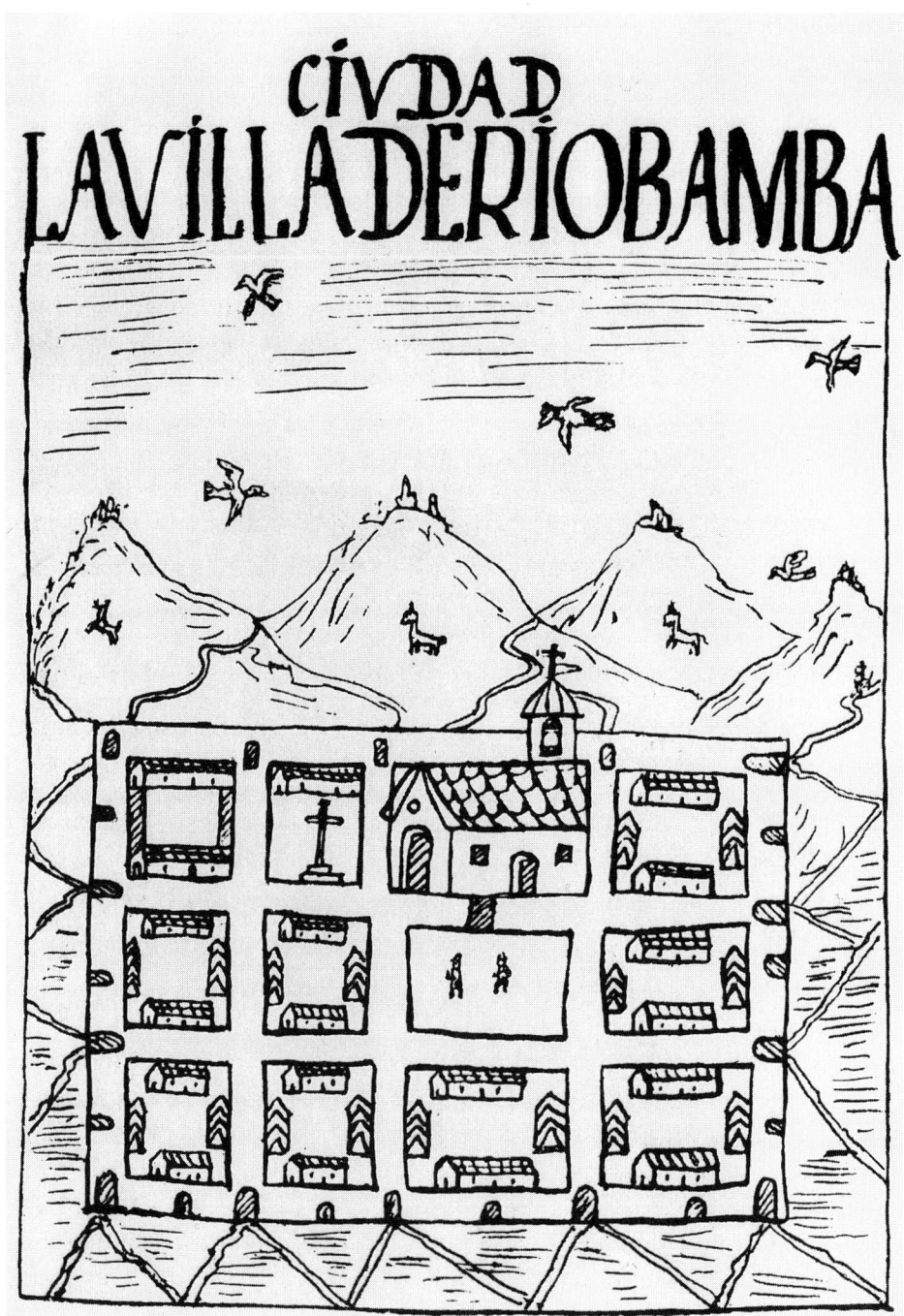

Plate 11 Plan of Riobamba, from Guaman Poma de Ayala, *Nueva Corónica*, p.995.

no doubt often performed in a highly ceremonial fashion, it existed beyond the ceremony itself, and as such could be adequately recorded by a scribe in the simplest of terms. In Arequipa, for example, the town was founded on Pizarro's behalf on 20 July 1540. The acting founder

set up the cross on the site which had been designated for the church, and he also set up the *picota* on the plaza of the said town.[13]

To erect a cross or lay a few symbolic foundation stones on the site of the future church, the *iglesia mayor*, of the town was of prime importance. Pizarro founded Lima on 18 January 1535, and in the record of the Act the order of events is clear.

And since the beginning of whatever town or city has to be in God and for God and in his name ... it is fitting to begin it with his church. He began the foundation and *traza* of the said city and named the church Nuestra Señora de la Asunción, to whom it was dedicated ... After he had marked out the plaza he made and built the said church, and placed with his hands the first stone and the first timbers ... And then he divided up the *solares* [plots] between the citizens, as will be seen on the plan of the said city which has been made.[14]

So in Pizarro's foundation of Lima the church and the *traza* of the new town go together; they are in fact inseparable. The main church in colonial Spanish American towns is always situated on the central plaza. This plaza is almost invariably square and so its dimensions determine the size of the blocks of the grid plan, the *cuadras* or *manzanas*. The width of the streets is also determined at the outset, at the central square. Each *manzana* can be divided into four equal plots (*solares*), the church usually being accorded two *solares* or half a block, either laterally along the whole of one side of the central square, as in Puebla in Mexico, or Quito, and as in many early plans (Plate 11), or with a frontage of half a block, so that the west portal opens on to the square, as for example in Trujillo, Ayacucho or Tunja (Plate 12). Once the church had been positioned, sites for other important buildings – the town hall (the *cabildo*), the governor's residence and so on were determined, either on or near to the square; monastic foundations were usually provided with sites a few blocks away from the central square.

This pattern is the norm in early Spanish American town foundations although the various royal ordinances concerning the foundation and lay-out of new towns are not the source of such unanimity. Those from the earlier part of the century are entirely non-specific, while the much fuller *Ordenanzas* of 1573 do not always correspond closely to American practice. There is, for

Plate 12 Lima, Plaza de Armas. View of the Cathedral and the Archbishop's Palace.

example, internal disagreement within the *Ordenanzas* about the position of the *iglesia mayor*, about whether or not it should be situated on the main square although there never seem to have been any doubts in practice.[15] More importantly, perhaps, the *Ordenanzas* do not recommend the square central plaza but, following Vitruvius, they recommend a rectangle with sides of a 2:3 ratio.[16] The conquerors' preference for a square plaza is, I feel, not simply a natural spill-over from the traditions of the military encampment – the conquerors were always self-consciously founding towns, not military bases. Even in the latter, but certainly in the former it is the sense of the historic significance of what they were doing that matters most, not mere pragmatism.[17] The grid plan is certainly the easiest and so the quickest form to draw up but, and much more importantly, a plan based on a square is unmistakably orderly both physically and conceptually.[18] A grid plan based on a square can be extended regularly without need for further planning decisions. With a rectangular central plaza there would always be questions about how to extend the town, how big to make the blocks in, for example, the areas extending from the corners of the plaza, and where to place the streets. The positioning of the church on the main square, too, is inherently orderly, both spatially and ideologically, and also in terms of the initial ceremonies of foundation. Both Church and State are represented at the heart of the new town, founded together at the same time and in the same place.

## The *picota*

Ecclesiastical authority was formally instigated by the erection of a cross either on the site proposed for the *iglesia mayor* or in the main square. The instigation of civil government was symbolized by the erection of a pillar of justice, most commonly termed the *picota*, but also known as the *rollo*, or more rarely the *cuchillo*. The exact function of this monument in the Possession or Foundation ceremonies seems to vary. When Pizarro took formal possession of Cuzco he did so by cutting a knot from the wooden *picota* which had previously been set up on some stone steps. A few years later, in 1541, Mariscal Robledo's foundation of the town of Santa Ana de los Caballeros in central Colombia (now called Anserma) included setting a tree trunk in a deep hole in the main square; he then struck it several times with his sword, unchallenged.[19] In Buenos Aires in 1580 justice was formally instituted as the *picota* (here called the *rollo* and Tree of Justice) was erected in the square, and Garay solemnly declared that death would be the punishment to anyone who struck it, moved it, or tore it down.[20] Some such symbolic monument was expected in a new Spanish town. Pedro Simón considered the foundation of Bogotá by Jiménez de Quesada to have been inadequate precisely because he did not erect either a *picota* or gallows.[21] Conversely, a *picota* could not be abandoned: if for some reason the site of a town had to be moved after its formal foundation, then the *picota* was carried to the new site and ceremoniously re-erected.[22]

Once the town was founded the *picota* often came not only to symbolize justice but also to demonstrate its execution, serving as the town pillory, and in some cases even as the gallows. In 1541, for example, the Ayacucho cabildo decreed that Indians should not work during the night (for fear of disturbances) and the penalty for non-compliance was a hundred lashes *en la picota*.[23] Guaman Poma illustrates the administration of Spanish justice with a drawing of a half-naked Indian tied to a masonry column, being whipped. In the text this structure is referred to as the *rollo*.[24] Sometimes the foundation of a town and instigation of justice is marked by the erection of both a *picota* and *horca*, gallows, as was the case in Cáceres, Honduras.[25]

Few *picotas* survive today. Indeed most of them probably disappeared relatively early on because once justice was well-established and, for example, a prison had been constructed, then the *picota* was rendered redundant. In

Plate 13 Chucuito, Plaza de Armas. The *picota* or *rollo*, now converted into a sundial; 1567.

Lima, for example, the *picota* erected by Pizarro in the main square in 1535 was moved to the entrance of the city in the early 1560s where perhaps it continued to serve its purpose in attenuated form, demonstrating to visitors the justice to be found within the city limits.[26] There is no record of what this particular *picota* looked like but we can assume it was a standing pillar of wood or stone. Many documents refer to the *picota* as a tree trunk but early town plans often show it as a classical stone column.[27] A stone *picota* still stands in the main square of Chucuito and consists of a truncated fluted column shaft set up on some stone steps which, although it has been converted into a sundial, is still referred to locally as the *rollo*[28] (Plate 13). It is possible that the wooden tree trunk used in many of the initial ceremonies was subsequently replaced with a stone version shortly afterwards, but because early town plans show the *picota* as a classical column this suggests that this was how it was envisaged even if in practice it was not always achieved (Plate 14). It is surely not coincidental that one of the iconographic accretions to the bare Gospel story that Pilate had Christ flogged, is that Christ was tied to a classical column, a pillar of justice, representing Roman law.

The *picota* and the cross were the first permanent symbols of Spanish control, of the introduction of *orden y justicia* into the territory. The choice of the classical column, the central element of the classical architectural system, is wholly appropriate in this context. The general theoretical connections which the Spaniards regularly made between classical architecture, civility, order and justice would thus be manifested in the *picota* itself.

As with the rituals associated with possession and foundation, the origins of the *picota* are obscure, but are probably very ancient. They are not necessarily even European: in Inca Peru an upright stone in the centre of a square, called an *usnu*, was a symbol of justice and in Cuzco at least it seems to have been directly replaced by the *picota*.[29] But this was not the first use of the *picota* in America and in any case, and for reasons that will become clear in due course, it seems highly unlikely that the Spaniards would simply borrow an Amerindian form outright unless they were predisposed towards it in some way. In the *Critias* Plato describes how in the Temple of Poseidon, at the centre of Atlantis, a column was placed on which the laws were engraved and at which the ten kings gathered to discuss the government of the island and the administration of justice.[30] This is suggestive but unusual. The *gnomon* which Vitruvius proposes in the centre of a new foundation is designed to calculate the directions of the winds, not to symbolize justice. In dealing with the foundations of towns or cities Vitruvius and indeed most classical authors

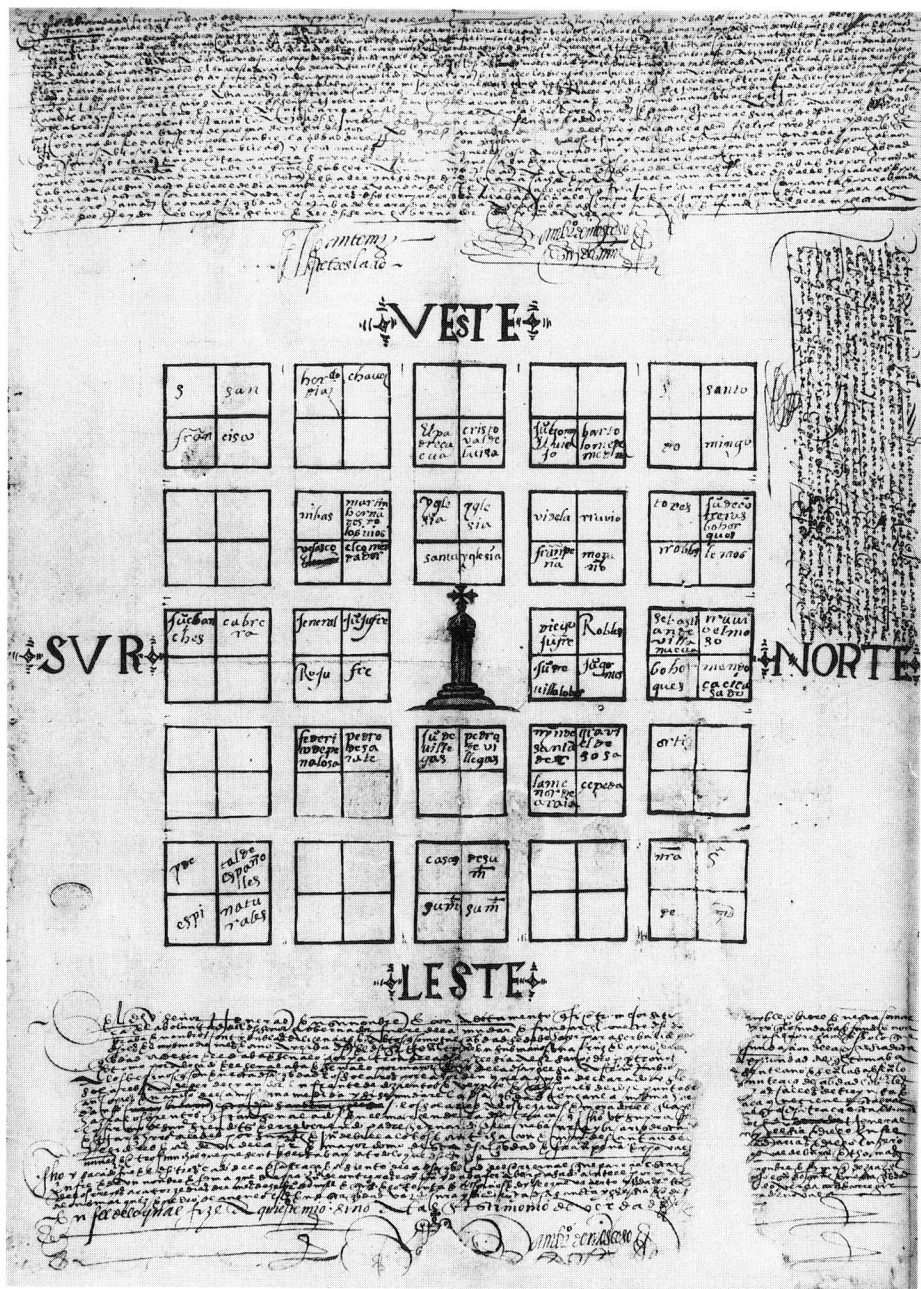

Plate 14 Plan of Mendoza, Argentina, 1562, showing the *picota* in the form of a classical column in the centre. The surrounding blocks are quartered, with the names of the settlers inscribed on some of them. The cathedral is positioned on the square with further churches in what at this point are the corners of the town.

are much more concerned with defining the outer limits, with the boundaries, walls, gates and *sulcus* of a new town than with identifying a ritual centre. Similarly, in the ideal town plans of Renaissance architectural theorists, it is the outline, the geometrical shape, which defines the town and which is to be formed by its walls, that is of supreme importance.[31] In the foundation of a new town in America it is never its limitation which is important; it is the centre, the point from which the new colony will grow and from which its influence will spread that matters. There are other possible sources for the *picota*. Kubler notes the use in Castile of classicizing columns called *rollos*, but again these were traditionally erected not in the centre of a town but on the edges, as boundary markers.[32] Various sorts of stone, especially upright stones marking a centre and a periphery, have been used in Europe since prehistoric times, and a centrally-placed mark stone – at a crossroads, for example – was sometimes the site of open-air courts or other aspects of the administration of secular justice.[33]

But none of these seem sufficient to explain the appearance of the *picota* in America. In fact the term only really occurs once it already exists, once it is a *fait accompli*. In other words, although the roots of the use of the *picota* no doubt lie far back in European semi-mythic history, there is no tidy line of descent down through an intellectual élite who can then be seen or even supposed to have reformulated and revitalized the tradition on behalf of the conquerors. The conquerors themselves dig the tradition out of their own consciousness and put it into practice. The practice evokes only the most cursory of explanations or justifications from those who record it, at least before the later sixteenth century, but its almost universal occurrence in early town foundations suggests most forcibly that all concerned knew what a *picota* was, why it was needed, where it should be placed, and in general what it should look like. Significantly, unlike some other aspects of the foundation of towns in America, the *picota* does not even receive the retrospective sanction of inclusion in the 1573 *Ordenanzas*; the authorities in Spain remain silent on the issue of a monument to civic justice.[34]

This tidy sequence – the selection of the site, and the formal acts of possession and of foundation, the symbolic institution of both ecclesiastical and secular juridical power, with the attendant delineation of the town plan – does not always marry with the actual facts. Often towns were already populated, and therefore to some degree planned, before the official foundation, or sometimes, as in the case of Buenos Aires, even before the official possession.[35] Sometimes, although a town might be formally founded, it was recognized that the site, and the foundation, were provisional, as in the case of Jauja, the first capital of Peru.[36] In the case of Quito there were two foundations: the modern town of Riobamba was founded as the provincial capital with the name of Santiago de Quito, but was soon deemed unsuitable, and the present city, formerly the capital of the northern part of the Inca empire, was officially founded as San Francisco de Quito, even before the Spaniards had gained possession of the site itself. The Act of Foundation took place in Riobamba, as it were by proxy, Riobamba itself later sinking into relative obscurity as the definitive Quito grew.[37] In some cases a site was populated but never founded, as at San Gayán near Pisco, which was the intermediate site for the Peruvian capital between Jauja and Lima. According to Cobo the inhabitants of San Gayán had to move up the coast to Lima after they had already made hundreds of adobes and had started to build their houses.[38] This was not a period of stability and permanence. In the circumstances it is all the more astonishing that so many towns were successfully founded, and that they all conformed so closely to the same pattern.

Once a site had been accepted as convenient in general terms, what factors conditioned the precise location of the central square and the church? The Acts of Possession or Foundation and the various other contemporary records all either fail to mention altogether or leave very understated the fact that in the majority of cases the site chosen was not virgin territory at all: in effect these Acts almost always constituted the ritual appropriation and reconsecration of an existing indigenous settlement. Cuzco, of course, is a major exception, just as Mexico City had been: no-one could have pretended or indeed would have wanted to pretend that the Spanish city had not been grafted on to the fabulous Inca capital, but even in this case there is a curious contradictory ring to the official documentation. Pizarro took possession of the city, as we have seen, on the steps of the *picota*. The Acts of Possession and Foundation are elided, and he appropriated a large Inca hall, a *galpón*, on the main square, to serve as the church. The following day he appointed the members of the *cabildo*. This is followed, extraordinarily, by the official division of the city into equal blocks and *solares* irrespective of where the existing Inca houses and palaces began and ended.[39] This could never have been perceived as anything much more than a theoretical plan; in effect the various existing buildings were distributed to particular conquistadors. In the same document Pizarro advised that building materials be taken only from unoccupied palaces and storehouses, and that inhabited housing should be allowed to remain intact, in the hands of the indigenous owners. The result was that although many of the buildings were wholly or partially rebuilt, especially after the Inca rebellion in 1536 in which the city was almost burned to the ground, the lay-out of the centre has not changed substantially since the days of the Incas (*see* plate 8). It is a grid plan, but not the perfectly regular grid Pizarro had in mind. Lizárraga is one of the few early commentators who was not impressed by Cuzco: he felt that it lacked the order and regularity necessary for a city, and in this he was criticizing the Inca plan which did not quite conform to the European ideal.[40]

In a great many other cases the appropriation of an existing Indian town or village seems to have been the normal procedure, especially in those areas where there was a substantial Indian population as in the territories of the Inca and Chibcha peoples, but the early official records are almost entirely silent about this. In the record of the foundation of Lima, for example, mention of an existing Indian settlement occurs only as a preliminary to the Act of Foundation, in a passage describing the search for a suitable site. The three officials sent to reconnoitre the lands of the local lord, the *curaca* of Lima, testify that they walked for six days throughout the land around the *pueblo* of Lima and ended up deciding that much the best spot was the chief's own seat, the *pueblo* itself (as always, the term *pueblo* could mean anything from a small village to a good sized town). All the usual reasons are given for this choice – there is plenty of wood and water and arable land, it is close to a good seaport, it is breezy and healthy (it is an old joke in Lima that they would not have chosen the site had they not visited it in January – from March to December the climate on this part of the coast is humid and heavily overcast) and because the Indians who would have to work in the new city to serve the citizens would not be put to much trouble because they are already in the vicinity.[41] The Act of Foundation itself gives no hint that Pizarro is standing in the middle of one of a group of several not inconsiderable townships. Bernabé Cobo, writing about a hundred years later, refers to this quite openly:

The city was positioned and laid out in accordance with the plan and drawing which had been executed on paper for this purpose in the same place as the Indian town called Lima, which was on the bank of the river on the south side, in the same situation and place (*sitio y lugar*) which the plaza and royal residences occupy today.[42]

It appears from the archaeological as well as from other documentary evidence that Lima was a substantial town and ritual centre and that both the orientation and general lay-out of the centre of the city were probably determined by existing adobe structures.[43] The *iglesia mayor* (soon to be elevated to a cathedral) was placed on an adobe pyramidal base, perhaps that of an Inca temple, the *plaza mayor* in front was already a plaza, and opposite the church was another indigenous structure involving a large adobe platform which Hernando Pizarro claimed for himself, and which later became the site of the *cabildo* and municipal offices (which it still is). Other evidence supports Cobo's assertion that there were other structures along the north side of the square towards the river, the site assigned for the royal residences. In practice the precise grid plan of the Spanish foundation seems only to have been imposed gradually over these, and over some other buildings slightly to the west; the central square and the siting of the main colonial buildings as well as the orientation of the streets would therefore appear to be derived from the Indian town.

Pedro Simón's account of Jiménez de Quesada's dramatic Act of Possession of the site of Bogotá does not suggest that he was taking over anything other than a grassy plain, but again it is clear that there were numerous settlements in the area including the seat of the local chief. As in the case of Lima it was on this last that the Spaniards decided to settle themselves, and again, although the earlier sources are vague and imprecise, later ones are quite explicit. Alonso de Zamora's account from the end of the seventeenth century upsets the picture present in the earlier accounts, of Jiménez's tidy group of twelve brave straw houses (twelve according to Simón to stand for the twelve apostles; according to Juan de Castellanos, the twelve tribes of Israel).[44] In fact twelve was far too few to be more than symbolic; in practice there would have been no question but that the settlers would use other existing buildings too. Once the site had been deemed suitable, says Zamora, they founded the town with twelve large and spacious houses *amongst those belonging to the Indians*.[45]

Tunja was also founded on the site of the seat of the local chief.[46] The colonial town of Quito, after an abortive start in Riobamba, was refounded on the site of Incan Quito, which had been elevated to the status of northern capital of the empire by Huayna Capac.[47] Tumbes, Trujillo, Cajamarca, Ayacucho, Arequipa, La Paz and Sucre were all appropriated from the Indians and formally founded as Spanish towns. No detailed study has been done on this question, probably because in most cases the pre-conquest origins are obliterated, but also because many still consider these settlements not to have been towns at all, but conglomerations of insignificant huts, especially, of course, if they were built of mud.[48]

Within these new towns the positioning of key features was often related to the original spatial lay-out: the founders would utilize the main square, for example, and more particularly, the churches seem wherever possible to have been placed on the site of an indigenous focus of either worship or power, or

Plate 15 Quito, San Francisco; late sixteenth century. The whole complex – the church, the monastery buildings to the right and the subsidiary chapels to the left – was built on to the remains of the palace of the Inca Huayna Capac.

both. Again there is often a lack of specific reference to this practice especially in the early years of the conquest. In Lima, as has been mentioned, the cathedral site may have been a pre-hispanic temple; evidence of similar practice elsewhere would support this suggestion. Mexico City, where the cathedral and central square were placed over the religious heart of the Aztec city, is prototypical, but the extent of the temple complex has only become clear during the archaeological work of the past ten years or so. In Cuzco the conquistadors simply appropriated the Inca temple to Viracocha as their cathedral. In Quito the Franciscans were awarded the prime site in the newly laid-out town, that of Huayna Capac's palace. In this and in many other cases, the partially destroyed buildings served as good, solid foundations so that the church could be elevated above its surroundings, 'so that it can be more splendid and have greater authority', *por que se pueda ornar mejor y tenga más autoridad*, as the 1573 *Ordenanzas* were to put it; this is certainly achieved with San Francisco (Plate 15), as it is with perhaps the most famous of all such

Plate 16 Cuzco, Santo Domingo, with the curved Inca wall from the Inca temple of Coricancha supporting the apse of the church.

Plate 17 Jauja; remains of a small sixteenth-century chapel on Inca foundations. From Torres Saldamando [Lima Cabildo], *Libro primero*, II, Appendices, 2nd series, plate 183.

examples, that at Cholula in Mexico, although of course neither is as a result of the *Ordenanzas*. The church of San Juan Bautista at Vilcashuaman is positioned on the remains of an Inca temple of the Sun, and the church at Chincheros near Cuzco on the foundations of an Inca palace (*see* frontispiece). In these and in other examples within Inca territory there are sections of Inca masonry to prove the point, as there are at perhaps the most famous example of this practice in South America, the Dominican church and monastery in Cuzco, placed on the remains of Coricancha, the principal Inca temple to the Sun (Plate 16). In some cases the foundations were disproportionately large (Plate 17). There are many other cases where because the indigenous shrine or palace was constructed of materials which were less durable (and which the Spaniards disdained) no visible evidence remains apart from the suggestive elevation of the church above its immediate surroundings.

The only specific recommendation of the practice seems to be that which occurs in the directives issued by the first ecclesiastical council of Lima in

1551, where in the section about how to combat idolatry they passed the following ruling:

> We decree that all idols and sanctuaries in those villages where there are Christian Indians should be burnt and torn down; and if it is a fitting position a church should be built there, or at least a cross erected.[49]

This legislation is concerned with the suppression of idolatry within Indian villages, not with the design of Spanish towns, but the underlying motivations are not dissimilar. In the early sixteenth century the Spaniards built their towns on Indian towns, their churches on Indian temples, as a matter of course, without comment, and in so doing they effectively suppressed not only idolatry but native culture and society as well. It is left to later generations to rationalize the practice. In the seventeenth century the Dominican historian Juan Meléndez defends the particular case of Santo Domingo in Cuzco, and in so doing draws a reflected glory to Christianity for having appropriated such an important site. The rich temple and the adjoining royal apartments, he says, were given to the Dominicans so that

> what had been a shrine of the devils, and consecrated to their infamous cults, should be consecrated to the truth of our Lord and God.[50]

In the sixteenth century this may have been so obvious that no-one bothered to record the fact that this is what they were doing as they placed their church on the foundations of an Indian temple. But the positioning of a church on a temple was the result of positioning the Spanish town on an Indian town, and the apparent conspiracy of silence on this matter may be at least in part related to the whole prickly question of the Spaniards' right to conquer by force of arms.

Successive sovereigns, from Ferdinand and Isabella onwards, reiterate that the Spaniards must not inconvenience the native inhabitants in any way; they must not take anything, nor occupy any territories without the Indians' consent.[51] All parties concerned were probably more or less aware that this was idealistic, and indeed contrary to the interests of the Crown as well as the colonists; but it was preferable not to put the case explicitly, not to boast about their regular displacement of the Indians. Noam Chomsky has suggested a general historical principle by which 'every action of every State is claimed to be undertaken solely for defensive purposes and with awesome nobility of intent' but that in practice 'planning is generally rational in the short term and [that] its goals relate directly to the interests of those who own and manage the domestic economy and who employ state power to realise their interests' which are termed 'the national interest'.⁵² This was said particularly of US imperialism in the twentieth century, but is equally true of Spanish in the sixteenth. It was expedient to skate over the existence of large Indian towns full of civilized Indians, it was expedient to skirt round the Spanish appropriation of such towns, and it was expedient to appropriate them because not only did they provide temporary accommodation and a supply of Indian labour to hand, together with ready-made foundations for the new colonial buildings and a large, levelled central plaza, but also because once appropriated by the Spaniards they of course no longer existed as Indian towns. Once this was safely past history then it could be openly referred to, but not before.

To begin with, these newly-founded 'Spanish' towns would not have been recognizably very Spanish, and they were certainly a long way from the general Spanish concept of what a town ought to be like. They were, for a start, full of Indians and of Indian houses. The Indians were usually only slowly squeezed out, their style of housing, used by conquerors and conquered alike, was sometimes not replaced with European-style buildings with neatly matching stone frontages in a noble (i.e. classical) style for many years, even in the town centres. In many cases a permanent, suitably imposing *iglesia mayor* was not begun until the last years of the century. The grid plan might be drawn up on paper, and in practice perhaps a few divergent buildings around the central square would be pulled down, but beyond the centre the grid would only gradually have emerged as a visible reality.

A fundamental problem was the difficulty – once the glamour of the Act of Foundation was over – of keeping the new citizens in the town. The lure of the unexplored territories and the ever-present dream of El Dorado attracted settlers away from their dusty plots of land in the newly-founded towns. In some cases they were required to go and fight in the army of one of the various factions struggling for control over Peru during the middle years of the sixteenth century,⁵³ many died or were killed, many went on to settle in greener pastures, some even succeeded in making a fortune and returning to Spain. In 1536 a royal decree recognizing this problem was sent to Pizarro as governor of Peru:

We have been informed that those Spaniards who up until now have gone out to this province, as they neither had nor have any intention of living and settling there, but rather of accumulating a quantity of gold and silver with which to return to Spain so neither do they build houses in which to stay and live, from which cause not only has arisen and arises hindrance to the settlement of the said province, but also for this reason the instruction of the natives is not receiving the attention it requires.

Pizarro was accordingly ordered to see to it that the colonists build houses of stone, or at least of mud, in as durable a form as possible, and that they settle down and turn their attention to the instruction of the Indians.[54]

The early records for the city of Quito illustrate this aspect of Spanish colonization. The town council in 1539 records a series of requests from citizens to leave the city. On 14 June 1539 it was ruled that anyone who left the town without permission was liable to a fine of 50 pesos in gold.[55] On 13 September 1544 all absent citizens were required to return to Quito immediately,[56] and so on. One of the problems was the lack of family ties; Spanish women were few and far between,[57] and although those Spanish settlers who had wives in Spain were required to send for them as soon as they had established themselves in a new colonial town, the evidence suggests that either the men were unwilling to send for their wives, or the women were unwilling to leave Spain for the unknown Americas. In Quito in 1556, for example, a carpenter who had lived in the city for three years was fined for not having sent for his wife to come from Spain and join him.[58] As with so many of these little documentary details we cannot tell whether it was she who was unwilling to come, or he who was unwilling to send for her, nor do we know the outcome; all we can tell is that this was an area of concern for the colonial authorities.

As well as the lack of a family, another related disincentive to a settled lifestyle was the practical discomfort of incipient urban existence. After the excitement of the initial conquest is over the general impression of the formative years of a Spanish colonial town is one not of civility but of primitive conditions and often considerable hardship – worse, for many settlers, than the conditions in which they had been living in Spain, and worse than those of the majority of the Indians whom they were supplanting. In theory, as we have seen, it was all very fine. The Crown required that governors in Spanish America see to it that in all the new Spanish towns proper houses were constructed as soon as possible, ideally of stone and with tiled roofs, and such instructions were passed on by the various town councils to the citizens. The plots of land allotted to the first settlers were generous and were intended to provide space for stock, gardens and orchards as well as for the family house and housing for the servants, and for barns and stables, along the lines of a mediaeval Italian *palazzo*, but such a haven was not established overnight. In practice, town councils had difficulty getting settlers even to build walls around their plots, and there are repeated threats of forfeiture if the land is not at least enclosed within a certain time. In Arequipa, for example, in 1550, ten years after its formal foundation, the *cabildo* declared that 'those plots which are not yet built on should be enclosed within three months'.⁵⁹ This ruling had to be repeated word for word in 1556.⁶⁰ Even Lima, the Viceregal capital and so the focus of great political and mercantile activity, had problems with wayward settlers. In 1538 a decree ordered that each citizen should build a house of stone,⁶¹ but in the following year a warning was issued that unless the owners built something, *anything*, in the near future, then their *solares* would be confiscated.⁶² In around 1540 we must imagine a Lima with for the most part very rudimentary housing of reeds and mud, with pigs, dogs, hens and children running in and out, and streets of earth, pock-marked with large holes where people had excavated soil with which to make adobes. There was always a serious shortage of timber for building or for furniture, let alone for fuel, and there were constant problems with both the water supply and the drainage system.⁶³ Not exactly a state of *policía*.

To begin with, of course, the citizens tended to use existing Indian buildings where available. In Jauja, for example, the temporary capital of the Peruvian Viceroyalty from 1533 until the title was transferred to Lima in 1535, various Inca buildings were assigned for use as the town hall, the church and the conquerors' houses.⁶⁴ In Cuzco the *iglesia mayor* was first established in an Inca temple on the central square, and despite various different proposals it remained there until the present cathedral was finally completed on an adjoining site 120 years later, in 1654.⁶⁵ The documents about this particular building make interesting reading. In 1539 the Bishop of Cuzco, Fray Vicente Valverde, wrote to the King about his new Bishopric, and described the church as very fine, 'for the Indies'.⁶⁶ He does not appear to have been worried that it was in effect still an Inca temple. The building seems to have undergone a gradual transformation: first it was converted to Christian use simply by swapping the Inca furnishings for Christian, in particular the Inca idol for a Christian image. During the years 1540 to 1570 it was gradually enlarged, the walls rebuilt, the straw roof replaced with tiles, and chapels, altars and a sacristy added. Portals, were built on (*portadas*, which in Spanish usage must mean portals of brick or stone; a doorway of wood would not count as a *portada*) and a wooden choir was installed.⁶⁷ In 1568, despite all these improvements, the then Bishop of Cuzco wrote to the King complaining that his cathedral was no more than an Inca *bohío*;⁶⁸ tastes and expectations had changed since Valverde's day.

If there were no suitable existing Indian buildings in a new town that could be converted into churches or houses for Spaniards then initially the

Spaniards made do with whatever they could get the Indians to build for them as quickly and easily as possible and so these too would be in the traditional local Indian style. They were, of course, usually of the much-disdained mud, reeds, straw and wood and so they are always called *bohíos*. Pedro Simón, talking of a new Spanish town in the northern Colombian region, recognizes the advantages of the local system of constructing houses in *bahareque* or woven reeds, which needs no nails and no carpentry but is simply tied to a wooden framework with reeds or bindweed: it is quick and easy.[69] But everyone's intention is always to get out of a *bohío* as fast as possible into something more substantial, more civilized, with a tiled roof and a proper door with a doorframe and hinges and a lock, and if possible with brick walls, although even mud was deemed a considerable improvement on straw and woven reeds.

All this takes time. In a letter of 1589 the writer complains bitterly about the state of the churches in the Bishopric of Caracas:

The churches in this Bishopric are all of straw and very poor, which is shameful, and the Cathedral and head of this Bishopric is . . . a *bohío* and straw house which is falling down.[70]

A series of testimonials assembled by the Dominicans of the New Kingdom of Granada during the second half of the sixteenth century to demonstrate their extreme poverty contain many similar examples where the word *bohío* is used expressly to denote inadequacy. In Bogotá there was no church, but rather a *bohío* covered with straw, in Pamplona the friars lived in a *bohío* which had no more the form of a monastery than some Indian *bohíos*, in Mariquita the monastery was no more than a group of *bohíos*, covered with grasses and without any appearance of a monastery, *cubiertas de hierbas sin forma alguna de monasterio*, and so on.[71] In Quito in 1573 it was reported that two of the city's parish churches, San Blas and San Sebastián, 'have not got the plan (*traza*) of churches because they are of straw and *tapias*' (large adobes).[72] Here the implication of the Dominican complaints about their churches and monasteries in Colombia is made explicit: they are of the wrong materials to be classed as churches. As we shall see, the ground plan of these early churches was very simple regardless of the materials from which they were constructed and so it is essentially the materials which condition whether or not a building can be considered to have a proper *forma* or *traza*.

From the council records of the newly-founded Spanish towns one gets a picture of a gradually emerging grid-plan town, but a grid plan that is not arrived at without regular civic intervention. In most cases a plan was kept in the council offices, with the names of the citizens and of the churches and monastic foundations written into the appropriate squares (*see* plate 11), and there are frequent commissions for an officially appointed person to go out and check that the plan was being adhered to. In Arequipa in 1549 a citizen asked the *cabildo* to send someone to check the width of the street between his house and the church – whether he thought the church was encroaching or whether he was afraid of getting into trouble himself is not stated, but in any case the street in question was found to be thirty feet wide and *conforme al plano de la Ciudad*.[73] Again in Arequipa in 1556 Francisco de Cháves was sent to inspect the buildings to see if they were being continued *en línea recta*.[74] In Lima there are constant worries about the regularity of the town and about the straightness and width of the streets.[75] On 1 October 1549 the magistrate (*regidor*) and the civil engineer (*alarife*) were sent out together to inspect the streets and check that they were straight and in accordance with the city plan.[76] On 6 November 1551 it was ruled that since many buildings had been found which did not conform to the plan they would have to be pulled down as they were disfiguring the city and 'the straightness and clarity of the streets'.[77] On 13 November 1551 the blame for the *diformidad de la traza* was placed on the failure of the *alarife* to go out and measure the streets at frequent intervals, and it was agreed that he should be paid one peso for every *solar* that he measured.[78] The monastic orders were always troublesome in this respect: rich and relatively autonomous, they were often guilty of disrupting the regularity of the town plan, but there was little the *cabildo* could do to enforce their various rulings. The early history of Lima provides several examples, as, for instance, in 1552, when the Augustinians were accused of having built right across one of the city's streets and of having opened up a new street elsewhere, both of which were considered to be *en perjuyzio de la traça y puliçia* of the city.[79] As early as 1549 a slightly different problem is already in evidence: the city council had requested that the Dominicans prove their title to some *solares* on which they were building, a question that was to recur for years without, apparently, ever being resolved.[80] In some instances the *cabildo* did relax its strict view of the plan, as in the case, again in Lima, of the influential Licenciado de Santillán, who argued that a house he owned that was blocking a street along the riverside was in fact a public asset; and after some debate the *cabildo* ended up by agreeing that it was indeed an ornament to the city.[81] What pressures were brought to bear we can only imagine.

Generally, despite the slight fluctuations in practice, the principle of a regular grid-plan town – with straight streets and stone portals to the houses and so on – was adhered to with remarkable tenacity, and defended as a necessary condition of civilized existence, of *policía*. The centres of innumerable colonial towns and cities – Tunja, Quito, Trujillo, Lima, Ayacucho, Huancavelica, Arequipa, La Paz, Potosí and Sucre, to name but some in the Peruvian Viceroyalty alone – testify to the strength of this belief.

Initially, although there may have been a shortage of resident Spanish citizens in these new towns, there were plenty of resident Indians. This, as has been seen, was because in many cases they were already living there when the Spaniards moved in, and in any case the availability of native labour was a prerequisite for the foundation of a Spanish town. Only as the new Spanish towns became better established and the numbers of Spanish citizens grew were the Indian residents gradually eased out. Documentary evidence of the Indian presence in early colonial towns abounds but it is almost always tangential to the substance of the documentation. In Lima in 1544, for example, a citizen requests the city council for more lands; his request is granted on condition that he

> enclose and do with them that which the city ordinances require, and that they are not detrimental to the streets of this city and are in accordance with the Indian settlements and the streets which run through those said settlements.[82]

Here it is apparent not only that there are Indians resident within the city, but also that the council accepts them and does not want to disrupt them. It is not long, however, before their presence becomes a source of irritation. In 1551 the Lima *cabildo* recorded with distress that there was a serious lack of plots within the city to assign to all the decent married Spaniards who were then requesting them, because so many plots had originally been assigned to Indians.[83] The truth of the matter is perhaps not that the plots had originally been assigned to Indians, but rather that they had never been taken away from them: the Indians had been allowed to continue to live in or near their traditional homes after it had been founded as a Spanish city because land was not scarce, because their labour was required, and also no doubt because the Spaniards did not want to jeopardize their control of this labour by forcing the entire population of the original native township to move elsewhere and so create even greater hostility towards themselves than they were already doing.

The town council records from other places also demonstrate that to begin with there were numerous Indian residents in Spanish cities and that gradually the Spanish authorities found ways of getting rid of them. In

Arequipa on 1 May 1546 the *cabildo* decreed that those Indians who were living in gardens (*huertas*, kitchen gardens or orchards) belonging to the town should clear out immediately.[84] Perhaps what had happened was that at the time of the foundation of the town in 1540 areas had been generally designated as *huertas* which were either empty plots into which Indians had subsequently moved or were originally areas of Indian habitation; perhaps, on the other hand, at the time of the foundation nothing was so clear cut and the *cabildo* of 1546 was simply using 'city gardens' as a formula for justifying the expulsion of the Indians from their homes. Whatever the case it is clear that the *cabildo* wanted to find a formula for getting rid of the Indians and for appropriating their housing as well. On 9 June of the same year the *cabildo* reported that some of these gardens – by now vacated of Indians – contained houses with tiled roofs, and ruled that these should be rented out, but that they should not be rented to Indians. This suggests that some of the resident Indians had been becoming relatively prosperous, no doubt a further source of irritation to the Spaniards.

Elsewhere too gardens, *huertas*, are a pretext for the increasing hispanization of the new towns. In Quito in 1538 individual citizens requested the land occupied by Indians so that they could use them for gardens,[85] and an earlier ruling by the Quito cabildo of 1535 required that all citizens who had Indians living in their gardens should get rid of them, the reason given here being that the Indian *bohíos* or *ranchos* (huts) were a fire hazard.[86]

Once the colonial town is well established and control over the Indians assured, then they can be moved out. By referring to the plots of land as city gardens this process is more easily justifiable: the Indians are by implication usurping or squatting on the land. They are moved out not primarily so that the so-called gardens can be planted or developed, but rather so that the town can assert full control over the land, and can rent out the more substantial of the appropriated Indian housing to new Spanish immigrants.

*Reducciones*

To begin with, the displaced Indians settled where they could, usually around the outskirts of the town, but as the colonial settlement expanded these lands too came to be required by Spaniards. As a town grew in self-confidence and pride, the citizens came to want to see the Indian populations better organized and better controlled, and removed from the confines of their own town. As suggested in the previous chapter, from the point of view of these new Spanish towns, orderliness, straight streets and so on were held to be manifestations of civility, of the superiority of the Europeans; on the other hand, from the point of view of the native populations it was constantly stressed by both the Crown and the governing authorities in Spanish America that if the Indians could be settled into similarly orderly environments, then this would have an actively civilizing effect upon them. The theoretical aspects of the various Royal and Viceregal mandates that required governors to organize the Indians into new orderly towns have already been discussed; the practical achievement of these, as with the Spanish towns themselves, was not so straightforward, but the underlying ideals are always present.

The first new towns for Indians were not founded with a view to gathering them together from their remote hamlets and scattered farms amongst the mountains, nor with a view to instructing them more efficiently in the Christian faith, which was how the Crown had originally seen it; they were for the Indians who worked for the Spaniards in the new Spanish towns, and they were primarily a means of exerting greater control over them. The case of Lima is well documented. Initially the Indians had lived scattered throughout the town, with a particular concentration around the area of San Lázaro on the north bank of the river Rimac outside the original limits of the city.[87] The road out of the city to the north ran through the parish of San Lázaro and during the 1550s and 1560s the Spanish authorities in Lima were anxious to construct a solid stone bridge linking this with the centre of the city.[88] As this became a real possibility, so too they turned their attention to the parish itself. In 1568 the Licenciado García de Castro arranged for the Indians from San Lázaro and elsewhere to be resettled in an area to the northeast of the city, to be called the Cercado or enclosure, as it is still known today. In the following year the new Viceroy Francisco de Toledo arrived in Lima and his indefatigable efforts saw the building programme through, so that it was more or less complete by 1571.[89]

According to Cobo the Cercado was everything a new, European-designed settlement should be. It was on a very healthy site, with fertile lands around and a plentiful supply of water; plots were laid out in an orderly fashion (grid plan, of course), good houses were built, and it was provided with its own church and hospital, and its own government, 'own government' in the sense in which the Bantustans in South Africa have their own government. It was, as the name suggests, enclosed within a high wall with three gates which were locked at curfew every evening in order, so Cobo puts it, to protect the Indians from molestation by either Spaniards or negroes or mestizos, although surely it was really for fear of Indian uprisings.[90] By no means all the Indians in Lima were moved into the Cercado; many continued to live in San Lázaro and others were scattered throughout the city, including a large number who lived in with their Spanish employers. Nevertheless the practice of collecting as many Indians as possible into a special enclosed area outside the immediate confines of the Spanish town was widespread, although as with Lima, there was a time lag between the initial foundation of the Spanish town and the formal establishment of *cercados* for Indians.

The Licenciado Salazar de Villasante sent the King an account of his efforts in this direction in Quito, where in the 1560s he had created two Indian villages, one on each side of the colonial city:

I founded them with vagrant Indians who wandered about like gypsies ... I made them lay out the streets *por cordel* (and I myself levelled them) and the blocks, all in good order.

He reported that he had arranged the water supply, and the lay-out of the squares, and he had built the houses and council offices, as well as a church in each village:

I left them in such *pulicía* that since then other Indians from badly organized villages have 'reduced' themselves into [similar] settlements and are building orderly houses.[91]

How close this was to the truth of the matter I cannot say but it seems unlikely. Certainly in the territories away from the Spanish towns the reorganization, the 'reduction' of the Indians into large, orderly villages or towns was far from voluntary.

The real drive in this direction was made by Toledo in the early 1570s;[92] by 1573 perhaps one and a half million people had been resettled into tidy little grid-plan townships where they could be more easily controlled, particularly with regard to the compulsory work in the mines (Toledo was responsible for introducing forced labour as well as for organizing the *reducciones*); where they could be more easily assessed for tax purposes and where they could be more easily educated in the Christian faith. The *visitadores*, the officials usually responsible for organizing the *reducciones*, seem to have followed the pattern laid down by Matienzo and Toledo. A suitable site was chosen, the town was laid out, a church and houses were built, and then the Indians from the surrounding area were moved in, but whereas for the Spaniards their new towns conformed to an ideal type which they were generally only too happy to espouse in practice, for the Indians the *reducciones* represented a devastating upheaval in their lives on all levels: economic, political, cultural, spatial and ideological.[93]

To begin with, the sites which the Spaniards chose were in fact not always suitable. Because the principle behind the reduction of the Indians – the practical principle that is, not the ideal – was to render them more accessible to the Spaniards, the new townships tended to be positioned where they could be reached on horseback. This meant that many communities were moved from one ecological zone to another, from, say, cool dry mountains to warm wet valleys; they had to walk vast distances to reach their traditional fields and pastures and the more remote of these were quickly abandoned. In outlying areas irrigation systems, essential to fertility in much of highland Peru as well as to the coastal desert, fell into disrepair. Some of the chosen sites for new settlements were subject to natural disasters such as floods and avalanches, and the new towns themselves must have seemed wholly alien. People who had spent their lives in isolated farmsteads found themselves cheek-by-jowl with dozens of strangers. Few of them can have recognized the benefits of a well-planned urban existence which the Spaniards felt to be so self-evident.

Even the shape of their houses was often forcibly changed. In the *reducción* of Huancayo in 1572, which conformed closely to Toledo's instructions, the Spanish official in charge forbade them to build houses in the round, conical shape traditional to the *huanca* people of the region.[94] In several other places Spanish commentators note with approval that the Indians now no longer live in round houses, which the Spaniards considered to be primitive, 'de rústica proporción',[95] as one man put it, but in little square houses 'imitando á las de Castilla'.[96] How far the Spanish authorities managed to enforce their ideas about the internal arrangements of houses, with separate bedrooms and so on, is difficult to assess but merely to change a round house for a square would have necessitated considerable changes in the domestic arrangements. It is unlikely, however, that even had they chosen to, the Indians could possibly all have acquired tables and chairs and beds, another of the standard requirements of instructions such as Matienzo's. A high proportion of Indians still have little or no furniture today, and sit on the ground much more readily and comfortably than most Westerners.

But the cause of most distress was that of the physical dislocation not only from their fields and homes but rather from their spiritual roots. This was, of course, yet another reason why the Spaniards saw the *reducciones* as essential to the well-being of the Indians, but in a culture where spirits inhabit or rather are inherent in every rock, cave, tree, spring or mountain, to be removed from these and from the tombs of their ancestors was to be removed from the sources of life.[97] Most Andean peoples held their own place of origin, known in Quechua as their *pacarina*, in particular veneration. Pablo José de Arriaga, investigating the many idolatrous practices in Peru in the early seventeenth century, saw this loyalty to the *pacarina* as one of the reasons why 'they resist the consolidation of their towns, and like to live in such bad and difficult places'.[98]

Sometimes the *reducciones* did fail: Antonio de Cháves y de Guevara wrote of the province of Huamanga (now Ayacucho), that

> the towns that have recently been reduced are for the most part not permanent, because after the said resettlements, and the difficulties involved in moving from different climates and to unhealthy sites far from their fields, many villages have been repopulated in their original locations and in other places, with the permission of the governors and the knowledge of the *corregidores* of their districts.[99]

But by and large Toledo was successful. The *reducciones* played an incalculable part in consolidating colonial rule and in disrupting the traditional Inca and pre-Inca administrative districts. There were dissenting voices about the real benefits of forced reduction among the Spanish officials of the day and modern writers such as Wachtel and Duviols have recognized the enormous, agonizing disruption they caused to the Indian populations, but generations of European historians have endorsed and continue to endorse Toledo's ideals if not his practice.[100] Culture, civility, economic growth and social order are still, for many people, essentially dependent upon an urban lifestyle; the ramifications of this idea in practice can still be recognized in many parts of the world, in countries of as widely differing political colour as Guatemala and Tanzania. It is perhaps not entirely coincidental that both these countries were colonized by Europeans.

## Summary

Both the new Spanish colonial towns and the Indian *reducciones* owe their origins to the general idea of a town, of a civilized society and of a civilized style of architecture which the Spaniards carried with them across the Atlantic. This is self-evidently true of the physical lay-out of such new towns, but it is the ideas that lie behind the practice that are more important. It is because the Spaniards were so confident in these ideas that they carried them through into practice without hesitation, often regardless of the empirical realities of the case.

As I have tried to demonstrate, many early travellers in South America were impressed by indigenous towns and indigenous architecture, but this seems not to have weakened their confidence in the superiority of their own culture. Not surprisingly they scarcely ever use their observations of indigenous culture to reassess their own,[101] but they regularly use their own to reassess, or rather to assess, that of the American Indians. As the Spanish colonies are consolidated, so this cultural confidence is in fact strengthened rather than weakened. Once the Indian towns have been appropriated and recognizably Europeanized then there is less evidence of a non-European urban society to upset this confidence. The unsettling possibility that a completely different, non-European people might also have developed a form of town based on straight streets, square blocks and a central plaza surrounded by important political and religious buildings could be set aside, to be dealt with by later historians. So too, the displaced Indians who lived in and around the Spanish towns, and who were progressively squeezed out during the course of the sixteenth century, became a lesser rather than a greater threat to European cultural hegemony: they could quite accurately be described as living in a disorderly fashion, their orderly towns subsumed into the Spanish, their new homes poor and ramshackle. Not only would the materials have been those for which the Spaniards had least regard – straw, reeds and mud – but they cannot have been large or elaborate; the Indians would have had neither the time nor the space nor the resources, nor even the desire, perhaps, to build the large palaces and halls which early commentators describe of pre-conquest cultures in so many parts of South America. These Indians lived in effect in shanty towns. *Ergo* such disorder was a sign of backwardness, primitiveness, and so provided further encouragement for the drive to 'reduce' the Indians into *policía*.

The Spanish predilection for urban living and their confidence in their own style of town means that South America becomes in colonial eyes firmly divided into Spanish-urban-civilized on the one hand, and Indian-rural-primitive on the other; this attitude contributes to the view of the Indians as simple savages, like children in need of guidance and organization. One does not have to posit an exceptionally cynical, long-term scheme on the part of the Spaniards to explain their attitudes and practices. Their practice alters the Indian reality so that it comes more nearly to approximate the Spanish idea of what the Indians are like, which in turn confirms the Spaniards' self-confidence. As the Indian world becomes increasingly disrupted, so the Spanish colony becomes stronger and more efficient. It develops the ideological security to exploit the Indians further under the aegis of the ideals of civilized society: to help them grow into good, civilized Christians by keeping them busy so that they have no time to indulge in vices, by teaching them to say their catechism in Spanish, by making them live in square houses in grid-plan towns, and by encouraging them to eat off tables and to sleep in beds.

# 3

# The builders

Buildings, expecially churches, were often the first permanent manifestations of colonial culture which the indigenous Americans encountered. The churches represented, of course, the new spiritual order but they also represented the new social, political, economic and architectural forms of colonial rule. The church was the ideological as well as the geographical focus of both the new Indian *reducciones* and the new colonial towns. As an institution, represented by the building, the church was the chief weapon in the colonial government's drive to civilize and to Christianize the native populations. And whether in Spanish or in Indian towns and villages, the labour required to construct such churches was provided by the native populations under the administration of the Spaniards, so that the Indians' first experience of working within the new regime was almost always with the construction of a church. Such labour was generally organized as a form of tribute and the way in which this resembled pre-conquest systems of labour tribute and communal work is one of the reasons for the Spaniards' success, not just in constructing churches throughout the continent, but in consolidating colonial rule as a whole.

## Labourers in Indian areas

Towards the end of the sixteenth century a Mercedarian friar, Diego de Porres, wrote to the King asking for recognition of his thirty-three years' work in Peru and Upper Peru (an area included in present-day Bolivia). As well as baptizing between seventy and eighty thousand Indians, marrying over thirty thousand, organizing many into orderly and civilized *reducciones* and founding seven Mercedarian monasteries, he claims to have built over two hundred churches.[1] What does this mean? Is it anything more than an imaginative boast? All the evidence suggests that it is, and that Porres' claims are probably reasonably accurate. Many of these churches would no doubt have been rudimentary constructions – a small chapel with adobe walls and a thatched roof – of the sort which churchmen constantly describe in their appeals to the Viceroy or to the Crown for better funding, and some were perhaps simply conversions of existing buildings,[2] but nevertheless, even allowing for this, the construction of churches in Spanish America during the early years of the conquest remains a remarkable achievement. By the end of the sixteenth century there were churches in most of the Indian towns and villages throughout the Spanish territories. Writing in the 1620s the Franciscan friar Pedro Simón estimated that 70,000 Christian churches had been built in the Indies.[3] With a total, even at this date, of only a few thousand Spanish settlers, most of whom were concentrated in a few dozen Spanish towns, how was this achieved?[4] How could a solitary missionary such as Diego de Porres have built, as he claims, churches in dozens of villages in remote parts of the central and southern Andes? It would be difficult to identify any surviving church as one of those built by Porres, but village churches survive all over Spanish America which can be dated to the sixteenth century and it is clear that by no means all of them were *mal hecho y de adobes*; on the contrary, many were substantial and durable structures with at least some details – doorways and a chancel arch, for example – in brick or stone.

In practice a friar such as Porres would not, of course, have built these churches himself: they would have been initiated by him but were executed by the Indians, probably within some version of the *encomienda* system. Introduced by Isabella in 1503, *encomienda* was to form the basis of the colonial exploitation of native labour at least until the eighteenth century.[5] An *encomienda*, sometimes loosely referred to as a *repartimiento*, was a grant to an individual conquistador as a reward for his services, and consisted of the right to the tribute labour from the Indians living within a certain area. The grantee, the *encomendero*, could use this labour in various ways, ways which were designed to strengthen and benefit the colony. In return, the *encomendero*'s principal duty to the Indians was to see that they were adequately instructed in the faith by providing a church, a priest and images of Christ and the Virgin in each village within the designated area.[6] Under the system of *encomienda* neither the *encomendero* nor any other Spaniard had rights, in theory at least, over the lands on which the Indians lived nor other controls over their lives. The uses and abuses of this system varied throughout Spanish America, but because the *encomienda* grant was originally envisaged as being temporary, and not of long duration – to give initial economic security to the

Spanish settlements while at the same time ensuring the civilizing and religious indoctrination of the native inhabitants – the tendency was for the *encomenderos* to exploit the Indians in their charge as much and as fast as possible, all the while seeking to convert their grants of Indian labour into control over the land on which the Indians lived, in order to secure their own and their families' futures.

The *encomendero* was entitled to exact taxes in kind from the Indians – food, cloth, pottery, firewood and, where possible, minerals. These were often demanded at levels that far exceeded personal requirements, but the *encomendero* could then sell the surplus to Spaniards who lacked *encomienda* Indians, or in many cases would sell it back, often forcibly and at hugely inflated prices, to the Indians themselves. An *encomendero* also required a tribute in the form of labour – to build his house in the local Spanish town (and to provide the necessary materials), to pasture his flocks and herds (generally on the Indians' own land) and to work any lands which he, the *encomendero*, had been granted or which he claimed as his own. In addition, the *encomendero* was sometimes required by the colonial administration to provide Indians from his *encomienda* to help with public works, road repairs, bridge building, street cleaning, and so on, as well as with the construction of churches.

In the Indian areas the *encomendero*'s primary responsibility to the Indians was to facilitate their conversion and to arrange for the construction of a church in each Indian settlement. This was first spelled out in the 1513 *Leyes de Burgos* and was repeated frequently in the official legislation.[7] In 1553, for example, a royal decree required that in each local *cabecera* or principal village a church be built, and that this be effected by taking as much as was needed from those tributes which the Indians owed both to their *encomendero* and to the Crown.[8] In effect, this meant that the Indians were responsible for providing the materials and labour for such churches as a part of their labour tribute, but they were also indirectly responsible for meeting whatever other costs were involved: items of their tribute in kind would be sold either by the *encomendero* or by other officials to raise cash in order to buy items which the local population could not supply for themselves. Gerónimo de Mendieta, writing in the early days of the Spanish colonization of New Spain, asks rhetorically:

Who has built so many churches and monasteries as the friars possess in this New Spain, if not the Indians themselves, with their own hands, their own sweat? ... And who has provided the churches with ornaments, with silver vessels and with everything else with which they are furnished and adorned, if not the same Indians?[9]

Mendieta sees this as a result of the Indians' extraordinary religious zeal and does not mention the question of taxes and tributes, but that he credits the Indians with entire responsibility for erecting and equipping churches is no more than the truth, whether their contribution was direct or indirect. The European settlers' financial contribution to the Church in America was in the form of tithes which principally went to pay the salaries of the Bishop, Dean and Chapter, and the parish clergy.[10] A small percentage went towards the construction and repair of churches, but this would naturally tend to be spent on grander churches in Spanish towns rather than on parish churches in Indian towns and villages. Such tithes were, of course, paid out of the profits which the colonists made – largely from the exploitation of the native populace. Various official attempts were made to define the finances of church construction, and these reflect perceptions shaped by the European economic system within which such undertakings would necessarily require a supply of cash. In theory, the construction of churches in Spanish America was seen in terms of the monetary costs and was therefore generally referred to as a tripartite system whereby the Indians, the *encomendero* and the Crown all contributed equally.[11] This fair-mindedness is more hypothetical than actual; the Indians always supply by far the greater part whether directly or indirectly in the form of their own labour, while the moral and especially financial responsibilities for building churches are the source of frequent tensions between the different colonial power groups.

The *encomenderos* were not on the whole particularly assiduous about their duties with regard to the building of churches and the conversion of the Indians. A letter of 1549 from Juan Solano, Bishop of Cuzco, to the Crown explicitly blames the conquistadors for the lack of churches in his see. There are, he complains, only five churches in the whole bishopric and those are not properly constructed because the conquistadors never think of building churches nor of complying with the King's rulings.[12] This, even allowing for the standard rivalry between the Church and the secular colonists, seems a common complaint, although an occasional *encomendero* seems to have taken his Christian duty seriously: in 1565 the Bishop of Coro (Venezuela) wrote to the King about a settler from Seville who lived in Curaçao, who never paid his tithes and who had done nothing about providing a priest in his area, but who nevertheless had had a church built which the Bishop believed had not cost him ten *ducados*, 'because he built it with the Indians'.[13] This is a rare case and no doubt a complicated wrangle lies behind the bare documented outlines. In practice the construction of churches was almost always initiated and supervised not by *encomenderos* but by clerics.

So the Church, or rather individuals like Fray Diego de Porres, were primarily responsible for the construction of the first churches in Spanish America. As soon as there was some sort of geographical understanding of the extent of the newly-discovered lands (albeit often very approximate) the Church divided them into Bishoprics which in turn were subdivided into *doctrinas*, the equivalent among the Indian neophytes of parishes.[14] Generally, an area comprising many *doctrinas* was first designated to a particular monastic order, the members of which were responsible for the initial proselytizing, after which they were expected to move on to other regions, leaving the work of consolidation to the secular clergy.[15] The first missionaries in the field would, where possible, arrange with the local *encomendero* for a church to be built.[16] These missionaries would usually tend to establish a church of their own order, with a monastic residence attached. While there certainly were zealous friars in South America there were also many who found preaching to the Indians uncongenial – if done properly it was an arduous and lonely existence – and who wanted to return to the conventual life for which their training in Europe had prepared them.[17] Thus in due course, when the secular clergy moved into the area, they would find that the friars were reluctant to pack up and move on. They wanted to stay in their new monastic houses and churches over which, in any case, they claimed jurisdiction. The local Indians, meanwhile, would be required to build another church to serve as a parish church to the community. Already by 1559 the Crown wrote to the Archbishop of Lima condemning the practice whereby in Indian regions the regular clergy were establishing churches which they termed monasteries, and were using Indian contributions to equip them with plate and ornaments which they – the mendicants – then regarded as the property not of the parish but of the Order. In the King's opinion the Indian communities, in having to build and equip a parish as well as a monastic church, contributing both goods and labour twice over, were being put to unreasonable trouble and expense.[18] As with the odd case of the settler in Curaçao who paid no tithes but who had had a church built at no cost to himself, one way or the other it was always the Indians who paid.

The Indians paid because, despite the relative scarcity of Spaniards to exact such tributes by force, the *encomienda* system was in outline not dissimilar to traditional forms of tribute, or at least it could be interpreted as such by the native populations when much else in their world was severely disrupted. This is true of Mexico and of northern South America,[19] but it is especially true of the territories that had been under Inca control before the arrival of the Spaniards. The Inca system of taxation extended to all major subject groups and included a tax in goods and a tax in labour. Tributes were paid both to the local chief or *curaca* and to the Inca state. Each group or settlement was divided, in a system which long pre-dates Inca social organization and seems common to all Andean peoples, into a number of clan-like groupings or *ayllus*, under a single *curaca*, and each *ayllu* was divided into family units under a single tribute-paying head, an adult married man. Each tribute-paying head was liable for *mita* labour duties as well as for tributes in kind. The *mita* consisted of work for the local community or for the state for a certain period annually – building roads, fortresses, temples or irrigation systems, working in the mines or serving in the army. These *mitayos* would often be required to work away from home, although generally within their own region; they would often work together in gangs, and food, tools and materials would be provided for them from the public stores.[20] Betanzos' description of Pachacuti's rebuilding of Cuzco includes numerous references to the organization of *mita* labour, to the supplies of food and equipment, including, for examples, the provision of specially made heavy-duty mantles, *mantas*, with which the Indians could carry stones and earth without spoiling their own clothes.[21] In other words all the *mitayo* contributed was his labour. In return he and his family had the right to cultivate sufficient lands for their needs, and the right to supplies from the communal or state storehouses in times of hardship or famine. He also received various gifts of food, cloth, *chicha* (maize beer) or coca, and what Murra calls 'institutionalized hospitality'[22] – feasting, music and dancing organized and provided for by the beneficiaries of the tribute labour, the local *curaca* or the Inca nobility.

Under the Spaniards, who were quick to recognize the advantages which the *mita* tribute offered them and to assume what had been the Incas' rôle at the top of the political hierarchy, the *mitayos* soon found that the bargain had become very one-sided. They received none of the – to Spanish eyes very insubstantial – benefits of pre-conquest days, the little gifts or the organized festivities. They had to provide their own tools and materials, their own food and clothing and, as the exploitation of the mineral resources expanded, many were having to travel far from their homelands in order to fulfil the work demanded of them. Under colonial rule *mita* duties that involved the construction of houses or churches in their own towns and villages were considerably less disruptive to traditional patterns than was the work in the mines of Potosí or Huancavelica. This is certainly an important part of the explanation for the many large churches in the Chucuito region[23] and must also help to account for the successful church-building programmes of men like Diego de Porres.

## Labourers in Spanish towns

The situation concerning the construction of buildings in Spanish towns is rather more complex, and represents a major break with tradition: the introduction of waged labour.[24] The *encomenderos* could be required to provide Indians from their *encomienda* grant to help construct the *iglesia mayor* for example, but there was generally a feeling that the Indians ought to be paid for such work.[25] Traditionally this sort of task would have come under the regular *mita* duties: gangs of workmen would have been called up from the country to work on Inca building projects in Cuzco or Quito, for example, and payment in the European sense did not enter into it. The question of payment of wages under early colonial rule does not really arise in relation to the construction of churches in Indian areas because they were for the Indians' own use. In Spanish towns, however, the question does arise and arises forcibly because the European monetary system was central to the organization, indeed the concept of, a European town, and the payment of wages for labour was (and is) an integral part of that system. Generally speaking it was thought beneficial to teach the Indians to work for regular payment – it of course clarified the mechanism of control, making it explicit and more readily comprehensible to the Spaniards than *mita* labour which, as many contemporaries noted, was open to abuse. As the century progressed the expanding colonial economy required that increasing pressure be placed upon the Indians to work, or to work harder within the colonial system, particularly in the mines: the development of forced labour is closely connected with the development of waged labour, the argument being that if they had to be forced to work, then at least they should be properly paid. Another not unrelated reason which is often given is that payment would be an incentive to work, and so would encourage the Indians not to be lazy, a vice commonly attributed (all the evidence to the contrary notwithstanding) to natives in the sixteenth as in the twentieth century.

During the sixteenth century, although wages for work on public buildings in Spanish towns becomes more and more common there is sometimes evidence of a degree of overlap between the old *mita* system and the new. In

Arequipa in 1591, for example, it was agreed that for a period of two years twenty Indians *de mita* should be supplied from the *encomiendas* of the Crown and of certain Spanish residents for the construction of the church and monastery of Santo Domingo.[26] They were to work for a month at a time, after which they should be replaced by another group and they were to be paid the fixed daily wage and to be treated well.[27] There is a further clause which suggests that the Spanish administration was in this case making some concessions to the traditional *mita* system: the *mitayos* were to be provided with leathers or sacking to carry materials so as not to spoil their own *mantas*. As has been seen Pachacuti made a similar provision for those working on the reconstruction of Cuzco in the previous century. There are other examples of employers supplying Indians with *mantas* in colonial times suggesting that this was a particularly sensitive area, an area in which the *mitayos* were reluctant to compromise. It is reasonable to assume that in this case the Spaniards had recognized the important place which textiles held in traditional Andean society.[28]

There was never any question but that manual labour was for Indians, not for Spaniards. And it was recognized too that without such manual labour the colony would collapse, as the Viceroy of Peru, Don Luis de Velasco, put it when writing to the King in 1603 about the need for legislation to impel the Indians to work. In this case he is arguing that they be made to cut wood from the forests around Guayaquil in order to supply Lima with timber for the city's buildings, but his justification is entirely general and unusually candid:

> Not one thing of the many which are necessary for the support and preservation of this republic, from the smallest to the largest, would there be nor will there be unless the Indians do or make it.[29]

## Labouring craftsmen

It is misleading, especially in pre-industrial societies, to draw a firm line between labour and craftsmanship. In pre-conquest times in the Andes there were, of course, professional artisans but the *mita* labourers themselves were by no means without certain skills, particularly basic building skills. Under the Inca regime almost all dwellings apart from those of the highest nobility were built by the community using communally held skills, and the building of a house was accompanied by communal feasting and celebration. A knowledge of how to construct a roof, using a framework of timbers lashed together with ropes and covered with thatch would have been widespread.[30] The making of adobes, sun-dried bricks, and the building of walls of adobes or *tapias* (similar to adobes but larger, and made *in situ* by erecting shuttering and packing the cavity with wet mud and stones) would have been more or less universal, and would not have been in the hands of professionals. Neither would the construction of walls of field stone set into mud mortar. In his account of tribute labour in Cuzco, Polo de Ondegardo implies that the labourers themselves were skilled in constructing the magnificent Inca walls: he does not mention professional stone masons at this point, and it seems probable that amongst a group of *mitayos* from any one village, some at least would have been relatively skilled in cutting and facing stone.[31] Particular provinces too were known and valued by the Incas for their skills: those from the southern Andes, the Collao, for example, were known for their skills as masons, and this area, not surprisingly, regularly supplied *mita* labourers to Cuzco 'to build houses and walls'.[32]

With this range of abilities available – although certainly with varying degrees of proficiency – in all Andean communities, and available from people accustomed to fulfilling regular labour tribute, Diego de Porres' claims are not necessarily that far-fetched. We do not need to find documentary evidence for specialist craftsmen to defend his case. He himself, and others like him, would have been responsible for choosing a site (which, as has been seen, would usually have been predetermined), for laying out a basic shape (probably simply a rectangle as wide as the available timber would span, with perhaps a rounded or polygonal end to mark the apse) and for supervising construction. Some sort of bell-tower or other form of support would have been necessary because one of the essential requirements for such churches was a bell to call the local people to prayer.[33] Adobe walls and a thatched roof: this is how many of the first churches are described, and although these materials were disparaged by the Spaniards it would be wrong to assume that such churches were all necessarily small and shabby. The example of Santo Domingo in Chucuito, discussed in the Introduction, is a good example of a very early monastic church of grandiose proportions that was built by the local Indians under the direction of the friars (*see* plate 2).

The Spaniards brought with them a new technology, but there is no reason to believe that this remained in the hands of skilled European professionals where it was found to be useful. Some skills were quickly disseminated from European craftsmen not just to Indian craftsmen but to the native populace in general. The making and firing of bricks and tiles, and the production of mortar, for example, did not long remain specialized skills, nor would the Spaniards have wished them to. The techniques of production were in any case only an extension of those used by potters on a larger and generally coarser scale, and it is not surprising to find that brick and tile were produced and used within the *mita* system from shortly after the conquest. The implication of the documents about Indian houses in Arequipa mentioned in the previous chapter is that they were building themselves houses with tiled roofs from a very early date, and tiles were being used in the mid-sixteenth century on the Inca palace at Vilcabamba, the centre of resistance to Spanish rule.[34] The advantages of fired clay building materials over the traditional adobes, especially in the wetter areas such as Vilcabamba, would have been immediately obvious. That brick has still not been taken up as a standard material for domestic dwelling in South America is a result not so much of the difficulty of the technique or of indigenous resistance to its use, but of its relative expense. Brick kilns require considerable quantities of fuel, a commodity that is in short supply in almost all the more densely populated areas of Peru and Bolivia.

One of the European building techniques which is always stressed in relation to the conquest of America is that of contructing arches and vaults out of stone. The conventional view, voiced in many twentieth-century accounts, is that the Indians were frightened of the unfamiliar vaulted interiors,[35] and while few authors deny that the Indians were quick to learn the technique, there is a contradiction in these two statements which is not confronted. It seems to me that this emphasis on the Indians' fear of stone vaults is on a par with those who attribute the success of the Spaniards in conquering America to the Indians' terror at horses and at firearms. Of course such novelties would have been astonishing and disturbing, especially when, as in the case of firearms, they were used against the native populations, but the implication of child-like simplicity and awe which lies behind such remarks is inappropriate, and merely upholds the traditional old-sophisticated-wise-advanced versus new-young-naive-backward view of the European–American contrasts.

There are, in fact, relatively few sixteenth-century accounts of the Indians' fear of the use of stone arches and vaults. Mendieta writes of the Indians' initial fear when the supports were removed from the first stone vaults to be constructed in Mexico, but his sentence continues,

when it was seen that the vault stayed firm, they lost their fear and shortly afterwards the Indians built two little vaulted chapels by themselves.[36]

In South America Acosta's reference to the Indians fleeing from the stone bridge at Jauja on the removal of the scaffolding is the only such story I know of.[37] It was repeated by Herrera who was writing at the end of the century without personal knowledge of America from whence it seems to have passed into European folklore.[38] The fear, if such there was, was very quickly overcome and the technique of building arches and vaults of stone thoroughly mastered. The European assumption that the technique of constructing an arch is an enormous leap both technologically and intellectually is based on an assumption of European technological superiority. The stone masons of the Inca state did use various forms of stone vaulting for covering small constructions, as in the palace buildings on the Isla del Sol in Lake Titicaca and in the nearby *chullpas*, the tomb towers of Sillustani, so it is not as if such a form of roofing had never occurred to them. And I find it hard to imagine that a craftsman who had worked on one of the walls of irregular shaped blocks so typical of Inca architecture could have been unaware that certain combinations of stones can tie together in such a way that stones below them can be removed without the whole wall collapsing, and that within a wall of irregular masonry certain stones are crucially weight-bearing and others not. The Inca walling of irregular blocks is relatively secure against earthquake damage precisely because the weight is distributed in a variety of different directions and also because it keys and locks together it can withstand a multiplicity of strains. It is a short step from this to a more regularized system, using a single central key-stone and leaving an opening below it, a system which, however, is considerably less stable in an earth tremor than the traditional lintelled doorways of Inca architecture, something the Spaniards were to discover to their cost. I prefer to see the Incas as not having developed, rather than not having discovered, the principle of the arch. In any event Indian stone masons soon put the technique into practice to produce arches and vaults at the behest of the missionaries or *encomenderos*. Both these two important new techniques introduced from Europe, the manufacture of brick and tile and the construction of arches and vaults, were quickly learnt and regularly used not by specialists or professionals but within the colonial version of the traditional tribute labour systems.

## Professional craftsmen

There were also professional craftsmen – Indian as well as European and African[39] – in sixteenth-century Spanish America. Those Indians who had been craftsmen before the conquest continued to pursue their craft under Spanish rule, adapting the forms and styles as required. Others who had not been full-time specialists under the Incas found that they could make a living as such after the conquest. There are numerous testimonies to the skill of the Indians both in adapting to European stylistic conventions and in learning new forms and new techniques. In Mexico Mendieta is among the most enthusiastic in this respect. He regards the Indians as responsible for 'almost all the fine and curious works in all manner of arts and crafts which are to be found in New Spain'. This is because, as he says, the Spanish master-craftsmen have to do no more than 'give the work to the Indians and tell them how to do it' and the Indians will promptly carry out the work so perfectly that in Mendieta's view it would be impossible to improve on it.[40] This opinion is also endorsed by many early commentators on the South American people. By the late 1540s Cieza de León observed that in Peru the Indian silversmiths were producing 'goblets, platters and candelabra' of a quality which he felt would have taxed a European craftsman to match, Indian sculptors were producing things which Cieza felt demonstrated their 'great wit'.[41] He also points out that the Indians were building the Spaniards' houses for them, using not only stone, but also brick and tiles which they were already making for themselves. Other sources too stress that the Indians quickly and easily picked up any *oficio o arte* which they were taught.[42]

There had been a wide variety of specialized artists in Inca Peru. Under the heading *oficiales* Morúa lists various occupations including *oficiales de albañería*, by which he means stone masons. These are specialists, professionals, who, he says, were housed, fed and clothed by the state and are thus distinct from the *mitayos* or tribute labourers.[43] Under the Inca administration these specialists were included in a class of people called *yana* or *yanacona* (the terms are interchangeable). The precise status and various duties of the *yana* in Inca times, and their position within the social hierarchy, is complicated, but it seems clear that there were various categories of *yana* including those who served in the Inca households and at the religious centres and those who worked as artisans. The *yana* lived outside the traditional clan-like structure of the *ayllu*, often far removed from their families and places of origin. They were therefore not necessarily answerable to a local chief or *curaca*, and were exempt from the various forms of tribute both at a local and at a national level.

Despite the variety of occupations in which its members were engaged the *yana* were apparently a relatively homogeneous group; in the confused aftermath of the conquest this became fragmented. They continued to be seen by the Spaniards as distinct from other Indians: in Arequipa in 1546, for example, the town council ruled that rooms were not to be let to Indians or *yanacona*, and in Quito the official documentation regularly makes this distinction, referring to 'naturales y yanacona', or 'indios y yanacona',[44] but economic differences quickly emerged within the *yana* group which were presumably not present in Inca times. Because they had been exempt from tribute under the Inca, initially they remained exempt under the Spaniards, and in some localities the *yana* used this to their advantage.[45] In rural areas especially, which were not strictly controlled by colonial government, they seem to have developed into a wealthy, independent and privileged class; elsewhere *yana* were often described by Spanish observers as being in a worse condition than slaves.[46] The artisan *yana* probably fall somewhere between the two.

After the conquest a great many *yana* lived in or in close proximity to the Spanish towns. References to *yana* in these towns often include a qualification to the effect that 'some of them are artisans'.[47] The others were household servants, imported from other areas or appropriated by the conquerors. From a European perspective these two types of employment – servants and craftsmen – are very distinct, and so it is perhaps not surprising to find that after the arrival of the Spaniards they are seen as separate entities and accorded different treatment.[48] The *yana* appropriated as servants are *ipso facto* socially inferior and subject to the Spaniards, unpaid and so outside the new economic order; the artisans on the other hand are employed by the Spaniards as a European craftsman would be employed: they are paid in cash for the goods they produce and so are integrated into the economy. A report from the end of the century covering various aspects of Indian tribute payments distinguishes *yanacona con oficio*, with a skill (among whom the writer includes painters, blacksmiths, tailors and shoemakers), from other types of *yanacona* and recommends that they be made to register themselves with the government officials of the town so that they can be taxed, and 'when they want to move' to another town or village they should report to the authorities.[49] The implication is clearly that some *yana* at least made a living as itinerant craftsmen.

The one craft which from a European point of view was considered essential to the building trade but for which there was virtually no indigenous tradition was that of carpentry. In pre-conquest South America roofing timbers were not jointed, but simply lashed together. Wooden furniture of any sort was extremely rare, doors and windows unknown, and the skills involved, particularly ways of jointing wood together, had never been developed. 'Doors' in Inca buildings, for example, consisted of removable panels of woven reeds. The *Relaciones geográficas* for Guamanga in 1557, working through a list of European crafts, classified Indian carpenters as those who made wooden beakers, *queros*, because there was no other activity involving wood which could be included under the heading: 'they do not use doors on their houses, nor even windows, nor benches, nor tables nor any other sort of carpentry'.[50] Of Inca carpenters Garcilaso de la Vega writes:

They did not know how to make a saw nor a drill, nor a plane nor any other instrument for carpentry work; and thus they did not know how to make chests or doors, but only to cut wood and trim it for their buildings. For the axes and adzes and the few tools that they made, silversmiths served instead of blacksmiths, because all the tools that they worked were of copper and brass. They did not use nails, so that whatever wood they put into their buildings was all tied with grass ropes.[51]

The Spaniards could not imagine a proper building without a proper door, and although some observers see the lack of doors as a sign of the Indians' great honesty,[52] others see it as a fault and yet another sign of backwardness – either they are simply lazy, or they have no property to protect.[53] Therefore, although the walls and roofs of the first churches could have been constructed using traditional building skills, the doors and doorframes could not. These were, however, seen as an essential component of a church: a church, it was decreed, should be shut and locked when not in use, so that it could not be used for profane purposes.[54]

The *yana* who had not been taken on as personal servants but who by virtue of being *yana* did not have traditional community roots nor duties to an *encomendero* and who did not have lands of their own would have had to find a way of making a living for themselves; they would no longer be supported by the state as they had been traditionally. The new colonial administration encouraged those with a particular skill to continue to practise it,[55] and in 1567 Juan de Matienzo recommended that those *yana* who were not servants learn a trade from a master.[56] Carpentry was perhaps the most common of these and a great many Indians – both *yana* and others – became skilful practitioners at an early date. Even a relatively brief apprenticeship with a European craftsman would have equipped an able man (always men) with a basic mastery with which to set up on his own. Indians were apprenticed to masters on the same terms – at least in theory – as Spanish, or as negro, mulatto or mestizo apprentices. In a document from the end of the century a

Spanish carpenter, Gabriel López of Lima, agreed to take on Juan, 'an Indian from Nazca', to teach him the trade. His apprenticeship was to last two years, he would be paid 24 pesos a year, he would be supplied with two new sets of ordinary Indian clothing of cotton, he would be fed and would be sent for religious instruction on holy days. At the end of the two years López considered that Juan should have been able to learn enough to become a master himself.[57]

There is no record of whether Juan did become a master carpenter, but many Indians did complete their training successfully. In Lima in 1557 Lucas Martínez Vargas contracted a Spanish carpenter Anton González to build him a mill, to help with the construction of which he agreed to supply the carpenter with thirty *indios de mita* and, as a separate category, four Indian carpenters.[58] Independent Indian carpenters are recorded in Quito in 1559,[59] and in 1572 Viceroy Toledo established a whole ward of Indian carpenters in the city of Cuzco, and another of silversmiths.[60] A large number of craftsmen with the status of *yana* would have been resident in Cuzco in Inca times, and the silversmiths would be survivors from these and their descendants; that the other group of artisans singled out by Toledo should be carpenters points both to the Indians' adaptability and to the high demand for this new skill.

Sixteenth-century Peru did not produce one of the big mission-based schools for training the Indians in both the liberal and mechanical arts which elsewhere in Spanish America offered an alternative to the apprenticeship system of learning a trade. At this time the Franciscan sphere of influence did not extend south of northern Peru, and it was the Franciscans who were responsible for establishing the most famous of these schools: Fray Pedro de Gante that of Tlatelolco in Mexico in the years immediately following the conquest,[61] and Fray Jodoco Ricke (also Flemish by birth) that in Quito which was properly founded in 1549.[62] In 1569 another was established in Bogotá, also by the Franciscans.[63] These schools, which were free, taught young Indian children to read and write and to sing or play musical instruments; older children were taught a trade – one that was of particular use to the church, such as painting or sculpture, or one which was of more general use such as cobbling, tailoring or carpentry.[64] Ricke's foundation, the Colegio de San Andrés attached to the Franciscan monastery in Quito, gave special attention to music and to painting and sculpture, but it also trained shoemakers, tailors, blacksmiths, carpenters and *albañiles* (masons in brick and/or stone).[65] The Peruvian Indian Jorge de la Cruz, having been taken by his *encomendero* first to Lima where he 'learned to make houses for Spaniards' and then to Quito along with the troops sent to suppress the rebellion of Gonzalo Pizarro, spent the rest of his life working for the Franciscans on the construction of their church, and perhaps in helping to train those attending the school in aspects of the building trade. His son Francisco Morocho followed in his footsteps working for the Franciscans both in Quito and in Riobamba, where he was responsible for their conventual church.[66] Quito, and the Colegio de San Andrés in particular, attracted Indians from a wide area, many of whom had been *yana* under the Incas, and they gathered in extensive settlements around the Spanish heart of the city. Despite the changing fortunes of the Colegio itself the traditions of craftsmanship it established persisted and Quito was to remain an important artistic centre throughout the colonial period.

At the beginning of the sixteenth century the Spanish attitude to Indian artisans was positive and encouraging. The 1516 instructions to the Hieronymites includes the recommendation that some of the Indians be taught trades so that they may become carpenters, tailors, stone-cutters, farriers, sawyers and so on, because such trades would be of use to the new republic, but also because this was seen as a way of encouraging the Indians to adopt a civilized way of life, to live in *policía*.[67] In 1518 the Spanish Crown wrote to the governor of Española that those Indians who had the 'capacity and ability' to live in towns in a civilized manner should be allowed to do so, as direct vassals of the Crown, and so independent of the *encomienda* system.[68] The implication of this, I think, is that such 'capacity and ability' would include a useful trade. The nascent colony had great need of skilled craftsmen and recruited them from among the Indians or negroes as necessary; where Indian craftsmen are concerned however, the encouragement offered is often couched in terms of the spiritual benefits of being gainfully employed. In 1550, for example, Charles V instructed the Viceroy of New Spain to see to it that those Indians who had useful skills be made to put them to good use, to ensure that they did not live in idleness.[69] Early attempts to train the Indians in the useful arts in this way received support from the highest levels, from the King and the Viceroy. In 1559 the Viceroy of Peru arranged for the Colegio de San Andrés in Quito to receive financial support,[70] and in 1562 King Philip accorded it a special grant in view of the good work it was doing, both in instructing the Indians in the Christian doctrine and in 'teaching them good customs and skills so that they can live in a Christian and orderly way'.[71]

But attitudes changed, or perhaps rather the balance of power between the local and the national ruling élite shifted in favour of the former. The Crown, as is often the case, tended to lag behind colonial opinion on such matters. The increased stability of the colony, together with an increase in the number of European craftsmen and the consolidation of craft guilds in the later sixteenth century led to a general hardening of attitudes towards the Indians. In Quito by 1567 there was apparently considerable hostility from the Spanish citizens to the liberality towards the Indians, and the Crown had to issue a statement in defence of the Indians' rights to attend the college.[72] Garcilaso de la Vega quotes a passage from Padre Blas Valera extolling the Indians' ability to learn but complaining about the Spaniards' reluctance to teach them:

> The clumsiness which they now exhibit is not a result of lack of skill or intelligence, but rather because they are unaccustomed to the ways and things of Europe and because they do not find people to teach the skills, but only things for profit and gain... Those who find a teacher or free time and liberty to learn, even if it be no more than imitating what they see without being taught, become skilled craftsmen in all the mechanical arts, and excel many Spaniards. And the same [is true] of reading and writing, and in music and instruments and other abilities, and even in Latin they would not be the worst if the Spaniards would only teach them.[73]

In New Spain there is a similar decline in interest in the education of the Indians as the century progresses.[74]

Interestingly, this shift of colonial opinion is not simply the result of the growing unity and strength of the European community, and a desire to clarify the racial boundaries; it is also the result of a desire to clarify social boundaries within the European community itself. In the same year in which the question of funding the Colegio de San Andrés arose, 1567, Juan de Matienzo, in his extensive report to the Crown on the state of affairs in Peru, suggests that he too is not entirely in favour of education for the Indians, but he also has strong views about the status of European craftsmen:

> In this Kingdom much disorder has arisen from allowing tailors, shoemakers, barbers, farriers, blacksmiths, carpenters, brick-masons and other artisans to go about as gentlemen; they do not ply their trades but rather they teach them to the Indians in their service, even though by means of laws and royal provisions Your Majesty has provided and ordered that they can be compelled to practise their crafts in new territories such as these, as is necessary.[75]

But he adds that there are exceptions, that some are very rich and live honourably and therefore do not need to be compelled to work. Evidently he is distinguishing between those craftsmen who he believes have genuinely achieved the status of gentlemen, and some who are imposters and upstarts.

His assumptions are that such distinctions would be obvious to the well-bred, and that such categories are real and should be maintained. Initially the colonies had offered ambitious settlers opportunities not only for making money, but also for social mobility; by Matienzo's time attitudes are changing, and the profoundly hierarchical social values of metropolitan Spanish culture are reasserting themselves.[76] In 1552 Prince Philip wrote to Viceroy Velasco in New Spain that it had come to his attention that craftsmen and other *personas bajas* had been appointed as *corregidores*, the local governors-cum-magistrates, and he ordered that no-one who was a brick-mason, or a tailor, or a potter, or any other practitioner of the mechanical arts should be eligible for such office, 'but only honourable people who have the necessary qualities'.[77] It should not be surprising to find that the Crown sometimes tends to be more liberal than the colonies on matters relating to the Indians and less liberal on matters relating to the colonists' own ambitions for social advancement. The wealth of the Indies reached the Crown principally through the medium of the colonists; it reached the colonists from the Indians, and the Crown, receiving reports of maltreatment of the Indians, tended to blame this on the colonists' greed and exploitative measures and also on their social flexibility and disorder. Potentially, of course, the colonists were a greater threat to the power of the Crown and consequently there was a greater need to keep them in check.

In the period under consideration there was a constant shortage of European-trained craftsmen in Spanish America. There are regular complaints about this from the colonies to Spain, and regular attempts on the part of the Crown and other officials to arrange for the need to be met. In 1508, 1509 and 1510, for example, the Crown repeatedly appealed to the Casa de Contratación in Seville (the governing body responsible for overseeing all American trade and emigration) to despatch *maestros canteros*, master masons, to the Caribbean, where there was little or no indigenous tradition of building in stone.[78] But the very reiteration of the demand demonstrates that the Casa de Contratación had difficulty in persuading people to go; they could offer no cash incentives – on the contrary, they would have had to finance themselves entirely until such time as they were well enough settled in America to start earning for themselves – and so for trained craftsmen already making a decent living in Spain the uncertainties of colonial life would not have had the same attraction as they did for soldiers, merchants and adventurers.

But those who did try their luck were in great demand. In 1536 the governors of Cartagena sent an account to the Crown of the difficulties they were experiencing in establishing proper towns for the European settlers. In Cartagena itself, the *iglesia mayor* was a dismal affair, only half finished. It had not been begun in stone because it was not possible to make mortar – there was no lime to be had locally – so the authorities said they would be forced to complete it as it had been begun, in straw and canes. They pointed out that it was difficult even to provide the necessary fittings such as doors, chairs for the clergy, and choir stalls, because not only were there no craftsmen, but neither was there a suitable local supply of wood nor any metal tools.[79] The construction of the fabric, given that it was in local materials, was evidently in the hands of the local Indian population. However inadequate, the governors recognized that this would have to serve for the time being, but for the church furnishings and fittings there were no local traditions which could be adapted: these required someone versed in the European technique of carpentry. 'By chance', the document rather ingenuously continues, a carpenter arrived, a resident of Santo Domingo, and the Bishop had asked him for an estimate of what it would cost to complete the church. Such costs would be those involved in hiring a European carpenter and in buying in those materials which could not be found locally, such as wood, nails, hinges and locks. The documentation only takes us to this point but it is reasonable to assume that the itinerant carpenter from Santo Domingo was in a good position to secure himself a highly lucrative commission. In the same year, 1536, Lima city council appointed two officials, one of whom was a carpenter, to inspect all the doors and windows and other work of carpentry carried out in the city, because there had been complaints about the exorbitant prices carpenters were charging.[80] There can be little doubt but that a carpenter's skill was highly marketable.

Initially there was very little division of labour within the two basic trades, the carpenters and the brick or stone masons. A carpenter such as the one who found his way to Cartagena in 1536 would have been able to construct a framework of timbers for a roof, make doors and windows and frames, wooden ceilings and floors, as well as basic furniture; such a range of skills would have been standard at the time. Most carpenters would also have been able to produce some sort of carved retable for an altar, but the sculpted image or images within it would usually have been produced by a sculptor.

As the number of skilled carpenters working within the colonial system increased (whether European, Indian, negro, mulatto or mestizo), specialists emerged, especially *carpinteros de lo blanco* and *ensambladores*.[81] *Carpintería de lo blanco* includes furniture but also, and more importantly from my point of view, ceilings made of small pieces of interlocking wood in either a *mudéjar* style, when they are termed *alfarje* and are the commonest form in the earlier colonial period, or a form of Renaissance coffering (*artesonado*), or a mixture of both.[82] Early sources suggest that this was the normal roof covering for richer churches in South America during the sixteenth and early seventeenth centuries, but surviving wooden ceilings suggest that this solution was especially favoured by the Franciscans. It occurs, for example, in the Franciscan churches in Bogotá, Tunja, Quito, Sucre and Potosí, and in Santa Clara in Ayacucho (Plate 18). The *ensamblador* was responsible for doors and windows, and for retables, and would tend to be more conversant with the classical architectural vocabulary than a *carpintero de lo blanco*, but the boundaries between the two categories remained flexible.

A carpenter provided the furnishings and fittings, and roof timbering for a building; the rest of the fabric, finances permitting, was built or supervised by a bricklayer or stone mason. The terms *albañilería* or *albañería* refer principally to work in brick but also often include work in stone, whereas the *cantero* appears to work exclusively in stone. The term *oficial albañil de la cantería* also occurs.[83] The work of the *albañil* or *cantero* could involve building walls, of course, but more importantly it involved the construction of vaults, and the distinguishing features and embellishments to buildings: portals and façades, balconies, arcades and grand stairways, where these were not made of wood. A basic knowledge of classical architectural mouldings would have been the stock-in-trade of an *albañil* or a *cantero*.

As with carpentry, the various subdivisions within these trades only begin to become apparent in America in the second half of the sixteenth century; initially there were simply builders who turned their hands to whatever was required. Work involving architectural mouldings in brick was common from an early date, especially along the Peruvian coast where there was a lack of good quality stone and it is in building in brick that the first subdivisions between builders occur. Classicizing portals of brick were made using pre-moulded bricks and by cutting or sharpening particular details *in situ*, and by the later sixteenth century this had become a distinct branch of *albañilería*. A *cortador de ladrillo*, strictly speaking a brick mason, was employed by the Franciscans of Lima in 1598 to execute a moulded cornice in the cloister.[84] Plastering, *yesería*, which would include work in moulded plaster, was also to become a specialist branch of *albañilería*.[85]

Another rather more general category in the building trade was that of *alarife*, perhaps best translated as a sort of civil engineer.[86] In 1537 Lima city

Plate 18 Quito, San Francisco. Detail of the *alfarje* ceiling of interlocking pieces of wood, painted and gilded, which decorates the gothic vaulting of the crossing; late sixteenth century.

council appointed Juan Meco as its first *alarife* whose job was to oversee the construction of the city.[87] He was a sort of supervisor and surveyor with responsibility for measuring out new *solares* as required, and for organizing the provision and distribution of water within the city. He is not referred to by any term that would suggest he had received a formal training or apprenticeship – only that he understood how to measure things – and his name suggests that he was of Indian blood. Meco remains a shadowy figure, his only other important duty apparently being his appointment in 1538 as superintendent, *mayordomo*, of the new hospital in Lima. His brief for this job is vague and may suggest that he was to be responsible for its design as well as for supervising its execution – certainly no other name occurs in this connection – but generally speaking a *mayordomo* would not have been involved in the practical aspects of building.[88] Within a few years the title *alarife* can be found applied specifically to a higher grade of builder than a simple *albañil*: in 1549 Diego de Torres, *alvanyr*, presented plans for the new council offices in Lima, the *casas de cabildo*;[89] by January of 1550 he is referred to as Diego de Torres *alarife*, and is found recommending a similar upgrading of Francisco de Valer from *albañil* to *alarife*.[90]

In all these trades there was – theoretically at least – a hierarchy from apprenticeship up through, say, *cantero* to master, *maestro cantero* or *maestro de cantería*, although in practice the title of master is rare in this period. Strictly speaking only accredited masters could take on apprentices, and the indentured apprentice was protected by law, the master undertaking to feed, clothe and teach him, and at the end of the allotted apprenticeship, to provide him with a set of tools.[91] But there were plenty of unofficial ways of learning a trade. If only masters could take on apprentices, those who were not masters could always take on assistants who in turn could set up on their own and do well. The first guild in Lima, for both carpenters and masons, was ratified by the city council in 1549, and was set up principally to ensure good quality workmanship.[92] In the sixteenth century its power even within Lima itself was very limited; with demand usually far exceeding supply, guild members could not enforce a strict monopoly. There were amateur craftsmen too, particularly among the clergy, from whom a dextrous assistant could learn a great deal. In Cuzco in 1585 for example, the Jesuit community consisted of nine Fathers and ten brothers, of whom one Father and four brothers were working on the construction of their new premises and were *oficiales*: two carpenters, one *albañil*, one painter and one blacksmith.[93] Many missionary friars, even if not themselves trained as practitioners of a particular craft, could have quickly learnt enough about the techniques of making brick and lime, of building a brick or stone arch or of simple joinery to have been able to direct others. It was the practical experience that counted in the end, and all the various ways of acquiring a skill in sixteenth-century South America were essentially practical, involving experience in a workshop and on a building site.

A confirmatory example can be found in the documents relating to the church of Portovelo in Panama.[94] In 1626 several carpenters and masons were called in to assess the cost of completing the church, and they drew up a detailed report of what had been built so far and of what remained to be done; this they submitted complete with an accompanying drawing. The text is thorough and knowledgeable: there can be no doubt but that these men knew their trade. The drawing, on the other hand, is crude in the extreme (Plate 19). It does contain the necessary information – the relative positions of the doors, windows and chapels and so on – but was evidently executed by someone who had not received even a rudimentary training in architectural draughtsmanship, someone who probably would not have recognized an accurately executed elevation if he had seen one, someone, in fact, who was not used to drawing things at all. And yet we must assume that the author was chosen as the most proficient of all the various assessors. It is worth noting that to give estimates, either of monies needed to complete a building as at Portovelo, or of expenses incurred so far as in the case of Cartagena discussed earlier, was a regular part of an accredited craftsman's work. It was probably reasonably well paid especially if the assessor were a master; it is also essentially an ability obtainable only through experience.

To become a master one had to be examined by another master of the trade. When the first guild was established in Lima in 1549 Gerónimo Delgado was appointed *hesaminador mayor* of the other *albañiles* and masters of the trade.[95] He presented himself to the council as a *maestro de cantería e geometría* with papers from Spain to prove it, and anyone with such credentials was automatically given preference over a master who had risen through the ranks in America. Delgado was, as he requested, appointed *maestro mayor* of Lima, the first to hold that office, and the top position in the trade. The city council would have been impressed by his credentials, but they would no doubt also have been attracted by the fact that he asked for no salary, only the honour of the position. He had also proved his ability: two years previously, in 1547, he had been appointed by the Dominicans to construct the vaulting over the crossing of their new church which was situated only a stone's throw from the

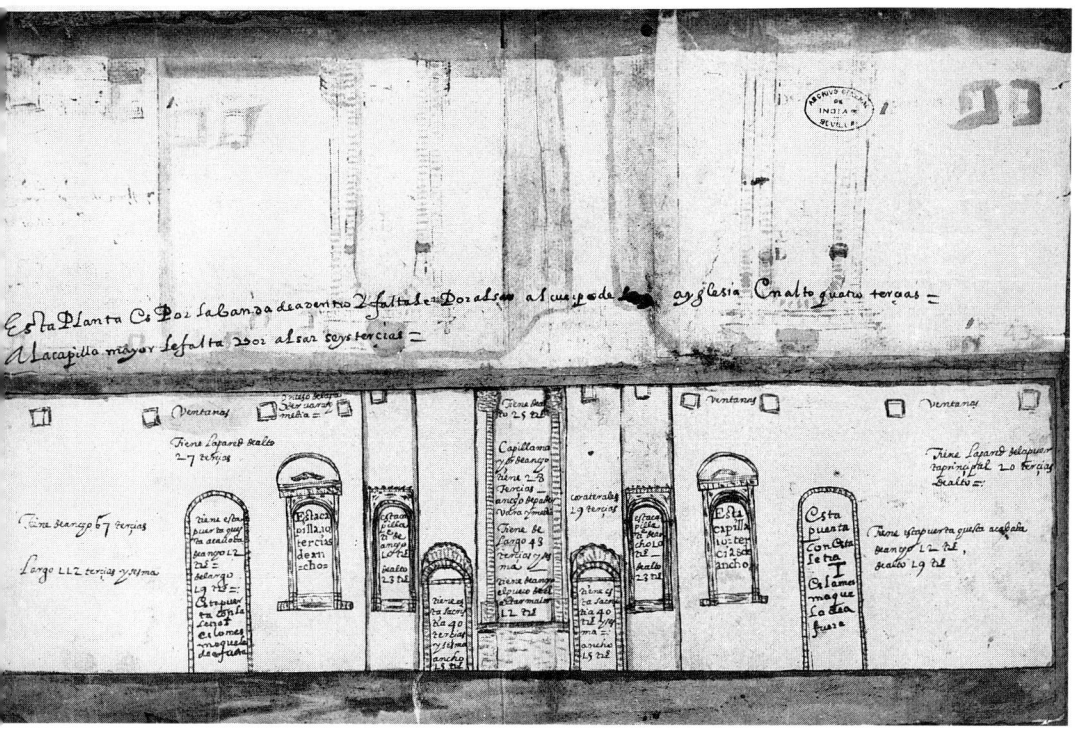

Plate 19 Portovelo, Panama. Elevations of the interior of a church; 1626. Archivo General de Indias, Mapas y Planos, Panama, 43v.

central square where the council met.[96] In 1550 he was also appointed *maestro mayor* of the cathedral,[97] a title which in relation to ecclesiastical buildings is sometimes replaced by *obrero mayor*.[98] The post of *maestro mayor* was perhaps at least as much honorific as practical because not all applications for the title were granted, even when a suitable candidate presented themselves and when there was apparently no-one holding the office at the time. In 1585 one of the most famous figures in the history of sixteenth-century Spanish American architecture, Francisco de Becerra, asked the Lima council to accept him as *maestro mayor* not simply of Lima but of 'all the Kingdoms of Peru'; the council were apparently not impressed, even though he was already *maestro mayor* of the cathedral, and they appointed him instead simply as the city *alarife*.[99]

The shortage of appropriately qualified personnel continues to be a regular complaint into the seventeenth century, but by this time the reality is rather more complex. In 1612, for example, the Archbishop of Lima begged the Council of the Indies to despatch a good *maestro mayor* for the cathedral, someone skilful and learned in the art of architecture because, said the Archbishop, there was no-one suitable to be had in the land since Becerra's death.[100] Becerra had died in 1605 and it seems odd that the by now rich capital of the Viceroyalty had not attracted a suitable replacement in the intervening seven years. In fact, in 1609 Juan Martínez de Arrona had submitted a report to the cathedral authorities on the damage caused to the fabric in the earthquake of that year, and he had called himself *maestro mayor de la fábrica de la cathedral*.[101] The ecclesiastical *cabildo*, however, recording their receipt of Arrona's report and those of three other experts, make no mention of Arrona as *maestro mayor* or indeed *maestro* anything.[102] Arrona evidently regarded himself as Becerra's natural successor, and given his experience seems the obvious candidate for the title but perhaps the other builders who reported on the earthquake damage also thought themselves eligible. The personal feelings which lie behind these documents can only be guessed at. The Archibishop, writing to Spain for a *maestro mayor* for his cathedral, was surely looking for the prestige which would come from such a direct import from Europe, but the appointment of an outsider would also avoid the problem of trying to make a decision between a number of local contenders. Arrona was in fact finally appointed *maestro mayor* for the cathedral in 1614 and was to be responsible for designing the central bay of the façade[103] (*see* plate 12).

Such confusions, rivalries and ambitions are very common especially where honorific titles or prestigious and lucrative commissions are concerned, but in colonial Latin America there is the added dimension of the peculiar snobbishness associated with things European. Those responsible for commissioning a prestigious building would not unnaturally have wanted to avoid trouble between local builders, among whom perhaps none had any formal qualifications, and few any recognized training. An outsider, preferably from Europe, whom they could believe to be superior even if in fact he was not, was always an attractive alternative.

## Architects

There were no architects in South America in the sixteenth century. The word *arquitecto* first appears in Peru in the 1620s in connection with the contract for the choirstalls of Lima cathedral. On 6 February 1623 Luis de Vargas submitted a tender for the work in which he called himself an *arquitecto*.[104] Not to be outdone, on 7 April 1623, Pedro de Noguera, who had been awarded the commission, called himself a *maestro de arquitectura*, though as with Vargas quite what this meant in terms of paper qualifications is unclear. On 1 August of the same year three jealous *escultores* claimed that Noguera was no more than a jumped-up carpenter, an *ensamblador*, and not even an *escultor*.[105] Perhaps the particularly prestigious nature of this commission was the catalyst which sparked off the use of the new term, a term still not common in Europe at this date, to signify an old and recognized art which had previously been practised by both amateurs and craftsmen under a variety of different labels.

The initial design of buildings, a task now usually associated with an architect, was in South America often the responsibility of the founder of the building or settlement. The founder was therefore often the architect of the new colony in a practical as well as in a metaphorical sense. In the case of Pizarro's foundation of Lima his physical involvement with the construction of the first cathedral is written into the Act of Foundation of the city: 'he made and built the said church, and placed with his hands the first stone and the first timbers'.[106] Given the order of the sentence the implication is perhaps that he 'made and built the said church' in a theoretical sense, but his involvement, ritual or otherwise, is deliberately stressed. In other cases the dual rôle of founder/designer is quite explicit. In 1572, for example, Jerónimo de Silva founded the new Indian town of Huancayo in accordance with the instructions which Viceroy Toledo had sent him the previous year. These stipulated that Silva himself was to lay out the streets, houses and plaza, and to see to the establishment of a Dominican church and monastery in the new *reducción*. For these too he was to draw up the plan which he was then to send to Lima to see if any *oficiales*, craftsmen, would be willing to undertake the work of construction.[107] In other cases the design of buildings was often drawn up by the patron or patrons in conjunction with the craftsmen.

Again and again the documentation makes it quite clear that the construction of the colony was not in the hands of theorists or highly-trained specialists, but was the responsibility of all colonists. The Spanish immigrants as a body brought with them a homogeneous set of ideas about towns, town plans, churches, government offices and private housing, about architectural style and architectural technique, and about Christianity and civility. They themselves turned these ideas into reality, sometimes with the help of European-trained craftsmen, sometimes with the help of Indian craftsmen who had acquired the necessary European styles and techniques, and sometimes with the help only of relatively unskilled Indian labour. The results are nevertheless astonishingly, unmistakably European in appearance.

# 4
# Questions of style

### The American contribution

The first European colonists firmly intended to introduce their own style of architecture and town planning into America. Two factors might be expected to have modified the results: first, the physical conditions of the American continent – how far, for example, did the climate, the geography or the available materials modify European building traditions? And second, to what degree did the artistic styles and traditions of the native peoples influence the appearance of the conquerors' architecture? Native Americans far outnumbered Europeans at all but the highest levels in the construction of the first colonial buildings in South America but to what extent is this visible? How far is the hand or mind of the indigenous craftsman identifiable in the forms of the buildings or in the style of their decoration? What, in effect, was the impact of America on the imported architectural forms? The answer to these questions is, in almost all cases: no more than the conquerors could possibly help.

To return again to the question of the building materials. The theoretical importance to the European settlers of the idea of a hierarchy of materials has already been discussed. In practice it meant that many of the traditional American building materials were despised, and although initially often unavoidable, colonists aimed to replace them as soon as possible with buildings of brick or stone, with roofs of wood and tile. The colonial authorities frequently tried to legislate to this end, as in Lima in 1538, when the citizens were required to build houses of stone, or in Arequipa in 1550 where it was ordered that thatched roofs be replaced with tile.[1] If brick and stone were desirable for domestic architecture it was considered essential – in principle at least – that high quality materials be used for churches. In Lima there was no stone to be had locally that was suitable for carving and polishing for use, for example, on church façades and it had to be imported from elsewhere. Incredibly, one of the sources was Panama, some 3,000 miles up the Pacific coast, a striking example of the strength of what was and what was not considered fitting in architecture.[2]

But despite the sometimes extreme measures to keep up standards certain concessions were made for both financial and practical reasons. Lima, the Viceregal capital and in many ways the most self-consciously European of the new colonial towns of South America, was forced to make more concessions than most, and today Lima and the other Pacific coastal towns of Peru, Chile and Ecuador, despite their relatively close and frequent contacts with Europe, are less European in appearance than most highland towns. A modern tourist's impression of the old colonial centres of highland Andean towns such as Quito or Ayacucho or Cuzco is of predominantly European building styles and traditional European building materials: imposing stone façades and red tiled roofs. Lima has never looked like this. The recurring complaints about the city during the first century or so after its foundation were that the buildings were only of one storey, that they were mostly of adobe, and that they had no roofs, pitched roofs that is, with gables and tiles. Today much of the housing in Lima and elsewhere in coastal South America is still only of one or two storeys, and tiled roofs are an extreme rarity, even an eccentricity.

The reasons for this have to do with climate, ecology and geology. Nowhere along the desert strip of the Pacific coast is there sufficient rain to warrant proper gabled roofs and so, given the difficulty of acquiring both tiles and timber for rafters strong enough to support them, there were strong incentives for using an alternative system of roofing. The indigenous inhabitants of the region used panels of woven reeds, *esteras*, to form flat roofs which were then covered with a thin layer of earth or ashes[3] to absorb the winter mists, and to offer some protection from the summer sun. Walls were traditionally made of *quincha*, panels this time of canes rather than reeds, and coated with mud in the fashion of European wattle-and-daub. These, despite the fact that they were considered of inferior quality, came to be the materials most commonly used in colonial housing throughout the desert coastal region: walls of *quincha*, sometimes in combination with wood and adobes in the manner of European timber-framing, with roofs of *esteras*.[4] *Quincha* also provides a suitable base for moulded stucco work, a common coastal substitute for carved stone on the façades of smaller parish churches. Only recently, with the introduction of cement and reinforced concrete, are such materials being superseded.

The use of such – to European minds – inferior building materials on the dry

Peruvian coastlands was largely because the preferred alternatives were extremely scarce and therefore expensive. But the danger from earthquakes would seem another obvious disincentive to constructing buildings of more than one or two storeys high and to roofing with heavy materials. The whole of the Andean region and western coastline suffer regularly from earth tremors of varying force and since structures of *quincha* and *esteras* can withstand considerable shocks their appropriation by the colonists for their houses seems only rational despite the low esteem in which these materials were held. Compromise in the realm of domestic housing was one thing, however; in public buildings, especially churches, it was quite another. Here the pressure to conform to European ideal standards was much greater, as, of course, were the resources to meet those standards. To Europeans a church scarcely even deserved to be so called unless it were of stone or at least of brick. Despite the earthquakes and despite the expense, during the second half of the sixteenth century many large stone or brick vaulted churches were begun on an ambitious scale. The tenacity of the ideas about architectural decorum was such that although the vaults of these churches came crashing down with monotonous regularity, and with devastating effects on the church furnishings below – and indeed occasionally on the population too – lighter, more flexible roofing materials were scarcely even considered for generations.

Take the case of Lima cathedral[5] (*see* plate 12). In 1606 the body of the cathedral, begun in roughly its present form in 1572, was half completed using brick groin vaults when it was seriously damaged by an earthquake; repaired, it was again damaged in 1609, and after various consultations it was agreed to change from groin to a form of rib vaulting as being stronger and lighter, and to reduce the overall height of the building by about a third. The interior was completed in this revised form in 1622 and was repeatedly reconstructed to the same design after serious tremors in 1630, 1678 and 1687. Not until after the disastrous earthquake of 1746 was it finally decided to replace the heavy brick vaults with a wooden framework covered in *quincha*, plastered and painted to give the appearance of vaulting. The walls and piers too were reconstructed with brick cores where necessary, but with an extensive *quincha* overlay. This is the form in which the cathedral stands today; the lighter roofing not only does less damage if it falls, but is less rigid than bricks and mortar, and in a light tremor the plasterwork may crack but the structure will survive when solid vaulting would not. Many other coastal churches that had been begun in brick in the sixteenth or seventeenth centuries were eventually provided with lighter roofings made from traditional local materials, but designed to give the appearance of vaulting. This compromise was only arrived at after about two hundred years' adherence to an inappropriate set of ideals and even then the aim was always to make such buildings look as if they were of stone. Even brick portals were often plastered and then painted to look like stone or marble, as was the case with the main portal of the hospital church of San Andrés in Lima in 1563.

In the highlands, where there was a plentiful supply of good quality stone as well as of skilled Indian masons, there are cases where the Spaniards were unmoved in their determination to vault their churches properly. Arequipa cathedral, which suffered from serious earthquakes during its construction in 1600 and 1604, was repeatedly rebuilt with stone vaults, although here the climate is such that false vaults of adobe and *quincha* would in any case have been unsuitable.[6] Cuzco has suffered badly from earthquakes over the centuries but the stone vaults of the cathedral are particularly strong and the walls thick and well-buttressed in a way that is comparable to the reinforcing anti-earthquake measures developed in church architecture in Guatemala.[7] Cuzco cathedral was in fact almost the only building in the city to survive the severe earthquake of 1650 with relatively little damage, so perhaps the Indian masons applied their inherited knowledge of earthquake-resistant structure to her huge stone vaults.

The climate and the available materials of South America certainly did affect the architecture, but on the whole the Spaniards resisted change, and tried to uphold their ideal standards at least in the outward appearance of their buildings, by making them look more substantial and of better quality materials than they often were. In other words, in this area their ideas and attitudes about architecture remained largely unaltered even though in practice some concessions did have to be made. The extent to which indigenous architectural forms and styles affected early colonial architecture is more complex but in the end I think the same is true: the conquering Spaniards did not deliberately borrow from native culture, but because some of their architectural innovations seem to have parallels in indigenous architecture the question of influence, whether conscious or unconscious, must be confronted.

The case of the open chapel and walled atrium is the most obvious of these.[8] The open chapel, developed in Indian communities in Mexico at the beginning of the colonial period, was, as the name implies, a relatively small, roofed structure open on one or more sides which offered the priest a distinct and protected location. Designed to cater, as is usually said, for the large

Plate 20  Andahuaylillas, near Cuzco; later sixteenth century. A balcony running across the whole width of the façade, is a common feature of Andean churches.

Indian congregations, it opened on to a large square and was usually raised up so that those gathered in the open air in front of it could be instructed in the fundamentals of Christianity, and could witness the celebration of mass. The open chapel was widespread throughout Spanish America in the sixteenth century. In South America none survive on the scale of those at, say, Actopan or Tlamanalco in Mexico, but smaller examples survive as at Copacabana in Bolivia, or alternatively highland Peruvian churches often have a balcony over the west portal which no doubt served the same purpose, as for example at Andahuaylillas, San Jerónimo and Urcos, all near Cuzco (Plate 20). In Cuzco itself in 1572 Viceroy Toledo reported that the church of La Merced on the main market square had a chapel 'built over the door of the church' where the priests say mass every day 'so that the Indians who are in the square may see it'.[9]

Whether or not something identifiable as an open chapel has survived in conjunction with an existing church, almost all churches in Spanish America still open on to a public space, a square or plaza of some sort. In some cases this is the main town square itself; in others it is carefully demarcated as an atrium or patio adjoining the church, often raised above the street level, approached up steps and with an enclosing wall topped with arches. In Indian parishes the population gathered in these patios to witness Christian services, as they did in the square in front of the church of La Merced in Cuzco, but more importantly, to be taught the Christian doctrine.[10] Bishop Loayza of Lima, in his instructions for 'curas de indios' of 1545 required that at least twice a week the missionary priest or priests should gather all the local Indian population together into the church 'or its patio' in order to teach them about Christianity and civility.[11] In the corners of an enclosed atrium there were often *posas*, small open-air oratories, where temporary altars could be erected for feast days, and the atrium would become the setting for colourful processions, music and dancing. Numerous atria with *posas* still survive in South America, particularly in rural areas.[12]

These, the open chapel, atrium and *posa*, are architectural forms without any very direct or obvious European antecedents. It is true that various forms of Christian teaching and preaching have traditionally taken place in the open air in Europe, in town squares and from open pulpits, but in Spanish America the space around a church is always deliberately and carefully organized with such purposes in mind, whether the space be in the form of a separate atrium or simply the town square. The *posa* too seems not to be a direct import from Europe. At first sight the wayside altars or small chapels (in Spain called *humilladeros*) at which religious processions in Catholic Europe pause for a blessing or prayer would seem a likely source, but this seems not to have been obvious to contemporary observers. In Cervantes de Salazar's description of Mexico City in 1554 the visitor from Spain is intrigued by the atrium with *posas* in front of the monastic church of Santo Domingo, and one of his guides has to explain the arrangement to him:

Because the cloister is too narrow to hold so many people, the devout and the multitude, who come here on such solemn, festal days as Christ's Nativity, Death, Resurrection, and Ascension . . . space was made so that, as they marched with the cross preceding and the images following, they might stop at each chapel to make offerings and to pray.[13]

Evidently this arrangement was a departure from European traditions.

It has been suggested that these distinctive features of colonial architecture, the open chapel, atrium and *posa*, were deliberately modelled on the forms of indigenous religious architecture in order to facilitate the conversion of the

Indians. Large walled or otherwise demarcated open areas were a feature of pre-conquest religious ritual in America. Worship for the majority of the population in the Mexican and Mayan areas, for example, took place out of doors, in large squares in front of the pyramids, while only the priests had access to the small temples above, a pattern which in some ways seems analogous to the Christian priest saying mass in an open chapel in front of a crowded atrium. Similarly in South America pre-conquest buildings large enough to contain the general populace are rare, but courtyards or open squares are an important feature of Inca religion as well as of the great pre-Incaic religious centres of Chavin, Tiahuanaco and Pachacamac. The residential complexes of the Chimu, Inca and Chibcha nobilities were often situated within spacious courtyards and enclosed within high walls, or, in the case of the latter, elaborate palisades. Cuzco's main square, the physical and metaphorical heart of the Inca state, was used for public ceremonies as well as for religious festivities. External space in Native American architecture is almost always as important as internal, and is often more so.

Can the prevalence of the open chapel and especially of the atrium in Spanish America therefore be seen as an example of the influence of Indian culture on colonial? The evidence is unconvincing. The missionaries to South America, particularly the Jesuits, were certainly aware of the need to take traditional customs into account in the conversion of the Indians, although I have not found much evidence of any equivalent to the elaborate adaptations of traditional rituals introduced by the church in Mexico.[14] José de Acosta, writing in the mid-1570s about the best means of converting Indians, was among those who stressed that it is important always to replace old pagan ceremonies with new Christian ones,[15] and José de Arriaga, a fellow Jesuit, repeatedly refers to the need for ceremonies, processions and music within the Christian ritual.[16] But no-one goes so far as to suggest that the pagans' use of space should be deliberately imitated in Christian architectural complexes in order to encourage them to espouse Christianity.

If this were indeed the case, it does not explain why these forms are not restricted to Indian towns and villages. Cervantes de Salazar's explanation of the atrium and *posas* in Mexico City does not suggest that these were for the use of Indians rather than Europeans; quite the contrary. In Lima the early seventeenth-century diarist Juan Antonio Suardo mentions numerous religious festivals where temporary altars were erected in the corners of the main square in the manner of *posas*.[17] There is no doubt from Suardo's diary that such festivals were intended for Christians, and were not understood as a means of winning over the Indians by providing open-air worship in a manner to which they were accustomed.

All of which supports the idea that such forms were not evolved in imitation of indigenous forms or at least not deliberately so. This is not to say that the location of the church and the atrium was not often determined by pre-existing structures, but this is not, it seems to me, the same as influence. There were various requirements from ecclesiastical authorities that in Indian areas pagan sites be consecrated to Christianity, by, if appropriate, building a church on the spot or at least by erecting a cross there.[18] This was no more than missionaries of the Christian church had done for centuries. Gregory the Great had first recommended the practice in the fifth century and it is not uncommon in other religions. The device by which the impact of a building can be greatly increased and its importance enhanced by including in the design a large open space in front is not the invention of any one culture either. It was exploited by the Aztecs and the Incas as by the Greeks and the Romans, and the question of influence is not helpful. The Spanish missionaries would naturally have wished to give their churches as much visual authority as possible and used large arcaded atria to good effect; that generally similar means of achieving this had already been used by the native Americans would not have surprised them. As with the town plan the indigenous structures and lay-out often conditioned the positioning of the main elements of the Christian complex: the church on the temple, the atrium and square on existing open spaces.

The Spaniards certainly made use of raised platforms, solid foundations, well-finished blocks of stone and so on, but this is not influence so much as appropriation for reasons of political and psychological as well as practical expediency. It is, I feel, misleading to talk about 'influence' in a case such as this, in the way one would talk of the influence of, say, Palladio on Inigo Jones or of African art on Picasso. Inigo Jones was happy, indeed anxious, to demonstrate his debt to his architectural forefather and his position in the classical tradition. Picasso too would have seen the notion of influence as appropriate to a discussion of his work in and around 1910 although in a different way. In Picasso's case it might be possible to argue that his use of African art was simply a manifestation of European domination of Africa but Picasso himself was not directly involved in this, and had no personal stake in controlling or exploiting Africans in the way the Spaniards did the Native Americans in the sixteenth century. In a situation not only of cultural but also of ideological and economic dominance, is it reasonable to expect to find evidence of Indian *influence* in this sense at any other than trivial or incidental levels? In Mexico the case can be put for a degree of visible Indian involvement in the appearance of early colonial art and architecture (although I am not sure this is the same as influence), and certainly in the seventeenth and eighteenth centuries, throughout the Spanish American territories, distinctive Latin American styles can be said to emerge that owe something at least to survivals or revivals of native forms. But in sixteenth-century Viceregal Peru this is rare. The Spaniards made use only of such Indian patterns and traditions as could easily be incorporated, or subsumed, within their own world view; they appropriated them as their own wherever possible.

The creation of large religious complexes, including a huge church, a walled atrium, *posas* and sometimes an open chapel as well represents the practical realization of generally-held notions about the importance and power of architecture to impress a public and, in the case of the Indians, to over-awe and impose upon them. These ideas are articulated very clearly in the 1573 *Ordenanzas* where it is assumed that when the Indians first encounter a Spanish town they will be amazed and realize that the Spaniards are there to stay, 'and they will fear them and will not dare offend them, and they will respect them and wish to have their friendship', but the same ideas are already present in some of the earliest legislation to deal with America – in the instructions to Pedrarias Dávila in 1513 – and are a part of colonial ideology.[19]

In the new Indian *reducciones*, for example, the church was the main instrument of moral and social control. An atrium in front of a church has the effect of extending the jurisdiction of the church out into the town, the main public square itself representing a sort of secondary atrium. In some cases this relationship is further emphasized by the addition of arches over the streets at the entrance to the square, as in the case of Tiahuanaco in Bolivia. Some of the surviving examples of arcaded atria in front of otherwise quite simple village churches, as at Chucuito in Southern Peru (*see* plates 2 & 4), produce an effect that is breathtaking in its grandeur. It is difficult to imagine that such dramatic effects were accidental, that they were not intended to impress. The regular spatial organization of church, atrium and public square is wholly in keeping with European ideas about order and civility, the architectural order representing the desirable ideological order. To suggest that such uses of external space demonstrate the influence of indigenous architectural traditions on Spanish would be to misunderstand the nature of the relationship between the two cultures.

Today we may sometimes recognize the pre-conquest elements in the lay-out of a particular colonial city, but it was not the conquerors' intention to preserve the memory of Indian towns and temples by basing their own upon them; such superimpositions are the tools of conquest and control, not of cultural exchange. And while the founding of Spanish towns on Indian does represent a degree of local spatial continuity, at a national and international level the establishment of colonial rule involved the political and economic reorientation of the whole South American continent. Power and wealth, instead of being concentrated in the highlands, moved to the coastal ports, to Cartagena and especially to Lima, through which the products of the country were funnelled *en route* for Europe where, ultimately, the real power base lay. Cuzco, the Inca capital and heart of the old state, becomes, as Wachtel says, a mere intermediary.[20] Indeed, as new routes to the coast were opened up, it became increasingly marginalized.[21]

So far, then, the question of the American contribution to the architecture of the Viceroyalty has only risen in relation to the materials and local conditions and to the positioning and lay-out of towns, spaces and buildings. But what of style? Can indigenous stylistic traditions be perceived in early colonial architecture in the way the Aztec style of sculptural carving can be identified on the façades of numerous sixteenth-century buildings in Mexico, for example? At the time of the conquest of South America there was really no equivalent native tradition of stone carving to that of the Aztec in Mexico, and the only significant style of stone architecture then current was that of the Incas, a style which is essentially architectonic rather than sculptural. Apart from the massive scale of so much of Inca architecture there are really only two other identifying features: trapezoidal doors, windows and niches and the patterns made by the blocks of stone themselves. Rows of niches are often used to articulate a wall surface in much the same way, as Cobo perceptively observes, 'as we use columns, cornices and other special mouldings and details'[22] (*see* frontispiece). The only other feature which could be considered decorative is that which pertains to the stone blocks themselves, or rather, to the joints between them, to which attention is almost always deliberately drawn. Sometimes the masonry is quite smooth, the mortarless joints almost invisible, but in most of the various styles of Inca masonry it is the quality of the masonry itself, the precision of the joints that serves to decorate or articulate the wall surface, whether it be the regular courses of gradated ashlars of the Amarucancha, the less regular but smoothly cushioned blocks of the sanctuary wall of Ollantaytambo, or the massive, aggressively coarse

Plate 21 Cuzco, Calle Zetas, no. 400. Inca-style colonial doorway; mid-sixteenth century.

boulders of Sacsahuaman (*see* plates 1, 9 and 10). In Inca architecture it is the technique which forms the basis of the style.

This distinctive style which so impressed the first European observers persisted after the conquest in a few buildings in and around Cuzco and, to a lesser extent, in Ayacucho (Plate 21). This small group consists of a number of private houses built for the conquistadors immediately after the conquest, all of which have as their distinguishing feature Inca-style doorways set into walls of Inca masonry. The convex blocks emphasize the mortarless joints of the stone walling, and the doorways are so overwhelmingly Incaic in appearance that, in Cuzco at least, they are often referred to as being of pre-conquest date. The craftsmen concerned must surely have been trained under the Incas. These doorways can, however, be easily distinguished from pre-conquest examples by the aperture itself, which is less trapezoidal, more nearly rectangular than traditional Inca doorways, and by the way the door jambs have been modified to accommodate hinged doors, opening inwards.[23] Doors, for the conquerors, were an essential component of any building and they scorned the removable panels of native tradition. These few transitional buildings in the central Andean highlands, perhaps better described as survivals of a pre-conquest style than as examples of a pre-conquest stylistic influence on post-conquest architecture, are, I believe, the only ones in South America where the hand of the indigenous craftsman is explicit, where the indigenous craftsman was employed by the conquerors to practise his craft in the traditional way.

Even more rare is evidence that would seem to point to a native craftsman attempting to follow the new requirements of the conquerors, but in the very failure of that attempt demonstrating a hand and eye trained to a different norm, a different system. A very small but telling example of this survives in the main square in Cuzco where the the west side is flanked by a colonnaded portico which must date back to the sixteenth century. The rough stone columns are surmounted by bracket capitals which support the wooden lintel. In one or two cases the capital is off-centre from the column, but this is not the result of careless assembly or of, say, earthquake-induced displacement: on close inspection it is clear that the capital and the top section of the column have been carved from a single block of stone, and so have been *carved* out of alignment (Plate 22). I feel sure that for a European mason, however rudimentary his training, the column and the capital were quite distinct elements and, especially in the case of bracket capitals, to be carved from two separate blocks, as they are elsewhere along the colonnade. The concepts,

Plate 22 Cuzco, Plaza de Armas, SW colonnade. Detail of bracket capital; mid-sixteenth century.

fundamental to the classical architectural tradition, not only that the column and capital are distinct elements, but that their assembly should be concentric, were not apparent to the author of these examples. They must therefore be the work of an Indian stone mason copying an example without comprehending the general rationale which lies behind it. I would not want to argue that all European craftsmen understood the theoretical principles behind the classical architectural system but rather that a distinction between column and capitals would have been taken for granted, one of those things which does not have to be said or even consciously learned.

Such small examples apart, in South America in the sixteenth century the involvement of indigenous craftsmen in colonial architecture is extraordinarily difficult to identify, presumably because, as many observers remarked, the Indians were so dextrous that they mastered new skills and new styles in no time. The particularly undecorated style of Inca stone masonry may have contributed to this: the various forms and decorative details of the classical architectural vocabulary of Europe had to be learned from scratch and could not be adapted from (and so confused with) an existing tradition, as is occasionally the case in Mexico, where, for example, a rosette used in a European architectural context may sometimes bear a suggestive resemblance to the form of the Nahua flower glyph. The surviving architecture from South America, far from demonstrating the involvement of the native craftsmen, seems on the contrary strikingly pure, classical and European. Considering the various problems – the lack of money and of traditional building materials, the difficulties of communication between one new Spanish town and the next, as well as the lack of appropriately-trained craftsmen – this is remarkable, too remarkable to be accidental.

## The Art of Architecture: a tradition transformed

The church is central to any discussion of architectural style in the early colonial period. It is in church architecture that we should expect to find the true expression of the conquerors' beliefs about style: the church was the spiritual, cultural and geographical focus of both Spanish and Indian communities, and so it is not surprising to find that it was also the visual focus. A church in Latin America is always visually unmistakable. It is the sheer size and dramatic positioning which initially sets it apart: a church dominates the square in front, the town round about, often the whole area.

On closer inspection, the church is distinguishable by a number of other

Plate 23 Cartagena cathedral, lateral portal; 1602–12.

features as well. Whether it be a cathedral in a new Spanish colonial town or a parish church in a remote Indian village it will be set apart from the surrounding buildings by a bell-tower, by the invariable use of the classical architectural vocabulary on the entrance, and above all by the use of a round-arched doorway. Throughout South America and, with some variations in arch form, in Mexico as well, the use of the arched entrance is reserved for ecclesiastical buildings, the lintelled for secular. The arch is always found in conjunction with at least some suggestion of classical mouldings: columns or pilasters supporting an entablature or at the very least impost and base mouldings on the door jambs to support the arch above. In other words, the two key features of European architecture, the technique of the arch together with the columns and capitals which are the mark of the one true Art of Architecture, are combined on each and every church façade. Only in the eighteenth century does this pattern begin to break up, and then only very slowly.[24]

The great and the small, the major cathedrals, the hospital, monastic and parish churches and the rural chapels all have classical, semi-circular headed entrances (Plates 23 & 24). Palaces, mansions, public buildings and private houses are all entered under an emphatically horizontal lintel (*see* plates 33–37) and the distinction is also often clearly visible in early town plans. The one grey area to this pattern is that of the entrances to monasteries and convents – in other words to the residences of ecclesiastics, as for example the lintelled entrance to the Dominican monastery in Ayacucho. But more often than not the arch is favoured: even when the use of monastic buildings has since changed, the arch is often an indication of their religious origins as in the case of the Mercedarian convent entrance in Quito or the entrance to the Jesuit college in Ayacucho, now a shop and a museum respectively.

The arch is reserved for church façades and it is invariably combined with at least some aspects of the classical architectural vocabulary: columns, pilasters and an entablature. This is the basic design in South America in the sixteenth and seventeenth centuries and within this there are two variants, one slightly more elaborate than the other. The more elaborate version is used for the façades of cathedrals and grander churches and consists of paired columns on either side of the aperture which support an entablature, usually with a small window or niche above, also with a classical surround, and with shallow shell-headed niches recessed into the wall between the columns. Examples of this design are to be found throughout South America: on the

Plate 24 Urcos, near Cuzco. Rural chapels; early seventeenth century.

Cathedral and the Dominican church in Cartagena which both date from the 1580s, on the main façade of the church of Santo Domingo in Cuzco,[25] and on the simpler pilastered version in the nearby village of Huaro (Plate 25). Other village churches in the Cuzco area follow roughly the same scheme, as at Andahuaylillas (*see* plate 20) and, behind their arcaded porches, at Urcos and San Jerónimo. In Potosí in Bolivia the façade of the otherwise ruined Augustinian church survives with the same paired columns and shell-headed niches intact (Plate 26). The proportions here are broader, less nearly square than either the Cuzco or the Colombian versions, and the few carved details place this firmly in the seventeenth century but the basic pattern is unchanged. Brick variants of the same design, with pilasters and topped with little pediments, are found on some of the churches in the province of Chucuito, such as the lateral portals of La Asunción in Juli and San Pedro in Acora (Plate 27) or, slightly to the north, that of La Inmaculada in Paucarcolla.

The most richly decorated version of this design to survive is that of the

Plate 25 Huaro, near Cuzco. Main portal; early seventeenth century.

Plate 26 San Agustín, Potosí. Façade; early seventeenth century.

Plate 27 Acora, San Pedro, lateral portal; c.1600.

cathedral façade in Tunja, begun by Bartolomé Carrión in 1598 (Plate 28). The overall arrangement is unchanged, but the carved details, the bucrania, the rosettes, the acanthus scrolls, the composite capitals with winged horses in the place of volutes, all give this portal a strong Plateresque flavour which is unique in South America. The contract for this façade, however, mentions none of these elements. It simply requires that Carrión adhere strictly to the overall proportions and the dimensions of 'bases . . . capitals, architrave and cornice' as laid out in the plan; what matters, evidently, is that it should conform to 'buena arquitetura', by which we must understand the basic structure of the classical system, not the relatively unimportant decorative details.[26]

The façade of the church of San Francisco in Quito deserves to be mentioned in this context (*see* plate 15). Begun before 1581 and rivalling Tunja as the most impressive surviving example of sixteenth-century colonial architecture in South America, it is really only an elaboration and expansion of the same motif set into a three bay design. The central round-arched doorway is flanked by paired Doric columns (this time without the

Plate 28 Tunja cathedral façade. Bartolomé Carrión, 1598.

Plate 29 Potosí, Santo Domingo. Main portal; 1606–9.

intervening niches) above which a pronounced cornice runs right across the façade, supported in the rusticated side bays by half-columns. The whole pattern is repeated in the upper storey, the central bay topped with a prominent curved pediment that is quietly echoed on either side.[27] The closer-packed columns and the emphasis given to the upper storey are the principal features which distinguish San Francisco and its successors (the Guápulo in Quito from the end of the seventeenth century, for example) from the Tunja cathedral type façade.

The second, simpler version of the standard church portal form consists of a round-headed entrance, flanked by pilasters or half-columns (rarely columns) supporting an entablature, usually with either a niche or a pediment above. In other words it differs from that of the Tunja cathedral type in that it has single instead of paired columns, and so lacks the intervening blind niches. Again, widely scattered examples can illustrate this. In Potosí, the Dominican church has an elegant little sixteenth-century portal with fluted Doric half-columns carrying an entablature and a small pedimented niche above (Plate 29). At the opposite end of the continent, a design for a Franciscan church in Caracas of 1593 contains the same features,[28] as does the very simple surviving portal to the church of San Francisco in Tunja, the sparse decoration of which includes the same form of diamond-pointed rustication as that found on San Francisco in Quito (Plate 30). In Ayacucho the portals of the Mercedarian and Franciscan churches are evidently closely related, despite the hideous restoration of the latter, and again they follow the general pattern. That of La Merced once had a classical framed niche above the doorway, while San Francisco has a pediment alone, framing a sculptured representation of St Francis receiving the stigmata (Plate 31). In Quito there are several variations on the same simple theme, most of them related to, although not necessarily derived from, the well-preserved portal on the church of Santo Domingo, which is unusual in that it includes some delicate Plateresque details.

It is sometimes possible to point to small groups of façades with family resemblances such as the two in Ayacucho which must come from the same workshop, or the widely separated Franciscan churches in Caracas, Tunja and Quito whose similarities point to an exchange or link within the order. Within Quito itself and within the province of Chucuito there are also suggestive similarities between a number of façades but despite such sub-groupings the overall impression is of uniformity and simplicity. Decoration on religious portals, beyond that included on the capitals and in the frieze, is

Plate 30 Tunja, San Francisco. Main portal; c.1610.

Plate 31 Ayacucho, San Francisco. Main portal; late sixteenth century.

generally very sparse: a few rosettes here and there, a cherub's head or a couple of ball-and-obelisk additions above the cornice are as much as most surviving examples run to. It is appropriate that the use of the Doric order, which has traditionally been viewed as the simplest and, within the Vitruvian anthropomorphizing system, the strongest and most sober of the orders, is quite common amongst these designs. Even if all the empty niches and bare acroterion had once been occupied by statuary (which is by no means clear), the overwhelming impression is of the bare bones of the classical architectural language.

It is the exterior, the public façade of a church which manifests this stylistic simplicity and uniformity. The interiors of early colonial churches are often extremely simple too, but they are rarely stylistically homogeneous or even stylistically classifiable. The roofing, in the case of the largest and most prestigious buildings, may be vaulted but in these cases it is the Gothic rib vault which predominates. This was favoured initially because for people unfamiliar with vaulting techniques it was easier to construct than barrel or domical vaults, and remained popular throughout Spanish America well into the seventeenth century partly, no doubt, because Gothic vaulting proved to be more resistant to earth tremors.[29]

An alternative form of covering, equally unclassical, was that of the elaborate *alfarje* ceilings of interlocking pieces of wood, the *carpintería de lo blanco* technique derived from and to a greater or lesser extent stylistically related to Moorish work. These ceilings, usually gloriously gilded and painted, are often accompanied at the crossing and between the nave piers not by classical semicircular arches but by pointed Gothic ones. This combination of Gothic pointed arches with an *alfarje* ceiling exists in San Francisco in Quito behind its uncompromisingly classicizing façade, although exterior and interior are coeval (Plate 18). In Tunja several churches were built in the late sixteenth century with this mixture of Gothic and *mudéjar* interior. It is true that by this date some citizens were beginning to feel that the Gothic style was outmoded: in 1600, when the smart new classicizing façade of the cathedral would have been complete, the *cabildo* of Tunja complained about the Gothic arches of the cathedral nave, calling them 'a very old order, crude and out of use',[30] but nothing was done about them and they survive in this form today. In smaller, poorer churches where neither vaulting nor a wooden ceiling were possible, the underside of the roof was sometimes decorated by pinning painted cloth to the beams, or sometimes the rafters themselves were simply painted and gilded.

Plate 32 Ilave, San Miguel, interior. Entrance to a side chapel, *c.* 1565.

Plate 33 Cuzco, Casa de los Cuatro Bustos; late sixteenth century.

Other ornamentation on the interiors of churches is usually very limited. The entrances to side chapels sometimes have an architectural frame, usually of approximately classical mouldings either in brick or stone, or, as in Andahuaylillas, in paint. In the case of San Miguel in Ilave however, mentioned at the beginning of this study, the four side chapel entrances are each framed with a different ogival arch (Plate 32). These are very pretty but could hardly be said to belong to the Art of Architecture as it was understood by people like Bernabé Cobo. In the interiors of early colonial churches it was only the retable that would unfailingly involve the elements of classical architecture, the paintings and sculptures framed by columns and an entablature of wood, perhaps gilded and painted. A classicizing retable, a *mudéjar* ceiling and Gothic vaulting: this combination is not unusual in churches dating from the late sixteenth or early seventeenth centuries in South America. Such variety is never found on the façades.

With secular architecture of the period the emphasis is again always on the façade, the ornamentation of the entrance being the main and in most cases the only important architectural feature. Secular buildings are distinguishable from religious above all by the use of the lintelled entrance but also because the decoration is sometimes slightly more elaborate and varied, sometimes slightly more unorthodox. A house in Quito on the Plaza Santo Domingo boasts a Plateresque portal that is unusually inventive for South America, the pilasters consisting of a series of superimposed elements topped with capitals with heads of goats and bearded men. In Cuzco too, apart from the Incaic-style portals, there are among the surviving secular buildings some examples from the late sixteenth or early seventeenth century with a Plateresque flavour that is absent in the religious architecture. These are decorated with the ubiquitous rosette, as well as with family crests and a few mythological beasts (Plate 33). In Tunja there are a couple of examples from the end of the century of portals in an unusually grand style: the portal of the Casa Mujica y Guevara (1592) (Plate 34) and the simpler but similarly rigorous arrangement of the Casa Mancipe (1597), both of which suggest the influence of Toledo, Herrera and the Escorial, as does the Estrada tomb monument of 1593 in Tunja cathedral. The Casa de Pilatos in Lima, dating from perhaps the beginning of the seventeenth century is equally sober and represents a sort of self-conscious tastefulness rarely apparent in ecclesiastical architecture at this date (Plate 35). But examples such as these, to which stylistic tags derived from peninsular Spain such as *estilo desornamentado* or Plateresque can be applied, are exceptions. Most of the conquerors' mansions

Plate 34 Tunja, Casa Mujica y Guevara; 1592.

Plate 35 Lima, Casa Pilatos; late sixteenth century.

are adorned with the simplest of architectural mouldings. Suárez Rendón, the founder of Tunja, built himself a large house on the main square. It has spacious rooms with ceilings painted with mythological scenes derived from European engravings, and elegant arcades and balconies on the side facing the garden, but the street façade is a sort of architectural understatement: the only decoration is that around the door: two little Ionic columns topped with no more than a dentilated cornice (Plate 36). Nearby, on one of the main streets, two houses have portals that consist of the shallowest of pilaster strips supporting an entablature above, both of which no doubt came from the same workshop (Plate 37). Again on these and on other contemporary Tunjan examples a rosette or patera-like motif is almost the only decoration other than the architectural mouldings themselves.

The problem about the neat visual distinction between secular and ecclesiastical architecture is that there is no European precedent either in theory or in practice. The various theoretical writings on classical architecture do not offer any comfortable explanation. Neither Vitruvius nor Serlio, nor any of their followers in sixteenth-century Spain mentions any preference for one or other shape, or suggests that their use ought to be restricted to certain types of building. In *De Re Aedificatoria* Alberti suggests that arches should be used on secular buildings and horizontal entablatures on religious ones,[31] but in practice in Pienza he was shortly to oversee an opposing scheme. In the later sixteenth century the Jesuit theorist San Carlo Borromeo is, with Alberti, one of the few who even posits a relationship between these particular forms and the functions of the buildings on which they are used. Partly no doubt to give added authority to the Gesù, the mother church of his order, Borromeo argues in favour of rectangular lintelled doorways for churches on the grounds that this was an early Christian form, whereas round arches had been used in pagan temples.[32] This, although it recognizes the possibility of distinct applications, is of course the opposite to the system as practised in colonial Spanish America.

Building practice in Europe is no more helpful in offering an explanation of the source of the colonial pattern. In sixteenth-century Spain architects used both forms for both categories of building. The main exterior façade of the Escorial has rectangular doorways, the church an arched narthex sheltering lintelled doorways beneath; the cathedral at Valladolid has lintelled entrances. Vandelvira's cathedral at Jaén (*c.* 1540–75) was probably the source for Becerra's ground plans for the cathedrals of Lima and Cuzco but the square-headed doorways of its façade were not to be influential in

Plate 36 Tunja, Plaza de Armas. Casa Suárez Rendón; mid-sixteenth century.

Plate 37 Tunja, house at Carrera 10, 21–04; late sixteenth century.

America. The university façades of Salamanca (*c.* 1525–30) and Alcalá de Henares (1540–53) use arched or suppressed arched portals; private houses throughout the country alternate between the two. In Seville, the last Spanish city the colonists would have seen before embarking for the New World, all the various permutations can be found in buildings dating from the sixteenth century. The cathedral itself includes both forms (as well as Gothic rib vaulting within, and Moorish horse-shoe arches in the patio and on the Giralda tower); the splendid private mansion, the Casa de Pilatos, has an ostentatious arched gateway (1529–33), Herrera's Exchange (1583–98) has rectangular entrances and Riaño's town hall, the Ayuntamiento (1527–*c.* 1546), combines both forms on the one façade.

In Italy the case is more unified but no more helpful in explaining Spanish American practice. Brunelleschi, the Sangalli, Bramante and Michelangelo all tended in practice to favour square-headed portals for churches. The extremely influential Gesù in Rome has lintelled portals both in Vignola's original design for the façade and in that as completed by Giacomo della Porta in 1584. This church is regularly cited as a prototype for Jesuit churches in the New World, but as far as the form of the entrance portals is concerned, the only important pre-eighteenth century example that follows the Gesù in this respect is that of San Ignacio in Bogotá: the façade has three lintelled entrances in a broad three bay design (Plate 38). San Ignacio is a particularly interesting case: begun in 1610, it was designed and its execution supervised by an Italian Jesuit, Giovanni Baptista Coluccini, a native of Lucca, who had been sent from Rome to the New Kingdom of Granada specifically for the purpose.[33] It is, therefore, the one major exception that proves the rule: that this isolated example, which has documented Italian origins, should have rectangular entrances is a clear indication that the designer was not influenced by, or perhaps one should say, not sensitive to, established colonial practice.

It is easy to see the benefits of such a simple binary scheme as the clearest of signifiers: this is a church; this is not a church. This is essentially an external, public language, a language of appearances. Inside the lintelled portal of a colonial house there may be an arcaded patio, even an arched doorway; inside a church, although a lintelled doorway is unusual, the true semicircular arch is by no means the rule; suppressed, ogival and especially Gothic forms are common. In South America at least the semicircular form of arch is the rule for church exteriors.

The use of the arch to give this special significance to a church is not

Plate 38 Bogotá, San Ignacio. Giovanni Baptista Coluccini; 1610.

Plate 39 Ayacucho, Plaza de Armas; late seventeenth-century *portales*.

confined to its appearance on portals: it is also used to the same end on atria walls. The usual form for an atrium wall is that of a continuous series of arches, often broken by one or more large arched gateways. These emphatically walled atria can, I believe, point to an explanation for the frequent use of arches in one very public but ostensibly secular context which has not so far been mentioned: the arcades that are sometimes to be found running around the central square of old colonial towns such as Cuzco or Ayacucho (Plate 39). The use of the arch here has the effect of extending the jurisdiction of the church into the secular domain; it is as if the main square were really the atrium, and indeed on religious festivals the church always appropriates the town square for processions and rituals. The erection of temporary altars in the four corners has the effect of sanctifying the area. The church spawns arches out into the public sphere whether it be town square or enclosed atrium, extending the civilizing influence of the church façade into the town itself. The worshipper, approaching the church across an open square, views the arched entrance of the church framed perhaps by the arch of the atrium gateway and flanked by rows of arches on either side. In the case of a longitudinally aligned church, on entering the door the view down the nave reveals further arches, in this case the arches of the crossing, and finally, the arched niche of the central image in the retable, focusing attention straight on to that image and on to the high altar below it. Even where the interior of the church includes pointed Gothic arches or vaults, the retable itself will reconfirm the rounded arch of the church door, and the visual impact is most impressive. How much more so must it have been to those whose eyes were accustomed to distinguishing the secular from the religious, accustomed to recognizing – instantly and automatically – the arch as associated with the sphere of religion.

But this innovative appropriation of the arched form to denote an ecclesiastical function is not the only way in which colonial architecture differs from contemporary European Renaissance architecture. The question of the particular use of the classical architectural vocabulary also needs to be considered. Before about the middle of the seventeenth century in by far the majority of cases the decoration on secular as well as ecclesiastical portals throughout the region is very restrained, not particularly modish. It is always secondary to the overall architectural structure which remains clearly and unmistakably classical, and permits of few variations. Such evidence does not fit with the general art historical assumptions that the further removed a community from the main cultural centre, the more provincial or peripheral it is, the more its artistic productions will tend to the decorative, irrelevant or trivial. Who, after all, would care if in rural Peru or Bolivia rich ornamentation were to flourish at the expense of the underlying rationale of the metropolitan models? Certainly not the Indians, so why such orthodoxy, and where does it originate?

The question is further complicated because the architecture of the period in Spain is in fact famous not for its stylistic unity but for its variety. The main stylistic groups, which have come to be known as the Isabelline, the Plateresque and the *estilo desornamentado*,[34] and which are understood as corresponding to the late Gothic, the early and the mature Renaissance styles respectively, are not neatly exclusive nor are they straightforwardly diachronic. The Isabelline merges with the early stages of the Plateresque in such a way that it is often difficult to classify works as one or the other. The later Isabelline style often includes classicizing elements within it, while the 'classical' architectural style diffused from Italy is apparently adopted initially in piecemeal form, as an ornamental style. In, for example, Alonso de

Covarrubias' façade for the hospital of Santa Cruz in Toledo (after 1515) he superimposes upon a classicizing portal two columns which follow the curve of the pediment for a while before resuming the vertical, a feature fundamentally at odds with the traditional Italo-Roman concept of classical architecture as essentially – albeit theoretically – structural. Another aspect of Spanish stylistic heterogeneity is the persistent popularity of the *mudéjar* style in Spain until well into the later sixteenth century; this is of course neither Gothic nor classical but is often found on the interiors, in the form of *alfarje* ceilings and stuccoed walls and patios, of buildings that are outwardly in a very different style. The *mudéjar* itself occasionally borrows details from both the Isabelline and the Plateresque.

Contemporaneous with the taste for richly decorated surfaces, the hallmark of the *mudéjar* style of ornamentation as of Isabelline and much of Plateresque architecture in early sixteenth-century Spain, there are a few isolated examples of a much more pure, Italianate style of classical architecture. Buildings such as Pedro Machuca's palace for Charles V in Granada begun in 1528 and the Tavera hospital on the outskirts of Toledo begun by Covarrubias in 1542[35] require, I feel, rather more of an explanation than that they simply represent isolated examples of enlightened, informed patronage in the midst of a society that otherwise fails to grasp the essential tenets of the classical system. This line of argument necessarily continues along the lines that only in the latter part of the century, when the King himself steps in and employs the Italian-trained Juan de Toledo on the construction of the Escorial do things begin to change and true, simple, unadorned classicism, the *estilo desornamentado*, really take a hold.[36]

The South American material focuses attention back on to the question of stylistic development in the Peninsula. Is it possible to see the relative simplicity and homogeneity of façade design in sixteenth-century Peru as the result of an enthusiastic espousal of at least some of the ideals of the *estilo desornamentado* as manifested in the Escorial? I believe not. It would in any case be unreasonable to assume that this style could have reached America much before 1580, and given that its diffusion within the continent would necessarily be slow, this makes the dates incompatible. But it is not just the chronology which seems to be wrong; it is, I believe, the premise on which it rests. To talk of stylistic diffusion implies taste; to talk of taste implies choice. When there is no church in an area at all, or where the existing church is of such poor materials and is lacking in all those features which would entitle it to the name of 'church', then choice, style, taste, are not what are at issue. These are the luxuries of an established and confident culture. This is why the only examples of early colonial architecture which can even tentatively be considered in these terms are to be found amongst buildings in the centres of the most securely European cities – Tunja and Lima – and above all in secular buildings. Here personal ambition and personal rivalries would seem to have resulted in some architectural designs which refer directly to current trends in Spain.

In religious architecture, even in the Spanish towns, rivalry between the builders or patrons of different churches, certainly up until the end of the century, cannot be considered a major factor in the style of the façade: there were very rarely enough substantial churches in close proximity for this to have been an issue. The urgent and overriding necessity was for something, almost *anything*, to be built, so long as it was primarily and unmistakably a church. To demonstrate the latest developments in architectural design, or to surpass in stylistic finesse the next church fifty miles down the road, or even to offer an inventive variation on the theme already established by another church within the same town was not what was needed: these considerations would have been not only irrelevant but inappropriate in the circumstances. It is uniformity, familiarity, standardization, which is required and this is unquestionably what is achieved. The overriding impression is that these façades represent a sort of distillation, a generalized ideal which has nothing to do with personal tastes, individual inventions or particular trends.

I want to argue that the designers of early colonial churches, from whatever their heterogeneous backgrounds, all turned back to the fundamentals of their culture for guidance, but that these cultural values were not learned in any formal sense. This is a difficult phenomenon to describe, far less explain, although at some levels it seems a quite obvious and familiar product of colonization: is it not simply an aspect of the expatriate syndrome so well described by Forster in *A Passage to India*, whereby those away from their home country adhere more strictly to traditional values than would be necessary or even appropriate when at home? Until the Spanish colony and Christianity along with it were really well established, then with hindsight at least, it seems obvious that diversity, invention or creativity would have been inappropriate, even a hindrance, especially in so important and public a field as architecture and town planning. This would help to explain not just the repetition of the basic classical format to frame an entrance, to present 'a church', but also the relative lack of ornamentation on early colonial buildings, despite the peninsular predilection for richly textured and ornamented surfaces: these

Plate 40 Juli, San Juan. Lateral portal; eighteenth-century refurbishing of a late sixteenth-century original.

would only have blurred the message. Only later in the seventeenth century does a taste for decorated surfaces develop, sometimes riotously and exuberantly; but a tradition so deeply engrained dies hard and the basic format of round-arched door, paired columns, intervening niches and strong entablature is almost always clearly visible beneath the vine-tendrils, the fruit, flowers, birds and monkeys of, for example, the lateral portal of San Juan in Juli (Plate 40). From the cathedral of Cajamarca to San Francisco in La Paz, Peru and Bolivia boast many more such examples where, despite the carved decoration, the overall impression is of soberly classical designs. In Santo Domingo in Arequipa, as if to ensure that there be no mistake, the pilasters are left bare amidst the carved surround (Plate 41).

In a culture which not only values but needs continuity rather than change, traditions rather than innovations, the apparent stylistic anachronism of the occasional appearance of Plateresque details as late as the end of the sixteenth century on, for example, Tunja cathedral façade, or even into the seventeenth century on the portal of the Casa del Almirante in Cuzco take on a different aspect. These cannot be interpreted as deliberately archaizing in the sense one might use the term in Europe, as a sophisticated joke, any more than the niched faces of the pilaster strips of the portal of La Merced in Quito can be seen as a deliberate piece of Mannerist wit (Plate 42). The former are, from a metropolitan point of view, out-moded, the latter merely a solecism. But from a contemporary colonial point of view, they all serve their purpose, they all operate within the narrow limits of established practice and expectations. In fact the problem with the Mercedarian example is that the designer *has* deviated from the established norm: he has recombined the accepted elements of a church portal in a new, unorthodox and, strictly speaking, illiterate way. That this design lacks successors or even very many parallels, surely suggests that there were those around who not only recognized that tradition and orthodoxy were preferable to innovation, but who knew within really very strict parameters what it was that constituted orthodoxy and literacy within the classical architectural style. Given the lack of skilled European personnel it is remarkable that such recombinations of the classical vocabulary are not more common; on the contrary, their very rarity points to the prevalence of a generally-held knowledge of the traditional architectural formulae, and to a recognition of their underlying significance.

The sources for the arch/ecclesiastical, lintel/secular system of architectural demarcation in Spanish America remain problematic. The question of exactly how this particular pattern evolved is not, I believe, really soluble

Plate 41 Arequipa, Santo Domingo. Lateral portal; 1677–80.

Plate 42 Quito, La Merced. Lateral portal; 1596.

within the normal theoretical and methodological parameters of historical investigation. There is no obvious European precedent. There is no mention of such a system in contemporary documentation, either in the form of official preliminary directions or, as there are for town plans, of *post facto* instructions, rationalizations and justifications; nor does there even seem to be a passing reference to the pattern as a recognized and established norm. If no-one said anything about it, and no-one wrote anything about it, did anyone think about it at all? May it, after all, be nothing more than a particularly happy coincidence? This question too needs to be answered.

In discussing the ways in which Spanish colonial culture differs from that of the metropolitan country, George Foster recognizes the considerable simplification which the latter undergoes in its journey across the Atlantic.[37] This he explains in terms both of the limited variety in the culture that was exported from Spain, and also in the process which he calls the crystallization of the culture in America, by which the first cultural arrivals quickly become the established pattern and so do not allow of later variation. In the case of architecture, this would mean that the first buildings to be erected in America established, by chance, a clearly visible distinction between secular and ecclesiastical architecture, and that all later architecture was derived from these models, thus creating a universal rule.

This explanation is not satisfactory at either the general or the particular level. On the one hand, I do not believe that something which determines the appearance of the most important buildings in society – its religious and political centres – could be introduced accidentally; unconsciously perhaps, but not accidentally. If this were the case then we must assume that the system could just as easily have been reversed, with the secular buildings carrying arches. This would be to suggest that the two forms of entrance were devoid of any meaning or resonance; that they were empty signifiers. This does not seem likely or even possible. On the other hand this explanation does not work precisely because most of the exceptions to the rule do in fact date from the earliest days of the Spanish settlement in America. One of the first major Franciscan churches on the mainland in Mexico has a lintelled west door: San Gabriel in Cholula was finished by perhaps 1552 and it would be reasonable to expect it to have been influential, at least within the order, but it was not. The façade of the first cathedral, that on the island of Santo Domingo, which was almost complete by 1541, consists of an unusual arrangement of two rectangular doors framed within a massive concave arch. That these designs, especially the latter, were to have no followers simply reinforces my contention that the system is far from arbitrary.

The simple pattern would have been quickly assimilated by Christians and non-Christians alike. As an integral part of the art of classical architecture, the arch is a manifestation of civility, and of culture; however distantly, for Europeans it will tend to carry the resonances of the classical triumphal arch as being a mark of power and military prowess. The arch immediately sets the church apart from other colonial buildings but also, and most emphatically, from Native American forms of architecture, and so from native traditions of culture and religion. The conquering Christians may have appropriated indigenous towns and cities, and indigenous centres of worship on which to build their own towns and churches; they may have had to make concessions to native beliefs and to native skills on occasion, but at least on this matter there could be no mistake, no confusion. The combination of arched entrance and classical architectural mouldings was peculiar to church portals and so distinguishes both the building and the institution from everything that had gone before: the Church demonstrably owed nothing to America. An Inca-style portal like those found on some private houses in Cuzco and Ayacucho discussed earlier in this chapter would therefore be inconceivable on a church façade.

It would seem that we are looking at something which works at a half-conscious, almost instinctive level, something so obvious and natural that it did not need to be articulated let alone justified or enforced. The conquering power immediately grasped the advantages to be gained from making a clear visual distinction between their religion and that of the American peoples, between their churches and the indigenous temples, between their technology as manifested in the Art of Architecture and demonstrated on their church façades and the skills of the native craftsmen, between, in the end, civilization and barbarism. I have to conclude that this pattern arose so naturally out of the general European attitudes and ideas about architecture and in response to the particular circumstances of America that it never evoked comment. It was simply adopted and assimilated into colonial culture throughout the continent. That it remained a peculiarly American perception, and did not enter into the metropolitan view of or understanding of colonial culture is, I believe, demonstrated by the single important exception of San Ignacio in Bogotá. It is difficult to imagine how this church was viewed by the colonists – did anyone even verbalize its uniqueness? – but as with the other significant exceptions, those which date from the very earliest period of the Spanish presence in America, San Ignacio did not inspire copies or variants; stylistically it was ignored, passed by. At some level it must have been seen to be an inappropriate outsider.

# Conclusions

What can all this tell us about the nature of colonial culture? The written record repeatedly confirms the colonists' interest in and respect for the culture of metropolitan Spain and indeed of Europe as a whole. At the beginning of the seventeenth century sculptors and architects trained in Spain were certain of making a good living in America; they were sought after precisely because of their European origins. Governors and leading churchmen wrote to Spain requesting that professionals be sent out to help with their building projects. The other side to this eurocentricism is that a great many people evidently felt cut off and isolated in Spanish America and wanted above all to return home, to spend their old age in Spain. Of the countless petitions to the King and the Council of the Indies requesting recognition for services rendered in America, many want no more than to be allowed to return to Spain; this is considered an adequate reward.

The evidence of early colonial architecture and town planning suggests, however, that respect for, even veneration of, things European does not necessarily imply that there was no room for originality, innovation, or improvisation. Even a cursory consideration will reveal that the colonizing enterprise was essentially one of improvisation. The New World was to the first conquistadors just that – new territories, new peoples, new cultures, and a whole set of new problems, new challenges and new requirements that had to be met if America were to be effectively conquered and controlled. This was a newness of such magnitude that there could not possibly be existing European patterns and procedures to meet every eventuality. People in Europe did not regularly found and lay out new towns, or erect churches, town halls and government offices; nor did they have to deal with large non-European populations, to organize, control and extract labour from them, to convert them to Christianity, and to teach them new skills and designs.

It is remarkable that throughout the continent the solutions to all these various challenges are so uniform. It is also remarkable that a number of these solutions seem to have been arrived at without recourse to discussion and debate. The grid-plan form for new towns was adopted from the outset without question; only eighty years later was it clearly articulated as official policy. The foundation ceremonies for new towns are repeated almost exactly time and again, with different personnel and in widely dispersed locations; again it is not until the end of the sixteenth century that instructions for how to proceed at an official foundation are detailed by experts in military affairs.[1] The contemporary record is similarly lacking in details about the *picota*: regularly mentioned in early descriptive sources and evidently a standard, if not indeed essential element in the foundation of a town, it is never described or explained in terms that would be of help to one unfamiliar with its form or function. And the choice of the church as the prime bearer not only of Christianity but also of classical culture in the form of both the Art of Architecture and the technology of the arch as combined on its public façade, this brilliantly original and at the same time profoundly traditional solution, this above all seems to be the result of some sort of collective intuition.

Colonial culture is remarkable for a homogeneity that comes not from the designs and plans of a single author or group of authors which were subsequently diffused across the land along with the conquerors, but from a whole series of more or less independent initiatives. This apparent paradox can only be explained if these various initiatives are seen as the product of the society and of the ideas and attitudes about architecture and civility which had general currency within that society. What a study of colonial architecture and town planning suggests is that there was some latent concept or tradition, or more probably a confluence of the traditions of the Roman Empire and the Christian Church which, under the particular conditions of the conquest and colonization of America, produced a set of more or less natural-seeming solutions. The uniformity of appearance of colonial architecture and town planning imputes to the conquistadors a single-mindedness of purpose, and a confidence in their own rectitude which perhaps can go some way to explaining their extraordinary successes in America. Even today, long after the end of colonial rule, and despite the pervasive influence of the United States, Spanish America is still united by language and culture to a degree that is like nowhere else in the world; perhaps only the Latin Middle Ages in Europe can be said to come anywhere near in the scale and scope of its cultural uniformity.

Latin America is united by its European heritage. What of course is left out of this equation, as it is so often left out of or at least marginalized in discussions of colonial architecture, is the whole question of indigenous culture. To return to one of my initial problems: where are the Indians? How are they present in colonial Spanish American architecture? The Spaniards considered the classical architectural style and the technique of constructing an arch as important marks of cultural progress; combined on a church façade they are signs of the civility and religion of the conquerors. The Indians quickly learnt how to construct arches and vaults, and must almost as quickly have grasped the essential elements of the classical style in order to build in accordance with their conquerors' wishes. But the restriction of the arch – a mark of cultural superiority – to the church effectively denied the Native Americans access to what was perceived as civilized architecture and to civilized society at any level other than the subservient. The Catholic Church in Spanish America did not go out of its way to establish racial equality. Only towards the end of the sixteenth century was the indigenous population admitted to sacraments other than those of baptism, marriage and penance: during the period under consideration, the Christianized Indians were almost entirely non-communicant. And, as they were considered unfit to take an active part in the mass it is not surprising that they were also excluded from taking Holy Orders. It was not until 1794 that the first Indian priests were ordained in Lima.[2] Therefore, during the early colonial period the Indians could not apply the new technique of constructing arches to buildings over which they had any real control. Production of churches was in the hands of Indians, but power remained with the Europeans.

Despite the fact that the very existence of these colonial churches is a result of colonial control over an Indian workforce, the peculiarly colonial features of the architecture lie not in the occasional intrusion of an indigenous motif but on the contrary, in the overall negation of any specifically American features. This seems to be the more true the greater the distance from the established centres of European civilization. The closer to the peripheries of the empire, the less there is architectural variety, the more strictly the church façades adhere to the central elements of the classical architectural system. This is especially true in Peru where the native traditions of grand stone architecture were so very strong, and yet the early colonial architecture is markedly more pure and classical than elsewhere. It seems probable that this was precisely because the Inca were a greater power on the Spaniards' own terms than any of the other cultures they encountered in America. The Inca were in a number of ways more deeply threatening than any of the other

Native American peoples but they lacked certain skills which to Europeans were fundamental to civilized society: in their architecture they had apparently no knowledge of the principle of the arch, nor of the principles of the one true architecture, the Art of Architecture extolled by chroniclers and demanded by patrons. The church façade combines the use of the arch with the classical architectural members and so constitutes a material manifestation of European cultural traditions.

In this context John Summerson's metaphor of architecture as a language with its own particular grammar and vocabulary is especially telling. To European observers one of the other most striking *lacunae* in Inca culture was that of a written language, without which they found it difficult to imagine how a people could have any real history. Classical architecture has both a history and a literature of its own; indeed its authority is rooted in traditions of literacy and history. An understanding of classical architecture is closely linked to a sense of historical time: the forms of the different members, the different orders and the different mouldings were explained by Vitruvius and his successors as the results of a series of developments through time. However esoteric, however unrelated to natural forms or technical solutions they may look, the columns, capitals and entablatures were all considered the end product of a process which began, as Vitruvius would have it, with the birth of human society. All the more appropriate, therefore, that the order particularly favoured on early colonial churches should have been the Doric, the strongest but also traditionally the oldest of the orders. The conquerors were establishing a Christian empire on solid foundations with ancient roots; with the Doric they were making a new beginning, preparing to rehearse history in the right order.

The architecture of early colonial Spanish America raises a number of broad questions about the revival of the classical tradition in the fifteenth century in Italy, and its gradual dissemination through other European countries. In Italy the initial revival of the classical style of architecture is seen as relatively straightforward. In the Old Sacristy of San Lorenzo, for example, Brunelleschi seems immediately to be using the basic vocabulary correctly according to established classical canons; such underlying principles as the theoretically supportive nature of columns and pilasters, or the need for an entablature to be supported, however non-structural it may be, are not in question. The Italians, as it were, get it right first time. Outside Italy however, the revival of the classical style of architecture is almost always presented as a struggle to comprehend the basic principles which lie behind the decorative details, or, in other words, understanding the structure of the grammar behind the surface vocabulary. This attitude is not always as explicit as it is made by Panofsky, for example in his essay 'On the first page of Vasari's *Libro*', but it is implicit in much of the writing on the classical tradition outside central Italy.[3]

The Plateresque style of architecture in early sixteenth-century Spain is a case in point. It is often seen by historians today as not-yet-classical: it is an 'untutored provincial extravagance',[4] in which classical elements are brought together in unorthodox ways and with an overlay of decorative ornament, as in the portal of the hospital of Santa Cruz in Toledo mentioned in the previous chapter. I would question whether this is always the result of ignorance. No-one, so far as I know, has suggested that Donatello's highly unorthodox usages on the Cavalcanti altarpiece in S. Croce are a result of ignorance; he manages, after all, to handle the classical vocabulary quite conventionally elsewhere. The usual approach to early sixteenth-century Spanish architecture is that, apart from the one or two intrusive Italianate exceptions, this 'provincial extravagance' was only finally tamed by Philip II, when his own personal, classicizing tastes in architecture were realized in the form of the Escorial. As I suggested earlier, the Escorial is clearly too late to explain the classicizing trends of Spanish America.

But one of these intrusive Italianate exceptions deserves closer attention. Charles V's palace in Granada was begun in 1528 to the austerely classical, geometrical designs of Pedro Machuca when all else was late Isabelline and Plateresque exuberance. It is situated in the middle of the Moorish palace of the Alhambra, part of which was destroyed to make room for it. Granada, the last capital of Moorish Spain, had finally been recaptured in 1492, an event of enormous symbolic significance for Christian Spain. The important point, I believe, is not simply the exact nature of Machuca's Italian training, but that such a classicizing building should have been placed in such a highly-charged position. Is it not reasonable to see this untypically classicizing palace as the clearest possible statement of the cultural and ideological values not just of the Spanish crown, but of Christendom? The relationship between the style of architecture and the act of Christian conquest could scarcely have escaped the notice either of the Christians or of the subjugated Moors. The plan of Charles V's palace is based on the square and the circle, the two purest and simplest geometrical shapes, the shapes with which writers always open their architectural treatises, it uses the Doric and Ionic orders, and it is built of stone and marble. The iconography, as Rosenthal makes clear, is unmistakably imperial throughout, in overall design, in detail and in materials.[5] The contrast between this and the surrounding Moorish palace buildings of intricate and irregular plan, decorated with moulded plaster, brightly coloured glazed tiles and *alfarje* ceilings could scarcely be more dramatic, nor more aggressive. Certainly no modern visitor fails to notice the visual discontinuity.

This is not to suggest that this palace served as the model for an architecture of conquest in America. As I have argued throughout this study, the roots of the colonial style of architecture lie not in specific sources but in generally-held ideas about civility and the Art of Architecture which surface into practical reality when the occasion demands: in Granada with the conquest of the Moors, and in America with the conquest of the Indians. The extension of this is that if untutored conquistadors can create a classical style in America when most of those at home were immersed in the solecisms of the Plateresque, then this must suggest that those at home were not necessarily ignorant. It suggests rather that although they *knew* deep down that the basic principles which were felt to underlie Christian society could be made manifest in a purist architectural style, their circumstances did not require that this be explicit in their own architecture. Only the challenge of conquest brings these principles to the surface.

One of the most striking aspects of the classical tradition in architecture and town planning is the way in which it has somehow managed to retain a monopoly on notions of civility and rationality. It is the classical tradition against which other styles have to define themselves. Since classical antiquity it has served as the representative architectural style of European culture, European civilization and European power in different countries at different times. Since classical antiquity it has played a part in the process of colonization as well as being one of its major visual manifestations. The regular recurrence of the classical style and the grid plan town in situations of political and social control testifies to the strength of the tradition, or rather to the strength of people's belief in that tradition, which amounts to the same thing. The idea of architecture as a method of social control was perhaps not very clearly articulated in the minds of the Spanish conquerors: they saw it more as a necessary improvement, one of the benefits of their regime, but at some level they must have grasped the effectiveness particularly of the grid-plan town in reorganizing people's lives and in making them more accessible, more easily organized and controlled, as well as less strange and alien. Building churches too introduced the conquered people to a whole range of aspects of the new political and economic system as can be demonstrated by returning again to the Province of Chucuito.

In the Introduction I posed a number of questions about the churches in the Province of Chucuito which can now be at least partially answered. These churches, as has been seen, were not small rudimentary structures, nor were they intended to be temporary, to meet the basic requirements of the evangelization programme until such time as more permanent buildings could be commissioned and financed. They suggest that the Spanish missionaries, as the representatives of European culture and colonial rule, wished at the very outset to make as clear as possible a statement of intent; that their churches be seen as a central and permanent part of the Indian community, both physically and ideologically. These churches and others like them must have involved enormous amounts of local labour and materials, and not inconsiderable organization and direction.

A survey of the area in 1567 – one of a number of such surveys commissioned at different times by both the government and the Diocesan church to investigate the disturbing wealth of the Dominicans in this particular province – reveals that during the 1560s the Dominicans undertook extensive church building projects as well as restoration programmes on their existing churches, sometimes, as at Acora, employing as many as 2,000 men at any one time.[6] After the expulsion of the Dominicans in 1572 there seems to have been a lull until 1590 when, as a result of pressure from the King, a new building programme was initiated. Two carpenters and a brick mason were commissioned to build sixteen churches in the seven main lakeside towns within the space of three years.[7] These were certainly not completed within the three years, and subsequent documentation concerning this commission is not always consistent about the numbers of churches involved, but there is no doubt that there was tremendous building activity in the region around the turn of the century. On 1 May 1603 the Viceroy, Luis de Velasco, sent the King a progress report:

In a letter of 28 December 1601, I wrote to Your Majesty about the need in the Province of Chucuito for churches to be erected in many pueblos which did not have them, and of the measures which were being taken to build them [that would be] of benefit to the Royal Estate which has to contribute two thirds of the cost, and without aggravation to the natives. Fifteen have been built according to the order ... as well as which the Indians at their cost have built another seven and have more under way.[8]

In other words, it seems from this letter that a total of twenty-two churches have already been built and there are yet more in progress. Even more interestingly, it sounds as if the initiative lies partly with the Indians themselves. In the earlier letter of 28 December 1601 Velasco had laid out the means by which the churches could be built at a minimum cost to the Crown, and with minimum aggravation to the Indians. The Indians, he writes, are very behind with their taxes – through no fault of their own, but rather because of bad administration – and they are now under pressure to pay up. He suggests with pride, as if it were highly original, that the solution to both problems is: for the Indians to build the churches themselves, for the value of their labour to be assessed on a daily basis, and the total deducted from their debt. The Crown for its part will contribute 1,500 pesos per church to cover the costs of carpenters, *albañiles* and nails.[9] In the letter of 1 May 1603 Velasco writes that the Indians are requesting that the churches which they have already completed be evaluated for tax purposes,[10] and in another letter on the subject of 10 October 1603 he again asks the King for a reply to these suggestions, but, he says,

although I have not yet had a reply, they go on building the churches, and will continue to do so until Your Majesty is pleased to send me an answer.[11]

'They go on building the churches'. Here, in part at least, must lie the explanation for the numbers and size of the churches of Chucuito. The evidence from this area suggests that far from being hopelessly bewildered in the face of their aggressive conquerors, the native population well understood at least some aspects of the colonial system and were capable of manipulating them to their own advantage. The taxes of which Velasco writes were due in cash. Traditionally, of course, there was no money and so no obvious ways of raising it, but by the later sixteenth century the Indians of Peru were under increasing pressure to work in the mines in return for wages, wages with which they could then pay their taxes. In the case of the Province of Chucuito thousands of men went off annually to work in the silver mines of Potosí nearly 1,000 miles away to the south; many never returned, many found that living in Potosí had its attractions, or more commonly, many found that in the inflationary cash economy of the booming mining town, they had to stay longer and longer in order to earn sufficient to cover the costs of the return journey as well as to pay their taxes. Chucuito may have appeared prosperous to the colonial officials but it was no longer flourishing as it had been in pre-conquest times.

The traditional Andean labour tribute requirement, the *mita*, had been of strictly limited duration, the work usually relatively close to home. It is easy to see how this system, together with the system of tributes in kind, could be adapted to the needs of the Christian missionaries. The Dominicans must have understood this almost from the outset, arranging via the local *curaca* for regular supplies of food for their kitchens, and for labour and materials for their churches and monastic houses. To the Lupaca all this would have been a familiar pattern. At the time of the arrival of the Dominicans in the 1540s the older inhabitants would remember the Inca conquest of their region fifty years previously, at which time the Inca had similarly required the construction of new temples dedicated to the new cult of the Sun. After the Spanish conquest the local Inca hierarchy was effectively replaced by the Dominicans who, anxious to establish their churches and houses in the area before the episcopal authorities could arrange for a permanent secular priesthood to be sent in, exploited the system for all they were worth. The Indians built churches for them as a part of their traditional labour tribute. In return, as always, they had the right to till their allotted lands and there is some evidence to suggest that the Dominicans were not unaware of the need for rituals and festivals to replace the way in which the *mitayos* had traditionally been rewarded by their *curacas*.

The expulsion of the Dominicans in 1572 (for assuming too much control over non-religious affairs)[12] was followed, or so it appears from absence of documentation, by a period of relative inactivity in church-building operations, and then from 1590 onwards until about 1610 there is a second great boom. This time, however, the local priesthood is not so centrally involved; it is the Royal officials who commission these churches and report on their progress although, as always, it is the Indians who build them. What must have happened is that the idea proposed by Velasco – that the value of the churches be offset against the Indians' tax arrears – was quickly taken up by the Lupaca because the concept of tribute labour rather than taxes in cash was a part of their traditional culture. They knew that the alternative was working in the mines of Potosí and so 'they go on building churches', and apparently even initiating them. Velasco's proposal was even more attractive than the system as operated by the Dominicans because the Indians no longer had to find the cash to pay for carpenters and ironmongery: that was to be provided out of the Royal coffers (in theory, at least). No doubt such evidence of enterprise and Christian devotion on the part of the Indians met with enthusiastic support from the local clergy who had nothing to gain from the annual exodus of large numbers of the local adult male population to the mines.

Juli exemplifies the results of the Indians' labours. Three of the churches in

Plate 43 Juli, La Asunción; between 1602 and 1620.

the town must date from this period: La Asunción, San Juan and Santa Cruz. The fourth church which survives in the town is now the cathedral of San Pedro which is an eighteenth-century renovation of that constructed by the Dominicans in the 1550s. The crossing of San Juan was completed in 1603, and work on La Asunción and Santa Cruz must have been begun shortly afterwards. These three churches in each of the three parishes of the town are good examples of the way in which a very small number of variables can produce three very different solutions. La Asunción and Santa Cruz, for example, are founded on identical ground plans but with the axis, and so the position of the principal façade, changed. La Asunción, which has a level atrium like a great Inca terrace in front of it, runs laterally, spanning the upper side of a sloping plaza so that its fine brick portal faces out over the town (Plate 43). Santa Cruz, across on the opposite side of the town, is positioned

Plate 44 Juli, view of the roofs of San Juan from the atrium of Santa Cruz.

longitudinally to the atrium and square in front, and the axis of the nave and main west door can be seen as continuing through the atrium arch, down the road in front and across the west end of the church of San Juan which is set at right angles a couple of hundred yards below (Plate 44). In other words, these sites are far from accidental. They reinforce, even define the axes of the grid plan lay-out of the whole town.

The portals on all three churches are of brick with stone details.[13] They are so similar, in fact, as to suggest that they are all variations of the same design and on close examination it is evident that one very limited range of moulds could produce the bricks for all the main features: an arched entrance with simple mouldings marking the jambs and voussoirs, flanked by pilasters, and with an entablature and shallow pediment above, with roundels in the spandrels, in the pediment and, in the versions with paired as opposed to single pilaster strips, between the pilasters (Plate 45).

These churches and all the other surviving sixteenth-century churches in the area would require only the most minimal involvement from European craftsmen. The brick portals at Juli would seem to be the result of a single expandable design. Assuming that brick kilns were available by the end of the century (the area around Juliaca to the north of the province is still a major

Plate 45 Juli, San Juan. Brick portal, west end; 1590.

brick-making centre, suggesting a good local supply of suitable clay) a few moulds could be used to produce all the basic elements, and would even condition the overall dimensions. Someone familiar with the classical architectural system would need to oversee the assembly of a portal like this but this would not necessarily need to be a specialist craftsman. Certainly once the basic design had been drawn up, the moulds made, and perhaps a prototype built, it seems entirely probable that a practical-minded Jesuit and/or some able native craftsman who had had experience working with a European brick mason could have overseen the subsequent versions.

Something similar must have happened in Acora where the two surviving churches probably also date from the 1590 initiative. Again, they are similar in plan, they are set at right angles to one another and in conformity with the lines of the grid plan of the town, San Juan end on, San Pedro laterally to their respective squares. As with Juli, the designs of their brick portals are closely related, those of San Juan being less ambitious and so presumably later versions of those of San Pedro (*see* plate 27). They almost certainly involved the same basic brick moulds and would not have presented problems to the craftsmen and labourers who had worked on San Pedro.

The way the churches of Juli and Acora are positioned to gain maximum spatial effect, emphasizing the axes of the grid-plan town, is clearly not accidental, nor are these isolated examples. The same is true of the town of Chucuito itself and of Zepita and Pomata as well as of towns outside the Collao region. In fact such dramatic effects are common amongst provincial churches in Indian areas. They demonstrate the way in which scattered missionaries responded to the challenge of confronting indigenous religion, indigenous architecture and indigenous society with something that, with the constant emphasis on the arch, the arched entrance, the arched atrium, even the miniature arches in the bell-towers, is visually entirely new, and, in the way the churches are aligned along the axes of a grid-plan town, visually highly ordered. At the same time, the construction of these churches provides an area of close contact between the two cultures: the main fabric, the adobe and stone walls and the thatched roofs, would have been well within the range of traditional local skills, while from occasional itinerant carpenters or brick or stone masons, the local craftsmen would have learnt the few necessary new techniques, of making bricks, of constructing regular arches in stone and of jointing timber to form doors and door frames. No doubt they would also have soon picked up the rudiments of the classical architectural vocabulary on which their conquerors laid such store. None of this need have taken very long, especially, perhaps, when the alternative to constructing these new style buildings dedicated to the new style cult was the untold misery of work in the mines of Potosí.

The church-building activity in the Province of Chucuito in the sixteenth and early seventeenth centuries is perhaps not entirely typical in the number and scale of its churches, but it is really no more than a sort of larger-than-life version of what takes place the length and breadth of the Spanish Empire in America: missionary priests, with a deep-rooted set of assumptions about what constituted the fundamental, the essential features of a Christian church, armed with the self-confidence of the righteous, embarked on the realization of a cultural ideal. Appropriating indigenous systems of labour tribute they organized the construction of massive churches in imposing positions, preferably on the site of a pre-conquest centre of worship, aligned in such a way as to suggest an overall orderly urban environment. They designed them on an ambitious scale and with two distinctive features: prominent bell-towers and arched entrances framed by at least some of the basic elements of the classical architectural vocabulary. These churches are the product of the indigenous people's first experience of working for the new power. Their construction serves as an introduction to a new culture, to a new style of architecture, and to a new set of materials and techniques, as well as to a new form of economy. Once completed these new churches and their atria are also and perhaps most obviously, the site of the new religion, of baptism and Christian teaching, and of instruction in the behaviour and morals required of Christian citizens. The architecture of sixteenth-century Spanish America is an architecture of and for conquest; it is instrumental in the construction and consolidation of the Spanish Empire.

# Notes

The original of a passage discussed in the text is given in the endnotes only where the specific meaning of words or phrases is important for my argument. Except where a published translation of a book is used, all translations are my own.

*Introduction*

1. Las Casas, BAE 110, p. 252.
2. In the sixteenth century – in theory at least – the Viceroyalty comprised the whole of the continent to the south of Panama with the exception of Portuguese Brazil; obviously my focus is on those areas which were colonized first and where buildings survive more or less in their original sixteenth- or early seventeenth-century form.
3. Quoted in Góngora, *Studies*, p. 35.
4. E. Baldwin Smith, *Architectural Symbolism*, pp. 3–4, describes a similar phenomenon in imperial Rome: 'During the Roman Empire, when the state was cultivating by every means at its command a kind of a monumental propaganda to impress the masses throughout the provinces, many of the accepted implications of architectural forms, which were based upon instinctive habits of thought, are only partially reflected in the literature.'
5. See Elliott, *The Old World and the New*, for one of the first such studies. Also Pagden, *The Fall of Natural Man*, and Barker *et al.*, *Europe and its Others*.
6. Pagden, p. 5.
7. Cieza de León, *Segunda parte*, pp. 240–1. Cieza comments on the roads in a similar vein on a number of occasions, as, for example, in *Segunda Parte*, pp. 51–2. Here the comparison drawn is with the Emperor Charles V, who, he says, would be unable to summon up the forces to build such a road. For a modern study of the Inca roads, see Hyslop, *The Inka Road System*.
8. Fraser, 'Architecture and Imperialism'.
9. For a detailed study of this province and its architecture, see Fraser, 'The Architecture of Conquest', unpublished PhD, University of Essex, 1984.

10 Meléndez, *Tesoros verdaderos de las Yndias*, 1, p. 318.
11 Marco Dorta, 'Iglesias renacentistas en las riberas del lago Titicaca'.

## *1 The idea of architecture*

1 Cobo, *Historia del Nuevo Mundo*, 2, p. 52.
2 See Porras Barrenechea, *Las relaciones primitivas*, for a classified bibliography on the discovery and conquest of Peru.
3 Porras Barrenechea, *Las relaciones primitivas*, p. 64. In this and other similar places I have retained the word *pueblo* deliberately, to avoid the clear distinction in English between town and village.
4 Porras Barrenechea, *Las relaciones primitivas*, p. 68: 'hay cuatro pueblos juntos todos de un señor . . . alli ay muchas ovejas y puercos y gatos y perros y otros animalias y ansares e palomas y halli se hazen las mantas . . . de lana y de algodon y las labores y las quentas y pieças de plata y oro y es gente de mucha polezia segun lo que pareçe tienen muchas herramientas de cobre e otras metales con que labran sus heredades y sacan oro y hazen todas maneras de grangeria tienen los pueblos muy bien traçados de sus calles tienen muchos generos de fortalezas y tienen mucha orden y justicia entre sy'.
5 Díez de Betanzos, *Suma y narración*, p. 11.
6 Díez de Betanzos, *ibid.*, p. 31: 'vio la mala reparación e arte . . . y las casas de los moradores della eran pequeñas y pajizas e mal edificadas y sin proporción de arte de pueblo'.
7 Zárate, *Historia*, F9v: 'Guanacava . . . fue el que mas tierras ganò y acrescentò a su señoria, y el que mas justicia y razon tuvo en la tierra, y la reduxo a policia y cultura, tanto que parescia cosa impossible, una gente barbara y sin letras, regirse con tanto concierto y orden'.
8 Morúa, *Historia*, p. 20. Before the Incas, the peoples of Peru lived 'sin haver pueblos en orden ni policía'. 'Los Ingas . . . como gente de tan gran valor y entendimiento, lo dispusieron y domesticaron, ordenando el modo de bivir y trazando y limitando los términos'.
9 Morúa, *ibid.*, p. 64: 'Hizo Tupa Ynga Yupanqui juntar los indios en pueblos, porque antes vivían en cuevas, cerros y laderas, donde más comodidad hallavan'.
10 Morúa, *ibid.*, p. 68: 'En fin, puso toda la tierra de su señorio en concierto y orden con tanta prudencia, que si ubiera leydo las Políticas de Aristótiles y todo lo que la filosophía moral enseña, no pudiera averse abentajado tanto'.
11 Fraser, 'Hierarchies and rôles of materials in building and representation' in *The Other America*, ed. Fraser and Brotherston, pp. 41–55.
12 E.g. 'Epitome de la Conquista del Nuevo Reino de Granada', printed in Friede, *Descubrimiento*, p. 265; Simón, *Primera Parte*, p. 295.

13 Gil Tovar & Arbeláez Camacho, *Arte colonial*, p. 10: 'el indio que formó la población básica – exceptuándolo en lo que tenía de orfebre – no mostró capacidades de trabajo artístico de gran altura... El gran templo de Sugamuxi no era sino una choza de barro y paja, por más que de sus paredes pendiesen láminas de oro.'

14 Simón, *Primera Parte*, p. 47.

15 Similarly, David Drew used the term 'Stone Age' without qualification of the Maya in the BBC TV programme, *Footsteps: Maudesley and the Maya*, 27 October 1987.

16 Garcilaso de la Vega el Inca uses it repeatedly, including in the extended title of the first part of his *Commentarios Reales* of 1609: *Primera parte de los commentarios reales, que tratan del origen de los Yncas, Reyes que fueron del Peru, de su idolatría, leyes, y govierno en paz y en guerra: de sus vidas y conquistas, y de todo lo que fue aquel Imperio y su Republica, antes que los Españoles passaran a el*. One of his chief sources, the lost manuscript of Padre Blas Valera of about 1590, was entitled *Historia imperii peruani*.

17 Pedro Sancho, in Ramusio, 3, F343r–343v: 'La città del Cusco per esser... cosi bella, & con tanti edificii, che saria stata degna da veder in Spagna, & tutta piena di casamenti di Signori vi fabricava la sua casa... & la maggior parte di queste case sono di pietra... & sono fatte con bell'ordine, fatte le strade in croce molto diritte, tutte immattonate, & in mezzo di ciascuna và un condotto d'aqua murato di pietra.'

18 Cieza de León, *Primera parte*, F230r–F230v: 'en ninguna parte deste reyno del Peru se hallo forma de ciudad con noble ornamento sino fue este Cuzco... El Cuzco tuvo gran manera y calidad, devio ser fundada por gente de gran ser.'

19 Acosta, *Historia natural*, p. 194: 'la labor es estraña, y para espantar; y no usaban de mezcla, ni tenían hierro, ni acero para cortar y labrar las piedras, ni máquinas, ni instrumentos para traellas, y con todo eso están tan pulidamente labradas, que en muchas partes apenas se vé la juntura de unas con otras'.

20 Pedro Sancho, in Ramusio, 3, F343v: 'le pietre sono cosi liscie, che paiono tavole spianate, con la ligatura in ordine all'usanza di Spagna'.

21 Cobo, *Historia del Nuevo Mundo*, 2, p. 261: 'aunque parecen las más toscas, a mi ver, fueron mucho más dificultosas de hacer que las de sillería; porque demás de la haz, que labraban tan llana como los sillares, no siendo cortadas a regla, y habiéndolas de asentar tan ajustadas unas con otras, bien se deja entender el trabajo que les constaría el haberlas de encajar como las vemos. Porque siendo, como son, unas grandes y otras pequeñas, y unas y otras desiguales en la forma y faición, están asentadas con tan sutil juntura como las de sillería.'

22 Cobo, *Historia del Nuevo Mundo*, 2, p. 188: 'No era este gran templo obra de los reyes Incas, sino mucho más antiguo, como los indios cuentan, y se echa de ver en la forma y calidad de su fábrica, que es muy diferente de las otras de los Incas, que casi todas eran de piedra labrada, y si esta lo fuera, pudiera competir con los más soberbios edificios del mundo.'

23 Pedro Sancho, in Ramusio, 3, F343v.
24 Cieza de León, *Primera parte*, F230r–F230v: 'las casas hechas de piedra pura con tan lindas junturas, que illustra el antiguedad del edificio, pues estavan piedras tan grandes muy bien assentadas'.

   It is interesting in this respect that when he is describing Coricancha, the temple of the Sun in Cuzco, Cieza says that he can only think of one modern building which is at all comparable: the Tavera Hospital in Toledo. This was an unusually classicizing building for its time, although Cieza is here perhaps thinking in general terms of its overall lack of surface ornamentation rather than of its classicism.
25 Polo de Ondegardo, *CLDRHP*, 3, p. 107: 'Digo quanto a la labor de las piedras, porque en lo demas, los edificios destos son sin horden ny proporcion y vajos e aun con poco cimyento.'
26 See Fraser, V., 'Hierarchies and rôles of materials in building and representation'.
27 Acosta, *Historia natural*, p. 194: 'pero aunque eran grandes estos edificios, comunmente estaban mal repartidos y aprovechados, y propiamente como mezquitas ó edificios de bárbaros. Arco en sus edificios no le supieron hacer, ni alcanzaron mezcla para ello.'
28 Morúa, *Historia*, 2, p. 52: 'Y es sin duda cosa certisima que, si el Ynga alcansara a entender la manera y arte con que se fabrican y lebantan los arcos para los puentes de piedra, las hiciera famosisimas.'
29 *Descripción*, p. 96: 'Si los indios hubieran alcanzado a saber el arte de la arquitectura y arte de fazer puentes y edificios se hubieran aventajado a todas las naciones del mundo.'
30 Cobo, *Historia del Nuevo Mundo*, 2, pp. 52–3: 'ni una sola piedra labrada al modo de Europa hemos hallado en las muchas ruinas de antiquísimas fábricas que vemos. Yo mismo muchas veces, y con más que mediana diligencia, he visto y considerado las ruinas de los mas suntuosos y antiguos edificios deste reino del Perú ... por ver si en algunas de las losas y piedras extrañas que dellos se sacan, hallaba señal de letras, carácteres o de alguna labor semejante a las nuestras fábricas, y por ningún camino tal cosa he hallado ni piedras labradas para arquería, ni con forma de basas, capiteles, columnas, ni de otras figuras que les suele dar el arte de arquitectura.'
31 E.g. Benevolo, *The Architecture of the Renaissance*, 1; Kubler, 'Ciudades y cultura'; Palm, *Los orígenes*.
32 *CDIRDCO*, 1st series, 39, pp. 280–98; the relevant passages are contained in paragraphs 6–7, pp. 284–5. A slightly expanded variant of these was repeated to Cortés on 26 July 1523, printed in *CDIRDCO*, 2nd series, 9, pp. 167–81.
33 There is some earlier legislation on this issue too: plots on Española had originally been divided up and distributed equally between settlers regardless of status, wealth or occupation, but in 1509 this democratic policy was revised by Isabella, because it was seen as the reason why 'this island has not grown nor been more

34 Konetzke, *CDHFSH*, p. 122.
35 Konetzke, *CDHFSH*, pp. 335–9: *Instrucciones para hacer nuevos descubrimientos y poblaciones*, Valladolid, 13 May 1556.
36 Kubler, *Mexican Architecture*, 1, pp. 69–80, discusses the foundation of Mexico City.
37 *CDIRDCO*, 1st series, 8; the paragraphs on the founding of new towns are pp. 497–531.
38 Stanislawski, 'Early Spanish town planning', published extracts from the Ordinances of 1573 alongside extracts from Vitruvius to demonstrate the dependence of the former on the latter. This method, however, by selecting only those passages which correspond, does tend to over-emphasize the similarities.
39 There is in fact internal disagreement within the 1573 Ordinances about which are the more salubrious winds, as there is between the various classical authors on the subject. See Rykwert, *The Idea of a Town*, pp. 41–2.
40 Lázaro de Velasco, in Sánchez Cantón, 1, p. 193: 'templos do se invoque el sancto nombre de Dios, ennoblecesen las ciudades con los sumtuosos edificios . . . fundanse muros conque se defiendan los pueblos, labranse casas donde moren y amparen de las injurias del tiempo los hombres'.
41 *Ibid.*, p. 205: 'I verá quanto bien se sigue a la republica christiana que aya hombres de buenas abilidades, ascentados juizios y de gran prudencia, experimentados, por aqui vengan a hazer las obras necessarias como son iglesias, templos acertados donde se invoque el nombre sancto de Dios monesterios de religiones, hospitales y los edificios necessarios para las ciudades concertadas y bien governadas. I para que si en algun tiempo ganen tierras de infieles aya por do regirse para el edificar los templos e iglessias.'
42 E.g. J.H. Elliott, *The Old World and the New*, especially pp. 8–16.
43 *CDIRDCO*, 1st series, 31, pp. 156–7.
44 *CDIRDCO*, 2nd series, 9, pp. 53–74. These seem to be identical, apart from some variations in orthography, with a set of instructions to the Hieronymites transcribed in *CDIRDCO*, 1st series, pp. 310–31, although in this case they are dated 1518.
45 Even in Europe the use of furniture was only just becoming relatively widespread at this date, but there is a tendency for those writing about other peoples to espouse customs or fashions of a class slightly higher than their own. I am grateful to Anne Laurence for drawing my attention to Quinn's discussion of this phenomenon in *The Elizabethans and the Irish*, p. 68.
46 Konetzke, *CDHFSH*, 1, pp. 335–9.
47 Other official documentation emanating from Spain demonstrates that this was not always the case; there is, for example, evidence of detailed understanding of the complexities of the traditional tribute systems.

48 See Gutkind, *Urban Development*, pp. 126, 212.
49 Matienzo, *Gobierno*, p. 3.
50 *Ibid.*, p. 48: 'naide ignora los inconvenientes que se siguen a los indios de estar apartados y escondidos en huaycos y quebradas, así para lo tocante a su policía como a su conversion, porque ni pueden ser doctrinados ni ser hombres perpetuamente, no estando juntos en pueblos, y en esto no es menester dar más razones de las que todo el mundo sabe'.
51 *Ibid.*, especially pp. 48–9 and pp. 54–5.
52 Toledo's instructions are discussed by Hemming, pp. 392–7, and by Moore, *Cabildo*, pp. 227–9. The various legislation has not been published in full: Lisson Chávez, *La iglesia*, 9, pp. 618–20, prints a document entitled 'Instrucciones en lo de la reducción de los pueblos de yndios' of 1572, which must originate from Toledo. See also A. Málaga Medina, 'Las reducciones en el Perú (1532–1600)'.
53 *Concilios Limenses*, 1, pp. 373–4: 'dexadas sus costumbres barbaras y de salvajes se hagan a vivir con orden y costumbres políticas, como es que a las yglesias no vayan sucios y descompuestos, sino lavados aderezados y limpios; que las mugeres cubran con algun tocado sus cabezas; que en sus casas tengan messas para comer y camas para dormir, que las mismas casas o moradas suyas no parezcan corrales de ovejas sino moradas de hombres en el concierto y limpieza y aderezo y las demas cosas, que fueren semejantes a estas'.
54 Quoted in Benevolo, *The Architecture of the Renaissance*, p. 451; italics mine.
55 Fernández de Oviedo, *Natural hystoria*, fivv–vr: 'las calles son tanto y mas llanas y muy derechas: porque como se ha fundado en nuestros tiempos ... fue traçada con regla y compas y a una medida las calles todas en lo qual tiene mucha ventaja a todas las poblaciones que he visto' (Quoted in Morse, 'Some characteristics', p. 319).
56 Cervantes de Salazar, *Life in the Imperial and Loyal City*, p. 38.
57 *Ibid.*, p. 42.
58 *Ibid.*, p. 48.
59 [Probanza], 'Sobre los monasterios e iglesias de Nuestra Señora del Rosario de la provincia de San Antonio, de religiosos Dominicos' in *Boletín de Historia y Antigüedades*, 45, 1958, p. 479.
60 Quoted in Vargas Ugarte in the introduction to his *Ensayo de un diccionario*, 1, pp. 24–5: 'La portada principal, hermosamente labrada de ladrillo, toda de movederas al romano con cuatro columnas sobre cuatro trascolumnas, hermosamente jaspeadas y entre las concavidades dellas pintadas las cuatro Virtudes Cardinales.' On this hospital, see also Castelli, 'La primera imagen del Hospital Real de San Andrés'.
61 Quoted by Gibson, *Aztecs under Spanish Rule*, p. 34.
62 By far the majority of members of the Consejo de Indios had never been to America. Góngora, *Studies*, p. 82.
63 MacAndrew, *The Open-Air Churches*, p. 44, includes a number of specific

contemporary references to the Indians as in a state of perpetual childhood.
64 *CDIRDCO*, 1st series, 8, pp. 530–1: 'Entre tanto que la nueva poblacion se acaba, los pobladores, en quanto fuere posible, procuren de evitar la comunicacion y trato con los indios; y de no ir á sus pueblos, ni divitirse, ni derramarse por la tierra, ni que los indios entren en el circuito de la poblacion hasta la tener hecha y puesta en defensa, y las casas; de manera que quando los indios las vean les cause admiracion, y entiendan que los espanoles pueblan alli de asiento y no de paso, y los teman para no osar ofender, y respeten para desear su amistad.'

## 2 First foundations

1 Moore, *Cabildo*, p. 34.
2 Gibson, 'Spanish-Indian institutions', p. 236.
3 Morse, 'Some characteristics', p. 317.
4 Martínez, *Apuntes*, p. 54.
5 Moore, *Cabildo*, ch. 3, pp. 48–64, 'The founding of the town'; Porras Barrenechea, 'La fundación de Trujillo', pp. 52–6, discusses the question of what constitutes a Foundation; Friede, *Los Chibchas*, p. 117, distinguishes two different stages for Foundations, the practical and the juridical; Guarda, 'Tres reflexiones', p. 91, discusses the difference between Possession and Foundation.
6 Friede, *Los Chibchas*, chs. 8 & 9; Martínez, *Apuntes*, ch. 3.
7 Quoted in Ariza, *Sitio de la fundación*, p. 12: 'se apeó del caballo, y arrancando algunas yerbas y paseándose, dijo que tomaba posesión de aquel sitio y tierra en nombre del invictísimo Emperador Carlos V, su señor, para fundar allí una ciudad en su mismo nombre, y subiendo luego en su caballo, desnudó la espada, dicidendo que saliese se había quien le contradijese aquella fundación, porque él la fundaría con sus armas y caballo; aun no habiendo quien saliese a la defensa, envainó la espada'.
8 Guarda, 'Tres reflexiones', pp. 89–93.
9 Ruíz Guiñazú, *Garay, fundador*, p. 54: 'E luego el dicho señor xeneral... tomava é tomó la poseción de la dicha ciudad é de todas estas provincias... y en señal de poseción hechó mano a su espada y cortó hiervas y tiró cuchilladas y dixo que si avia alguno que se lo contradiga y que parezcan presenten todas las dichas justicias y Regidores y mucha gente, y no pareció nayde.'
10 Ariza, *Sitio de la fundación*, p. 13.
11 Friede, *Los Chibchas*, ch. 9.
12 Porras Barrenechea, 'El acta perdida', pp. 89–90: 'en esta picota que pocos dias ha mande hazer y poner en medio desta plaça en las gradas de piedra que tiene que no estan acabadas de labrar con esta puñal que en my cinta trayo yo labró algo dellas y corto y labro un ñudo del madero de la dicha picota como a todos los que sois presentes do bien visto y hago todos otros autos de posesión e diligencias

de fundación desta cibdad que soy obligado e debía hazer . . . poniendo por nonbre a este dicho pueblo que he fundado la muy noble y gran ciudad del Cuzco'.
13 Arequipa, *Colección*, p. 198: 'puso la Cruz en el sitio que viene señalado para la Iglesia, y así mismo puso la picota en la Plaza de la dicha Villa'.
14 Cobo, *Lima*, pp. 289–90: 'Y porque el principio de cualquier pueblo o ciudad ha de ser en Dios y por Dios, y en su nombre . . . conviene principiarlo en su Iglesia; comenzó la fundación y traza de la dicha ciudad y en la iglesia que puso por nombre nuestra Señora de la Asunción cuya advocación será . . . después de señalada la plaza hizo y edificó la dicha iglesia y puso por sus manos la primera piedra y los primeros maderos de ella . . . y luego repartió los solares a los vecinos del dicho pueblo segun parecerá por la traza que de la dicha ciudad se hizo.'
15 *CDIRDCO*, 1st series, 8, p. 526; § cxxv recommends that the church should not be on the main square, § cxxvII that it should.
16 *CDIRDCO*, 1st series, 8, p. 522, § cxIII. Kubler, in Kubler and Soria, *Art and Architecture*, p. 13, notes that in Spain in the sixteenth century architects preferred the 'wide, heavy sesquialter (2:3) proportions . . . to the $\sqrt{2}$ rectangles and duple proportions of Italian taste'. Whether these 2:3 proportions derive from Spanish taste or from Vitruvius does not really matter; either way their appearance in the 1573 Ordinances is not surprising. Their absence in South American towns is further evidence that these were not laid out by trained architects or scholars.
17 Rykwert, *The Idea of a Town*, p. 68 suggests that military *castra* were not the source of the orthogonal plans of classical antiquity either but that, on the contrary, the camp was 'a diagrammatic evocation of the city of Rome'.
18 Durán Montero, *Fundación de ciudades*, especially p. 31; Morris, *History of Urban Form*, discusses the recurrence of the grid-plan form for new towns in Europe and the Near East from Sumeria to the nineteenth century.
19 Martínez, *Apuntes*, p. 81.
20 Ruíz Guiñazú, *Garay, fundador*, p. 54.
21 Ariza, *Sitio de la fundación*, p. 15.
22 Martínez, *Apuntes*, p. 83.
23 Ayacucho, *Cabildo*, p. 65.
24 Guaman Poma, *Nueva Corónica*, p. 796.
25 *CDIRDCO*, 1st series, 14, p. 57.
26 Cobo, *Lima*, p. 309.
27 E.g. plan of Mendoza (Argentina) of 1562, reproduced in Chueca Goitia and Torres Balbas, *Planos de ciudades*, 1, cat. 19.
28 This must be the monument referred to in a source of 1567. Garci Díez de San Miguel, *Visita*, p. 77.
29 Porras Barrenechea, 'El acta perdida', pp. 74–5.
30 Plato, *Critias*, p. 141.

31 In this context it is interesting to compare the utterly impracticable walled town fantasies designed by George Waymouth for New England in 1605, reproduced in Quinn & Quinn, *The English New England Voyages*, figs. 9–14, which owe far more to Filarete's Sforzinda or even Plato's Magnesia than they do to experience. The English colonizing efforts, succeeding the Spanish by almost a century, were necessarily shaped both by a knowledge of Spanish practice and by a desire to improve on it. Plans like these simply could not have been produced for the use of Spanish settlers at the beginning of the sixteenth century.

32 Kubler, *Mexican Architecture*, 1, pp. 210–11.

33 Watkins, *The Old Straight Track*, pp. 28–9.

34 At the end of the century handbooks for prospective conquistadors begin to appear and in these one finds the first prescriptive references to the necessary foundation and possession ceremonies and to the erection of a picota, e.g. Vargas Machuca (1599), F105v–F106v. As with the 1573 *Ordenanzas*, these instructions mirror established practice.

35 Ruíz Guiñazú, *Garay, fundador*, pp. 51–3.

36 Cobo, *Lima*, pp. 282–90; Porras Barrenechea, 'Jauja, capital mítica', p. 122, n. 13; Morse, 'Some characteristics', p. 322.

37 Porras Barrenechea, 'La fundación de Trujillo', pp. 44–7.

38 Cobo, *Lima*, p. 290.

39 Porras Barrenechea, 'El acta perdida', *passim*.

40 Lizárraga, *Descripción*, p. 79.

41 Cobo, *Lima*, p. 287.

42 *Ibid.*, p. 290: 'Fue asentado y trazado la ciudad conforme a la planta y dibujo que para ello se hizo en papel, en el mismo asiento del pueblo de indios, dicha Lima, que estaba en la ribera del rio, a la banda del sur, en el mismo sitio y lugar que hoy ocupa la plaza y casas reales.'

43 Harth-terré, *Lima, Ensayos*, pp. 17–28, 'El pueblo Yunga de Lima'. His evidence seems sound but his argument is not picked up by Rostworowsky, *Lima y Canta*, pp. 67–88, who unites a number of documents about the seat of Taulichusco, the *curaca* of Lima, nor by Agurto Calvo, *Lima Prehispánico*.

44 Friede, *Los Chibchas*, p. 108.

45 Quoted in Ariza, *Sitio de la fundación*, p. 14: 'doce casas grandes y capaces entre las que tenían los indios'.

46 Salamanca Aguilera, *Guía*, p. 12; only right at the end of the official document is it mentioned that the site chosen is 'encima de los dichos cercados que los indios tienen'.

47 Porras Barrenechea, 'La fundación de Trujillo', pp. 46–7.

48 Moore, *Cabildo*, p. 60, n. 22, remarks, for example, 'If the site chosen [for a new Spanish town] was already inhabited by Indians, their huts were torn down and the materials used for the settlers' homes.'

49 *Concilios Limenses*, 1, p. 8.
50 Meléndez, *Tesoros*, 1, p. 606.
51 E.g. the 1556 Instructions to the Viceroy of Peru, in Konetzke, *CDPHFSH*, 1, p. 336: 'elejáis sitios y lugares para poblar, teniendo respecto a que sea la tierra sana y fertíl . . . todo lo cual proveeréis que se reparta a los pobladores, no ocupando ni tomando cosa que sea de los indios sin voluntad suya'.
52 Chomsky, *New Statesman*, 29 July 1983, p. 16.
53 Zárate, *Historia*, f8r.
54 *CDIRDCO*, 2nd series, 10, pp. 347–9.
55 Quito, *Libro primero*, 2, p. 37.
56 Quito, *Libro segundo*, 1, p. 100.
57 Boxer, *Mary and Misogyny*, p. 35.
58 Quito, *Oficios y cartas*, p. 51.
59 Arequipa, *Colección*, p. 269.
60 *Ibid.*, p. 289.
61 Lima, *Cabildo*, 1, p. 251.
62 *Ibid.*, pp. 290–1.
63 Bromley, *La fundación*, pp. 141ff.
64 Hemming, *The Conquest*, p. 95.
65 Harth-terré, 'Las tres fundaciones'.
66 *CDIRDCO*, 1st series, 3, p. 95.
67 Harth-terré, 'Las tres fundaciones'.
68 Marco Dorta in Angulo Iñiguez *et al.*, *Historia*, 1, p. 696.
69 Pedro Simón, *Primera parte*, p. 384.
70 Marco Dorta, *Materiales*, p. 59.
71 [Probanza], 'Sobre los monasterios', pp. 478, 480 & 482.
72 Quito, *Oficios y cartas*, p. 584.
73 Arequipa, *Colección*, p. 265.
74 *Ibid.*, p. 289: 'Se comisionó a Francisco de Cháves para que vea si los edificios de la Ciudad están en linea recta, y si los vecinos no se han entrado terreno.'
75 Gakenheimer, 'Decisions of Cabildo', p. 249.
76 Lima, *Cabildo*, 4, p. 182.
77 *Ibid.*, p. 474: 'Eneste cabildo se acordo que por quanto en muchas de las calles desta çibdad estan fechas casas y tapiados solares en perjuyzio dellas metiendose en el sitio de las calles y atapando otras sin guardar la horden de la traça desta çibdad y viendo que todo esto es en tanto perjuyzio que si no se rremedia de derribarse e que no se haga mas sera mucho daño y fealdad de la traça y calles por tanto que cometian y cometieron a los señores geronimo de silva alcalde hordinario y a los señores martin yañez y hernando de mena diputados que tomando consigo al alarife desta çibdad y los negros o yndios que les paresçiere que son menester y saquen pormenores de las casas donde oviere perjuyzio en lo

suso dicho y a consta dellos se derribe y ponga en el termino que conviene conforme a la traça y a la derechura y claridad de las calles.'
78 *Ibid.*, p. 481.
79 Lima, *Cabildo*, 4, pp. 611–12.
80 *Ibid.*, p. 116.
81 *Ibid.*, pp. 332–3.
82 Lima, *Cabildo*, 3, p. 83: 'Con tanto que los çerque e faga enellos lo que es obligado conforme a las hordenanças desta çibdad e que sean syn perjuyzio de las calles desta çibdad conforme a los asientos de los yndios e a las calles que van por medio de los dichos asientos.'
83 Lima, *Cabildo*, 4, pp. 464–5.
84 Arequipa, *Colección*, pp. 258–9.
85 Quito, *Libro primero*, 1, p. 423.
86 *Ibid.*, p. 67.
87 Gakenheimer, 'Decisions of Cabildo', p. 250.
88 Harth-terré & Márquez Abanto, 'El puente de piedra'.
89 [Lima Cabilda], *Libro primero*, ed. Torres Saldamando, 2, Apéndices, 2nd series, Appendix 5, pp. 105–216.
90 Cobo, *Lima*, pp. 352–5. See also A. Málaga Medina, 'Las reducciones en el Perú (1532–1600)', p. 157–61.
91 *Relaciones geográficas*, 1, p. 25: 'Fundéle de indios derramados, que andaban como alárabes . . . híceles hacer las calles por cordel, y yo mismo las nivelaba, y por sus cuadras, con mucho ordén . . . tienen fuente de buen agua en mitad de su plaza. Híceles sus plazas y casas de cabildo . . . híceles dos iglesias, á cada pueblo la suya, y ansí serán bien doctrinados, y dejéles en tanta pulicía, que, despues acá, otros indios de pueblos mal ordenados se han reducido á poblaciones y hacen las casas por orden.'
92 Duviols, *La destrucción*, pp. 320–9.
93 Wachtel, *Los vencidos*, p. 216; Hemming, *The Conquest*, pp. 392–7.
94 Espinosa Soriano, 'La guaranga', p. 43.
95 *Relaciones geográficas*, 1, p. 176 (Province of Vilcas Guaman, 1586): 'Las casas desta provincia son pequeñas y bajas, hechas á dos aguas, y otras redondas de piedra y barro, sin cal, cubiertas con paja, de rústica proporción.'
96 *Ibid.*, pp. 88–9 (Province of Jauja, 1582): 'Las casas que van edificando despues de las reducciones son cuadradas y pequeñas, imitando á las de Castilla; porque ántes solian ser buhiyos redondos.'
97 Duviols, *La destrucción*, pp. 317–25.
98 Arriaga, *Extirpation*, p. 24.
99 *Relaciones geográficas*, 1, pp. 111–12: 'Y así, los dichos pueblos recien reducidos no son permanentes por la mayor parte, porque, despues de la dicha reduccion y verse los inconvenientes que hay en haberse mudado á diferentes temples y sitios

mal sanos y léjos de sus sementeras, se van vuelto á poblar muchos pueblos adonde ántes estaban y á otras partes con licencia de los gobernadores y con parecer de los corregidores de sus distritos.'

100 E.g. Martínez, *Apuntes*, p. 153; Moore, *Cabildo*, pp. 225–30; A. Málaga Medina, 'Las reducciones', p. 163.
101 Elliott, *The Old World and the New*, p. 15.

## 3  The builders

1 AGI, Charcas 142. Two loose unbound folios. Dated 1586 in a later hand, but probably written in the 1590s.
2 In Inca territories especially, the friars often converted the wayside *tambos*, inns that provided food and shelter for travellers, into chapels.
3 Simón, *Primera parte*, p. 24; for the achievements of the friars in Mexico, see MacAndrew, p. 50.
4 In the 1580s in the area covered by the modern countries of Ecuador, Peru and Bolivia, less than 8,000 Spanish settlers were recorded, fewer than 250 of whom had direct control over Indian labour within the *encomienda* system (discussed below). The figures are given in Zavala, *El servicio personal*, 1, p. 286, n. 665.
5 Konetzke, *CDPHFSH*, 1, p. 42, publishes Isabella's directive. See Parry, *The Audiencia of New Galicia*, pp. 9–11 and ch. 3, 'The Audiencia and the Indians'; Góngora, *Studies*, ch. 1, 'Conquistadors and rewards of conquest'; Gibson, *Spain in America*, ch. 3, 'Encomienda'.
6 *CDIRDCO*, 2nd series, 10, p. 34, Cédula Real of 1536.
7 These were the first general laws dealing with the native populations of America and their government, dated 23 January 1513. Published in Konetzke, *CDPHFSH*, pp. 38–57.
8 *CDIRDCO*, 2nd series, 10, p. 171, Cédula Real to the Consejo de Indias: 'vos mando y encargo que tengays mucho cuydado como en las cavezeras de todos los pueblos ... que se hagan iglesias y para ello hagays tomar y que se tomen de los tributos que los dichos indios an de dar a nos y a sus encomenderos los que fuere menester hasta que la iglesia sea acabada.'
9 Mendieta, *Historia ecclesiastica*, p. 422.
10 Haring, *The Spanish Empire*, p. 285. Tithes were divided into four parts: one went to the Bishop, one to the Dean and Chapter; the remaining parts were divided into nine (*novenos*) of which two parts went to the crown, four to parish clergy and three for church fabric. See also Gibson, *Aztecs*, p. 123.
11 An official instruction to this end is published in Lisson Chávez, *La iglesia*, 4, p. 189, and there are numerous references to specific buildings, e.g. AGI, Charcas 142, 1569, with reference to the Cathedral of La Plata (Chuquisaca); AGI, Charcas 142, 1586, with reference to the church of Tolu, Cartagena.

12 AGI, Lima 305, Letter from Juan Solano to the Spanish Crown, 20 December 1549.
13 Marco Dorta, *Materiales*, document 20, p. 7.
14 These ecclesiastical boundaries often differed from those of the secular administration. In Mexico the parish-like subdivisions are commonly termed *visitas* rather than *doctrinas*.
15 *Concilios Limenses*, 1, p. 24.
16 Tibesar, *Franciscan beginnings*, p. 62.
17 Tibesar, *ibid.*, pp. 37–8, and p. 49: Viceroy Toledo instructs Franciscans in Lima to go out to Cajamarca to the Indian *doctrinas*. Lisson Chávez, *La iglesia*, 5, p. 40: letter from the Dominicans in Lima to the Crown about the difficult conditions, and how the friars do not like being sent off into the provinces. AGI, Lima 270, vol. 2, F24v, letter from Audiencia of Los Charcas to the King of 1 March 1575, about how there are too many friars who do not work in the field.
18 Lisson Chávez, *La iglesia*, 6, p. 159.
19 Parry, *The Audiencia of New Galicia*, pp. 55–7; Kubler, *Mexican Architecture*, 1, pp. 135–42; Eugenio, *Tributo y trabajo*, especially pp. 235–51.
20 This is necessarily a summary of a complex system that has been the subject of much research in the last twenty-five years. See especially Murra, *The Economic Organisation*, and Wachtel, *Los vencidos*. The only group to whom the *mita* did not apply were the *yanacona*, to be discussed below.
21 Díez de Betanzos, *Suma y narración*, especially pp. 31–48.
22 Murra, *Formaciones económicas*, p. 31.
23 See Conclusions below.
24 Zavala, *Servicio personal*, 1, p. 251, n. 110.
25 Sections XXV and XXIX of Toledo's orders of 1572 concerning the government of Cuzco and the organization of the Indians include a requirement that they be paid; summarized in Zavala, *Servicio personal*, 1, pp. 138–40. The earliest legislation about Peru does not mention wages, e.g. Ayacucho, *Cabildo*, 1 January 1540, and Vaca de Castro's ruling, Zavala, *ibid.*, 1, p. 11.
26 BN 1591. A52. 'Provisión expedida por el Virrey Dn. García Hurtado de Mendoza para que los corregidores de la ciudad de Arequipa repartan de los Collaguas la cantidad de 20 indios.'
27 The wage would probably have been a *tomín*, the standard daily payment in sixteenth-century Peru. Zavala, *Servicio personal*, 1, p. 252, n. 121.
28 Murra, 'La función del tejido en varios contextos sociales y políticos' in *Formaciones económicas*, pp. 145–70.
29 AGI, Lima 34, Pt. 2, F104r, 10 October 1603: 'ninguna cossa de quantas son nescessarias para el sustento y conservaçion desta republica desde la menor hasta la maior se haria ni la havria, sino la hiciesen los Yndios – assi es forçosso y necess[o] el corte de la madera.'

30 Inca roofing techniques are discussed by Gasparini and Margolies, *Inca Architecture*, especially pp. 308–19.
31 Polo de Ondegardo, *CLDRHP*, vol. 3, 'Los errores', p. 106.
32 Díez de San Miguel includes several references to *mitayos* going to Cuzco from Chucuito, e.g. p. 39, p. 80.
33 Konetzke, *CDPHFSH*, 1, p. 43 (Leyes de Burgos, 1513).
34 Hemming, *The Conquest*, p. 499.
35 E.g. Santiago Sebastián, *Itinerarios*, p. 25; Gil Tovar and Arbeláez Camacho, *El arte colonial en Colombia*, p. 49.
36 Mendieta, *Historia ecclesiástica*, p. 410: 'Mas visto que quedaba firme la bóveda, luego perdieron el miedo, y poco después los indios solos hicieron dos capillitas de bóveda.'
37 Acosta, *Historia natural*, p. 194.
38 Herrera, *Historia general*, 5, p. 113.
39 Both black labourers and black craftsmen played an important part in the construction of the major Spanish cities, especially Lima. See e.g. Harth-terré and Márquez Abanto, 'El artesano negro', and Bowser, *The African Slave*, ch. 6, pp. 125–46, 'The Black artisan'. My prime concern here as elsewhere is with the relationship between indigenous American styles, materials and techniques and those of the conquering Spaniards.
40 Mendieta, *Historia*, p. 410: 'esto se puede entender por regla general, que cuasi todas las buenas y curiosas obras que en todo género de oficios y artes se hacen en esta tierra de Indias (á lo menos en la Nueva España), los indios son los que las ejercitan y labran, porque los españoles maestros de los tales oficios, por maravilla hacen mas que dar la obra á los indios y decirles como quieren que la hagan. Y ellos la hacen tan perfecta, que no se puede mejorar.'
41 Cieza de León, *Primera parte*, F269v–270r.
42 E.g. Quito, *Oficios y cartas*, p. 588 (from the 1573 *Relaciones geográficas* for Quito). Even Matienzo admitted that 'tienen habilidad en oficios mecánicos de todos géneros', Zavala, *Servicio personal*, 1, p. 51.
43 Morúa, *Historia*, 2, p. 87.
44 Arequipa, *Documentos*, p. 259; Quito, *Cabildos de la Iglesia Catedral*, p. 40; Quito, *Oficios y cartas*, p. 589.
45 The Crown's instructions of 1563 to Lope García de Castro, governor of Peru, include a requirement that *yana* be made to pay tribute (Zavala, *Servicio personal*, 1, p. 39) but the tradition survived, and in 1570 Viceroy Toledo wrote a report on Guamanga (Ayacucho) recommending that all *yana* be taxed like everyone else, because he believed that Indians were evading tax simply by calling themselves *yana*, Zavala, 1, p. 112. Wachtel describes a similar occurrence in the Valley of Yucay in 1572, *Sociedad e ideología*, pp. 150–1.
46 Bishop Valverde in a letter to the King, 1539, in Lisson Chávez, *La iglesia*, 2, p. 111.

47 Vázquez de Espinosa, *Compendium*, p. 353, of the *yanacona* of Popayan; *Relaciones geográficos* of the *yanacona* of Guamanga, 1, p. 129.
48 This distinction continues to colour twentieth-century studies of *yanaconaje*. The craft of running a household in Europe has, as the sphere of women, traditionally been disparaged, but cooking, cleaning and serving at table may, to the Incas, have been on a level with singing or carpentry or gold-smithing. Similarly, there is an art to being a good courtier in elaborate, ritualized courts such as those of Haile Selassie or Louis XIV.
49 Zavala, *Servicio personal*, 1, p. 221.
50 *Relaciones geográficas*, 1, p. 97.
51 Garcilaso de la Vega, *Comentarios*, BAE, 133, p. 126: 'No supieron hacer una sierra, ni una barrena, ni cepillo, ni otro instrumento alguno para oficio de carpintería; y así no supieron hacer arcas, ni puertas, más de cortar la madera y blanquearla para los edificios. Para las hachas y azuelas, y algunas pocas escardillas que hacían, servían los plateros en lugar de herreros, porque todo el herramental que labraban era de cobre y azófar. No usaron de clavazón, que quanta madera ponían en sus edificios todo era atada con sogas de esparto.'
52 Pedro Simón, *Noticias historiales*, 2, p. 66.
53 Meléndez, *Tesoros*, 3, p. 358.
54 *Concilios Limenses*, (1551), 1, p. 59.
55 Toledo's *Ordenanzas* of 1575, in Zavala, *Servicio personal*, 1, p. 143.
56 Zavala, *Servicio personal*, 1, p. 57.
57 Harth-terré & Márquez Abanto, 'Perspectiva social', p. 435.
58 *Ibid.*, p. 434.
59 Quito, *Oficios y cartas*, p. 146.
60 Zavala, *Servicio personal*, p. 113.
61 Kubler, *Mexican Architecture*, 1, p. 153.
62 Vargas, *Patrimonio artístico*, p. 5.
63 Lee López, 'La cofradía', p. 476.
64 Mendieta, *Historia ecclesiástica*, p. 408.
65 Marco Dorta in Angulo Iñiguez, *et al.*, *Historia*, 1, p. 591.
66 *Ibid.*, p. 602.
67 *CDIRDCO*, 2nd series, 9, p. 70: 'Y por que los pueblos se pongan en policia debeis trabajar que se muestren oficios algunos de los indios, asi como carpinteros, pedreros, herradores, aserradores de madera y sastres y otros semejantes oficios para servicio de la Republica.'
68 *CDIRDCO*, 2nd series, 9, p. 92: 'entre los yndios naturales de las yndias ay muchos que tienen tanta capacidad e abilidad que podran bivir por sy en pueblos politicamente como biven los cristianos españoles e servyrnos como nuestros vasallos syn estar encomendados a cristianos españoles.'
69 Konetzke, *CDPHFSH*, 1, p. 264.

70 Quito, *Oficios y Cartas*, p. 159.
71 *Ibid.*, p. 277.
72 Quito, *Audiencia*, p. 143.
73 Garcilaso de la Vega, *Comentarios*, BAE, 134, p. 139: 'La rudeza que ahora muestran no es falta de habilidad e ingenio, sino por estar desacostumbrados a las costumbres y cosas de Europa y porque no hallan quien les enseñe cosas de habilidad, sino cosas de granjería e interés ... los que alcanzan maestro o tiempo desocupado y libertad para deprender, aunque no sea más que imitando lo que ven, sin que les enseñen, salen oficiales en todas artes mecánicas y hacen ventaja a muchos españoles. Y lo mismo en el leer y escribir, en la música e instrumentos y otras facultades, y aun en el latín no fueran los peores sí quisieran los españoles enseñarles.'
74 Gibson, *Aztecs*, pp. 399–402.
75 Matienzo, *Gobierno*, p. 348: 'En este Reino hay muy gran desorden en consentir a los oficiales de sastres, calceteros, barberos, albéitares, herradores, carpinteros, albañiles y otros oficios mecánicos, andar hechos caballeros, y que no usen sus oficios y los enseñen a los indios que en su servicio estovieren, aunque por leyes y provisiones reales Su Magestad tiene bien proveído y mandado que puedan ser compellidos a usar sus oficios en tierra nueva como ésta, adonde tánto es menester.'
76 Góngora, *Studies*, p. 114.
77 Konetzke, *CDPHFSH*, 1, pp. 309–10: 'no proveáis a los dichos oficios de corregidores a ninguna persona de oficios de albañil, ni sastre, ni olleros, ni otros oficios mecánicos, sino a personas honradas y que tengan para ello las calidades.'
78 *CDIRDCO*, 2nd series, 5, pp. 126, 188 & 197.
79 Friede, *Documentos inéditos*, 4, pp. 96–7: 'no se hará en ella [la iglesia] de piedra cosa alguna, porque no hay cal ni otro aparejo para ello, y hay necesidad que se acabe como está empezada de paja y cañas, con que lo que toca a la capilla y coro y rejas y coro de clérigos y asentamientos de escaños y puertas con lo demás necesario, es muy costoso hacerse de madera en esta ciudad, porque no hay el aparejo de maestros y herramientas ni madera cerca del dicho pueblo, para que se pudiese hacer.'
80 Lima, *Cabildo*, 1, p. 133.
81 Harth-terré & Márquez Abanto, 'Perspectiva social', pp. 374–5.
82 Mariátegui, *Techumbres y artesonados peruanos*.
83 AGI, Panama 31, 18 March 1626.
84 Harth-terré & Márquez Abanto, 'Perspectiva social', pp. 373–4.
85 The carpenters and the *albañiles* both relied on a third craft – that of the blacksmith, who supplied the tools of both trades as well as nails, fittings such as bolts, hinges, brackets, and iron grills and railings.
86 Parry, *Cities*, p. 11, translates *alarife* as municipal architect; he also includes the

term *medidor*, meaning surveyor, but I have not found this post referred to in the early documentation concerning South American cities.

87 Lima, *Cabildo*, 1, p. 133.
88 *Ibid.*, pp. 216–17, 24 May 1528: 'Este dya los dichos señores dixeron que por quanto enesta çibdad no esta fecho el ospital . . . y porque hasta agora no esta nombrado mayordomo ny persona que entienda en que se haga ny haga las otras cosas que al dicha ospital convengan y Juan Meco es persona honrrada y que con toda fidelidad e como convenga entendera en myrar e proveer que se haga el dicho ospital en donde esta señalado que se haga por sus merçedes para que han dedicado y señalado dos solares dixeron que le nombraran e nombraron por mayordomo del dicho ospital.'
89 Lima, *Cabildo*, 4, p. 140.
90 *Ibid.*, 4, p. 236.
91 Harth-terré & Márquez Abanto, 'Perspectiva social', p. 361.
92 *Ibid.*, p. 357; Lima, *Cabildo*, 1, p. 44.
93 Vargas Ugarte, *Los Jesuitas*, p. 66.
94 AGI, Panamá, 31, 18 March 1626, for text; and AGI, Mapas y Planos, Panamá, 43, for accompanying drawing of exterior and interior elevations on obverse and reverse of a single sheet.
95 Lima, *Cabildo*, 4, p. 44, 11 January 1549.
96 Angulo, 'La iglesia de Sto Domingo', p. 233.
97 Harth-terré & Márquez Abanto, 'El puente de piedra', p. 101, n. 2.
98 Harth-terré & Márquez Abanto, 'Perspectiva social', p. 372. Parry, *Cities*, p. 11, translates *obrero mayor* as commissioner of public works.
99 Marco Dorta, 'Arquitectura colonial: Francisco Becerra', p. 15.
100 *Ibid.*, p. 15.
101 AGI, Lima 310, Auctos del audiencia y acuerdo sobre el reparo de la iglesia, F1r.
102 BN 1535. A 125, F40r.
103 Harth-terré, 'El imafronte de la Catedral de Lima'.
104 AGI, Lima 310, 16 February 1623, Memoria de las condiciones . . . F4v.
105 *Ibid.*, F19r–20r.
106 Cobo, *Lima*, p. 289.
107 Espinosa Soriano, 'La guaranga', p. 62.

## 4 Questions of style

1 Lima, *Cabildo*, 1, p. 251; Arequipa, *Colección*, p. 270.
2 Cobo, *Lima*, mentions several examples of stone imported from Panama: for San Lázaro, p. 399; for La Merced, p. 417; for San Agustín, p. 421.
3 Cobo, *Historia del Nuevo Mundo*, 1, p. 89, says earth or dung, *estiércol*.
4 Zárate, *Historia*, F6r, describes the internal and external appearance of pre-1555 houses in Lima in some detail.

5 The following details are taken from Cobo, *Lima*, pp. 360ff, from Wethey, *Colonial Architecture*, pp. 247–51, and from Bernales Ballesteros, *Edificación de la iglesia catedral de Lima, passim*.
6 Harth-terré, *Perú: Monumentos*, pp. 73–9.
7 Kubler & Soria, *Art and Architecture*, p. 83.
8 McAndrew, *The Open-Air Churches*; Palm, 'Las capillas abiertas'; Kubler, *Mexican Architecture*, 2, pp. 314–41.
9 Levillier, *Gobernantes del Perú*, 4, p. 117.
10 As with the open chapel, this was not necessarily because there was insufficient room for all the new converts in the church (as Mendieta, *Historia*, p. 418, and others following him have claimed) but because unbelievers, the not-yet-Christians, were not strictly speaking allowed inside a church. *Concilios Limenses*, 1, p. 33.
11 Mateos, 'Constituciones para indios del primer Concilio Limense', pp. 9–10.
12 See the many examples illustrated in Mesa & Gisbert, *Iglesias con atrio y posas*.
13 Cervantes, *Life in the Imperial and Loyal City*, p. 51.
14 Ricard, *The Spiritual Conquest*.
15 Acosta, *De Procuranda*, p. 565.
16 Arriaga, *Extirpation*, e.g. p. 108, and pp. 137–8. See also MacCormack, 'From the Sun of the Incas to the Virgin of Copacabana'.
17 Suardo, *Diario*, 1, e.g. p. 169 and p. 173.
18 E.g. *Concilios Limenses*, 1, p. 8.
19 Martínez, *Apuntes*, Appendix, p. 172.
20 Wachtel, *Los vencidos*, p. 154.
21 This privileging of the coast and Lima in particular is still very evident today: the main north–south coastal highway is metalled and well-maintained while inland even the main through-routes, however essential to the country's economy, are often little more than muddy tracks.
22 Cobo, *Historia del Nuevo Mundo*, 2, 188.
23 Harth-terré, 'Los últimos canteros incáicos'; Kauffmann Doig, *Influencias 'Inca'*.
24 Fraser, 'Architecture and imperialism'.
25 Although this presumably post-dates the earthquake of 1650 it appears to have been rebuilt to its original late sixteenth-century design.
26 Quoted in Marco Dorta, 'Tunja', p. 467.
27 The precise sources for the design of this façade have caused considerable problems. Kubler, in Kubler & Soria, *Art and Architecture*, p. 87, feels that 'no American façade of the 16th century is more Italianate', but adds that 'the accumulation of Italian forms is Flemish in its profusion'. Navarro claims it to be closely related to the Escorial, a claim that Marco Dorta, in Angulo Iñiguez *et al.*, *Historia*, 1, p. 612, feels is exaggerated, but he avoids suggesting any specific sources himself, offering a broad 'todo es clasicismo' instead. Bayón, *Sociedad*, pp. 39–41, has a range of possibilities; he finds it amazing that anyone should

recognize echoes of the Escorial, seeing the rustication as Nordic, and the whole as a Flemish-Dutch interpretation of the Italian Renaissance, while also recognizing the influence of Serlio. At the same time he is reminded specifically of Leyden Town Hall, p. 63, n. 9. For González de Valcárcel, *Architectural Conservation*, p. 123, the façade is Vignolesque, and for Kelemen, *Baroque and Rococo*, p. 158, 'the austere, late Renaissance design is given a Baroque touch by the paired columns and bands of rusticated stone work' although he does not commit himself to specific sources. One could expand this list of possible influences to include the Plateresque (the grotesque masks in the frieze), Philibert de l'Orme for the rustication, and perhaps Giulio Romano for the more eccentric handling of the classical architectural vocabulary, but the whole exercise is unhelpful.

28 Illustrated in Angulo Iñiguez, *Planos de monumentos*, 1, plate 7.
29 Kubler & Soria, *Art and Architecture*, p. 63.
30 Quoted in Marco Dorta, 'Tunja', p. 467.
31 Alberti, *De Re Aedificatoria*, Bk 1, ch. XII.
32 Borromeo, 'Instructiones', 3, ch. VII.
33 Arbeláez Camacho, 'El templo de la Compañía'.
34 All are disputed terms. See e.g. Kubler and Soria, *Art and Architecture*, pp. 1–21; Bury, 'The stylistic term *Plateresque*'; Rosenthal, *The Palace of Charles V*, pp. 241–5.
35 The plans were modified by the Italian-influenced Bartolomé de Bustamante, see Wilkinson, *The Hospital of Cardinal Tavera*.
36 Kubler & Soria, *Art and Architecture*, p. 11.
37 Foster, *Culture and Conquest*, especially pp. 227–34.

## Conclusions

1 Guarda, 'Tres reflexiones' in Solano, *Estudios*, p. 89.
2 Neill, *A History of Christian Missions*, pp. 173–5.
3 Panofsky, *Meaning in the Visual Arts*, pp. 206–65. His argument is based on an assumption of Northern incomprehension, of their appropriation of the superficialities of classicism rather than its essence. The practitioners of architecture in Northern Europe 'at first appropriated the decorative accessories of the new Italian style rather than its essential fundamental principles'. Summerson's language is similar: 'The Northern Italian Renaissance . . . grasped the ornamentation of the antique but not its bony structure,' *The Classical Language*, p. 8.
4 Kubler & Soria, *Art and Architecture*, p. 10. Kubler in fact attributes this attitude to the 'courtly class' of early sixteenth-century Spain, but the tenor of his writing suggests that this was his own opinion too: 'The expressive effect [of the Plateresque] is often extravagant and florid, suggesting great animation and energy, but at unexpected places and for unclear reasons. The ornament is never

delicate. If it could be described in sound, it would be loud, harsh, and intricate of rhythm.' Uncouth, perhaps? And here, as of course in architectural theory, classicism is closely associated with rationality.

5 Rosenthal, *The Palace of Charles V*, ch. VII, pp. 236–64. Interestingly, in view of the prominence of the Doric order in early Spanish American church façades, he notes that there is no evidence of opposition from the stone cutters to Machuca's Doric and Ionic details, even though these 'were certainly new to most of the Spanish craftsmen working on the Alhambra', nor, despite this newness, is there much evidence of the transformation or misunderstanding of these forms by the local stonecarvers, p. 239.

6 Díez de San Miguel, *Visita*, p. 158.

7 This contract is cited in Marco Dorta, 'Iglesias renacentistas', p. 704, who gives no source but perhaps follows Mendiburu, *Diccionario*, vol. 5, p. 329. I have been unable to trace the contract itself but there is plenty of documentary evidence to demonstrate its existence, particularly in AGI, Lima 34.

8 AGI, Lima 34, vol. 3, FF47r–48; 1 May 1603: 'en carta de 28 de diciembre de 601 años... di noticia a V.M. de la necessidad que havia en la Provincia de chicuto [*sic*] de la Real corona de hacer iglessias en muchos pueblos que no las tenian y del medio que se tomó para hacerlas en beneficio de la Real hacienda que havia de pagar las dos tercias partes de la costa y sin molestia de los naturales. hicieronse quince por el orden... de mas de los quales los yndios a su costa an hecho otras siete y tienen mas començadas'.

9 AGI, Lima 34, vol. 1, FF66r–66v; 30 December 1601.

10 AGI, Lima 34, vol. 3, F47v, 1 May 1603.

11 AGI, Lima 34, vol. 3, F159r; 10 October 1603: 'y aunque hasta agora no tengo respuesta se van haciendo las yglessias y se continuaran entre tanto que V.M. se sirva de mandarme responder'.

12 In 1572 Gutiérrez Flores, at the behest of Viceroy Toledo, secretly investigated a series of complaints against the friars (see Gutiérrez Flores, 'Resultas de la visita'); Toledo visited the Province himself and expelled the Dominicans on the charge of interfering with the course of secular justice (see Levillier, *Gobernantes*, for several letters to the King on the subject, especially *Gobernantes*, 5, pp. 111–13, where Toledo itemizes the immorality of the friars and 4, pp. 413–14, where he reports their expulsion).

13 That on Santa Cruz and the lateral portal of San Juan have both been faced with exuberant eighteenth-century façades but fragments of the originals are still visible beneath. See Mesa & Gisbert, 'Renacimiento y manierismo'.

# Select bibliography

It would be impossible to acknowledge all the books which have shaped my thinking during the research and writing of this book. Accordingly, in the bibliography the emphasis is on works on the colonial art and architecture of Latin America at the expense of other material, historical, archaeological and anthropological, but also at the expense of comparative material which has had a more general influence on my approach. This book does not attempt to catalogue early colonial architecture nor, except in a few cases, to document individual buildings. Nevertheless, despite various detours, my central concern has always been the architecture and the questions it raises, rather than, for example, the society or the political forces which produced it. For this reason it seems appropriate to offer the reader a reasonably thorough list of the literature on the subject. My arguments are based on a very wide range of visual examples, and as such need to be corroborated with reference to more illustrations than those that could be included in this book.

*Abbreviations*
*Archives*

| | |
|---|---|
| AGI | Archivo General de Indias, Seville |
| BN | Biblioteca Nacional del Perú, Lima |

*Collected Works*

| | |
|---|---|
| BAE | Biblioteca de Autores Españoles |
| *CDHIP* | *Colección de documentos para la historia de la Iglesia en el Perú*, ed. E. Lisson Chávez, 25 vols., Seville, 1943–5 |
| *CDIRDCO* | 1st series: *Colección de documentos inéditos relativos al descubrimiento, conquista y organización de las posesiones españoles de América y Oceania*, ed. J.F. Pacheco, F. de Cárdenas & D.L. Torres de Mendoza, 42 vols., Madrid 1864–84 |

*CDIRDCO*     2nd series: *Colección de documentos inéditos relativos al descubrimiento, conquista y organización de las antiguas posesiones españoles de Ultramar*, ed. A. de Altolaguirre y Duvale & A. Bonilla y San Martín, 25 vols., Madrid, 1885–1932

*CDPHFSH*     *Colección de documentos para la historia de la formación social de Hispanoamérica 1493–1810*, ed. R. Konetzke, 4 vols., Madrid, 1953–62

*CLDRHP*     *Colección de libros y documentos referentes a la historia del Perú*, ed. C. Romero & H. Urteaga; 1st series: 12 vols., Lima, 1916–19; 2nd series: 10 vols., Lima, 1920–35

## Periodicals

*AIAA*     *Anales del Instituto de Arte Americano e Investigaciones Estéticas*, Buenos Aires
*BCIHE*     *Boletín del Centro de Investigaciones Históricas y Estéticas*, Caracas
*RAN*     *Revista del Archivo Nacional del Perú*, Lima

## Primary sources (pre-1800)

Acosta, José de. *Escritos Menores*, BAE 73, Madrid, 1954
    *Historia natural y moral de las Indias* (1590), BAE 73, Madrid, 1954
    *De Procuranda Indorum Salute* (1596), BAE 73, Madrid, 1954
Alberti, Leon Battista. *De Re Aedificatoria*, London, 1965
Angulo Iñiguez, Diego. *Planos de monumentos arquitectónicos de América y Filipinas*, 4 vols., Seville, 1934
[Arequipa]. *Colección de algunos documentos sobre los primeros tiempos de Arequipa*, Arequipa, 1924
Arriaga, Pablo José. *The Extirpation of Idolatry in Peru* (1621), trans. L. Clark Keating, Lexington, Kentucky, 1968
Avila, Francisco de. *Relación de Idolatrías en Huarochiri* (1608) in *CLDRHP*, 1st series, II, Lima, 1918
[Ayacucho Cabildo]. *Libro de Cabildo de la Ciudad de San Juan de la Frontera (1539–1547)*, Lima, 1966
Benzoni, Girolamo. *La Historia del Mondo Nuovo*, Venice, 1565
Bertonio, Ludovico. *Vocabulario de la lengua aymara*, Rome [1612]
Betanzos, *see* Díez de Betanzos
Borromeo, San Carlo. 'Instructiones fabricae et supellectilis ecclesiasticae' (1570s) in *Trattati d'Arte del Cinquecento*, ed. P. Barocchi, vol. 3, Bari, 1962
Calancha, Antonio de la. *Crónica moralizada del Orden de San Agustín en el Perú*, Barcelona, 1638
Casas, Bartolomé de las. *Obras*, BAE 95, 96, 105, 106 & 111, Madrid, 1957–8

Castellanos, Juan de. *Primera parte de las elegías de varones ilustres de Indias*, Madrid, 1589
Cervantes de Salazar, Francisco. *Life in the Imperial and Loyal City of Mexico in New Spain and the Royal and Pontifical University of New Mexico* (1554), trans. M.L. Barrett Shepard, introduction & notes by Carlos Eduardo Castañeda, Austin, Texas, 1953
[Charcas, Audiencia de]. *Correspondencia de presidentes y oidores según documentos del Archivo General de Indias*, ed. R. Levillier, Madrid, 1918–22
Chueca Goitia, F. & Torres Balbas, L. *Planos de ciudades iberoamericanas y filipinas*, 2 vols., Madrid, 1951
Cieza de León, Pedro de. *Primera parte de la chrónica del Perú*, Antwerp, 1554
    *Segunda parte de la crónica del Perú* (1554), ed. M. Jiménez de la Espada, Madrid, 1880
Cobo, Bernabé. *Historia de la fundación de Lima* (1639), BAE 92, Madrid, 1956
    *Historia del Nuevo Mundo* (1653), BAE 91–2, Madrid, 1956
*Concilios Limenses* (1551–1772), ed. R. Vargas Ugarte, 3 vols., Lima, 1951, 1952, 1954
Cortés, *see* Pagden, A.
[Cuzco], *Anales del Cuzco 1600–1750*, Lima, 1901
    *Noticias cronológicas del Cuzco* (1571–95), Lima, 1902
    'Relación del sitio del Cuzco' (1535–39) in *Colección de libros españoles raros o curiosos*, ed. F. Ramírez de Arellano, vol. 13, Madrid, 1871
    'El acta perdida de la fundación del Cuzco' in 'Dos documentos esenciales sobre Francisco Pizarro y la conquista del Perú', ed. R. Porras Barrenechea, *Revista Histórica*, 17, Lima, 1948, pp. 9–95
*Descripción del virreinato del Perú* (early seventeenth century), ed. Boleslao Lewin, Rosario, 1958
Díez de Betanzos, Juan. *Suma y narración de los Incas* (1551), BAE 209, Madrid, 1968
Díez de San Miguel, Garci. *Visita hecha a la provincia de Chucuito por Garci Díez de San Miguel en el año 1567*, ed. W. Espinosa Soriano & J. Murra, Lima, 1964
Espinosa Soriano, Waldemar. 'La guaranga y la reducción de Huancayo. Tres documentos inéditos de 1571 para la etnohistoria del Perú', *Revista del Museo Nacional*, 32, Lima, 1963, pp. 8–80
Fernández de Oviedo y Valdés, Gonzalo. *Historia general y natural de las Indias*, BAE 121, Madrid, 1959
    *Natural hystoria de las Indias (sumario)*, Toledo, 1526
Fernández de Piedrahita, Lucas. *Noticia historial de las conquistas del Nuevo Reino de Granada* (1688), Bogotá, 1973
Friede, Juan (ed.). *Documentos inéditos para la historia de Colombia*, 10 vols., Seville and Bogotá, 1955–60
Garci Díez, *see* Díez
Garcilaso de la Vega, El Inca. *Los Comentarios Reales de los Incas* (1st part 1609; 2nd part 1617), BAE 133–5, Madrid, 1960
    *Royal Commentaries of the Incas*, trans. H. Livermore, London and Austin, 1966

Guaman Poma de Ayala, Felipe. *Nueva corónica y buen gobierno* (c. 1612), Paris, 1936
Gutiérrez Flores, Pedro. 'Resultas de la visita secreta lega que hizieron en la provincia de Chucuito (1572)', *Historia y Cultura*, 4, Lima, 1970, pp. 5–48
Herrera Tordesillas, Antonio de. *Historia general de los hechos de los Castellanos en las Islas i Tierra Firme del Mar Océano* (1559–1625), 8 Decads, Madrid, 1601–15, 1661
Konetzke, Richard, *Colección de documentos para la historia de la formación social de Hispanoamérica 1493–1810*, 4 vols., Madrid, 1953–62
'Letras Anuas de la Provincia del Perú de la Compañía de Jesús, 1620 à 1724', *Revista de Archivos y Bibliotecas Nacionales*, year 3, vol. 5, Lima, 1900
Levillier, Roberto (ed.). *Gobernantes del Perú, cartas y papeles del siglo XVI*, 14 vols., Madrid, 1921–6
— (ed.). *Organización de la Iglesia y Ordenes religiosas en el Virreinato del Perú en el siglo XVI. Documentos del Archivo General de Indias*, Buenos Aires, 1919
[Lima Cabildo]. *Libros de Cabildo de Lima*, ed. Bertram T. Lee, Lima, 1935
*Libro primero de cabildos de Lima*, ed. E. Torres Saldamando, 2 vols., Paris, 1900
Lisson Chávez, Emilio. *Colección de documentos para la historia de la Iglesia en el Perú*, 25 vols., Seville, 1943–5
Lizárraga, Reginaldo de. *Descripción y población de las Indias* (c. 1600), Lima, 1908
Lozano, Pedro. *Individual y verdadera relación de la extrema ruyna que padeció la ciudad de los Reyes Lima, 28 Oct. 1746*, [Lima], 1746
Marco Dorta, Enrique. *Fuentes para la historia del arte Hispanoamericano*, 2 vols., Seville, 1951
*Materiales para la historia de la cultura en Venezuela*, Caracas, 1967
Mateos, Francisco. 'Constituciones para indios del primer Concilio Limense' in *Missionalia Hispánica*, Year 7, Madrid, 1950
Matienzo, Juan de. *Gobierno del Perú* (1567), Paris and Lima, 1967
Meléndez, Juan. *Tesoros verdaderos de las Yndias*, 3 vols., Rome, 1681–2
Mena, Cristóbal de (attr). *La conquista del Perú* [Seville, 1534]
Mendieta, Gerónimo de. *Historia ecclesiástica indiana* (late sixteenth century), Mexico, 1870
Molina, Cristóbal de (so-chantre de la catedral de Santiago de Chile). *Relación de la conquista y población del Perú* (c. 1553), CLDRHP, 1st series, 1, Lima, 1916
Molina, Cristóbal de (el Cuzqueño). *Relación de las fábulas y ritos de los Incas* (1573), CLDRHP, 1st series, 1, Lima, 1916
Montesinos, Fernando de. *Los Anales del Perú*, Madrid, 1906
Morales Padrón, F. & Llavador Mira, J. *Mapas, planos y dibujos sobre Venezuela existentes en el Archivo General de Indias*, Seville, 1964
Morúa, Martín de. *Historia general del Perú* (1590), 2 vols., Madrid, 1962, 1964
Oviedo, *see* Fernández de Oviedo
Pagden, Anthony. *Hernán Cortés. Letters from Mexico*, London, 1972
[Peru]. *Nouvelles certaines des Isles du Peru* [Lyons, 1534]

Plato. *Timaeus and Critias*, Harmondsworth, 1971

Polo de Ondegardo, Juan. 'Los errores y supersticiones de los Indios' (*c.* 1560), *CLDRHP*, 1st series, 3, Lima, 1916

    'Instrucción contra las ceremonias y ritos' (*c.* 1560), *CLDRHP*, 1st series, 3, Lima, 1916

    'Relación de los fundamentos acerca del notable daño que resulta de no guardar a los indios sus afueros' (1571), *CLDRHP*, 1st series, 3, Lima, 1916

[Probanza], 'Sobre los monasterios e iglesias de N.S. del Rosario de la provincia de San Antonio, de religiosos Dominicos', 1550, 1571, 1579 in *Boletín de Historia y Antigüedades*, 45, Bogotá, 1958, pp. 475–98

[Quito]. *Colección de cédulas reales dirigidas a la Audiencia de Quito* (1538–1600), Quito, 1934

[Quito Cabildo]. *Libro primero de Cabildos de Quito* (1534–1543), 2 vols., Quito 1934

    *Libro segundo de Cabildos de Quito* (1544–51), 2 vols., Quito, 1934

    *Oficios y cartas al Cabildo de Quito por el Rey de España o el Virrey de Indias* (1552–68), Quito, 1934

[Quito, Cabildo ecclesiástico]. *Libro de cabildos de la Iglesia Catedral desta ciudad de San Francisco de Quito* (1583–94), ed. Jorge A. Garcés, Quito, 1947

Ramos Gavilán, Alonso. *Historia del célebre santuario de N.S. de Copacabana*, Lima, 1621

Ramusio, Gian Battista. *Navigationi et viaggi (1563–1606)*, 3 vols., ed. R.A. Skelton & G.B. Parks, Amsterdam, 1967–70

*Relaciones geográficas de Indias: Perú.* 4 vols., ed. M. Jiménez de la Espada, Madrid, 1881

Salinas y Córdova, Buenaventura de. *Memorial de las Historias del Nuevo Mundo Piru*, Lima, 1630

Sámano-Xérez, *see* Xérez

Sánchez Cantón, Francisco J. *Fuentes literarias para la historia del arte español*, 5 vols., Madrid, 1923–41

Santacruz Pachacuti Yamqui, Joan de. *Relación de antigüedades deste reyno del Pirú* [*c.* 1615] *CLDRHP*, 2nd series, 9, Lima, 1927

Santillán, Hernando de. *Relación del orígen, descendencia, política y gobierno de los Incas* (1563), BAE 209, Madrid, 1968

Sarmiento de Gamboa, Pedro. *Historia de los Incas* (1572), Buenos Aires, 1943

Simón, Pedro. *Primera parte de las noticias historiales de las conquistas de tierra firme*, Cuenca, 1627

    *Noticias historiales de las conquistas de tierra firme en las Indias Occidentales*, 2 vols., Bogotá, 1953

Suardo, Juan Antonio. *Diario de Lima, 1629–39*, Lima, 1936

Titu Cusi Yupanqui, Inca Diego de Castro. *Relación de la conquista del Perú y hechos del Inca Manco II* [1570], *CLDRHP*, 1st series, 2, 1916

Toledo, Francisco de, Viceroy. *Ordenanzas de Don Francisco de Toledo, Virrey del Perú, 1569–81*, ed. R. Levillier, Madrid, 1929

Ulloa, Antonio de. *Relación histórica del viage a la América meridional*, 5 vols., Madrid, 1748

Unanue, Hipólito. *Guía política, eclesiástica y militar del Virreynato del Perú para el año de 1793*, Lima, 1985

Valadés, Diego de. *Rhetorica Christiana*, Perugia, 1579

Vargas Machuca, Bernardo de. *Milicia y descripción de las Indias*, Madrid, 1599

Vázquez de Espinosa, Fr. Antonio. *Compendium and Description of the West Indies 1612–1630*, trans. Charles Upson Clark, Washington, 1942

Velasco, Juan de, *Historia del Reino de Quito en la América Meridional*, 3 vols., Quito, 1841–4

Xérez, Francisco de. *Verdadera relación de la conquista del Perú* (also known as the Relación Sámano-Xérez), Seville [1534]

Zamora, Alonso de. *Historia de la Provincia de San Antonio del Nuevo Reino de Granada del Orden de Predicadores*, Barcelona, 1701

Zárate, Agustín de. *Historia del descubrimiento y conquista del Peru, con las cosas naturales que señaladamente alli se hallan y los sucessos que ha avido*, Seville, 1577

Zavala, Silvio, *El servicio personal de los Indios en el Perú, vol 1: Extractos del siglo XVI*, Mexico, DF, 1978

*Secondary sources*

Aguilera Rojas, J. & Moreno Rexach, L.J. *Urbanismo español en América*, Seville, 1973

Agurto Calvo, Santiago. *Lima Prehispánico*, Lima, n.d. [c. 1984]

Angulo, Domingo. 'La iglesia de Sto Domingo de la ciudad de Los Reyes', *RAN*, 12, 1939, pp. 221–8

Angulo Iñiguez, Diego. *Bautista Antonelli; Las fortificaciones americanas del siglo XVI*, Madrid, 1942

Angulo Iñiguez, D., Marco Dorta, E. & Buschiazzo, M.J. *Historia del arte Hispanoamericano*, 3 vols., Barcelona, 1945–56

Arbeláez Camacho, Carlos. 'El templo de la Compañía de Bogotá', *BCIHE*, 6, 1966, pp. 87–104

see also Gil Tovar, F.

Ariza, Fr. Alberto E. *El convento de Sto Domingo de Santa Fé de Bogotá*, Bogotá, 1976

*Sitio de la fundación de Santa Fé de Bogotá*, Bogotá, 1976

Armas Medina, Fernando de. *Cristianización del Perú 1532–1600*, Seville, 1953

Barker, Francis, *et al. Europe and its Others*, 2 vols., University of Essex, Colchester, 1985

Bayón, Damián. *Sociedad y arquitectura colonial sudamericana*, Barcelona, 1974

Benavídez Rodríguez, Alfredo. *La arquitectura en el Virreinato del Perú y en la Capitanía General de Chile*, Santiago de Chile, 1941

Benevolo, Leonardo. 'Las nuevas ciudades en el siglo XVI en América Latina. Una experiencia decisiva para la historia de la cultura arquitectónica del *cinquecento*', *BCIHE*, 9, 1968, pp. 117–46

*The Architecture of the Renaissance*, 2 vols., London, 1978
Bernales Ballesteros, Jorge. *Edificación de la iglesia catedral de Lima*, Seville, 1969
Beyer, Glenn H. (ed.). *The Urban Explosion in Latin America*, Ithaca, NY, 1967
Blunt, Anthony. *Artistic Theory in Italy 1450–1600*, Oxford, 1978
Bowser, Frederick P. *The African Slave in Colonial Peru, 1524–1650*, Stanford, California, 1974
Boxer, Charles R. *Mary and Misogyny: Women in Iberian Expansion Overseas, 1415–1815*, London, 1975
Bromley, Juan. *La fundación de la ciudad de Los Reyes*, Lima, 1935
Bromley, J. & Barbagelata, J. *La evolución urbana de Lima*, Lima, 1948
Bury, J.B. 'Juan de Herrera and the Escorial', *Art History*, December 1986, pp. 428–49
    'The stylistic term *Plateresque*', *Journal of the Warburg and Courtauld Institutes*, 1976, pp. 199–230
Buschiazzo, Mario J. *Historia de la arquitectura colonial en Iberoamérica*, Buenos Aires, 1961
    *Estudios de arquitectura colonial Hispano-Americano*, Buenos Aires, 1944
Canny, Nicholas & Pagden, Anthony, *Colonial Identity in the Atlantic World, 1500–1800*, Princeton, 1987
Castelli, Amalia, 'La primera imagen del Hospital Real de San Andrés a través de la visita de 1563', *Historia y Cultura*, 13–14, Lima, 1981, pp. 207–16
Chacón Torres, Mario. *Arte virreinal en Potosí*, Seville, 1973
Cuentas, Alberto. *Chucuito, album gráfico e histórico*, Puno, 1928
*Documentos de arte colonial sudamericano*, vols. 8 & 9. 'La arquitectura mestiza en las riberas del Titikaka', Buenos Aires, 1952 & 1956
Duque Gómez, Luis. *Colombia: Monumentos históricos y arqueológicos*, vol. 2: 'Arte colonial neogranadino', Mexico, 1955
Durán Montero, María Antonia. *Fundación de ciudades en el Perú durante el siglo XVI*, Seville, 1978
Duviols, Pierre. *La destrucción de las religiones andinas*, Mexico, 1977
Elliott, John H. *The Old World and the New*, Cambridge, 1972
Eugenio Martínez, María Angeles. *Tributo y trabajo del indio en Nueva Granada*, Seville, 1977
*Forum et Plaza Mayor dans le Monde Hispanique* (Colloque interdisciplinaire, Casa de Velázquez, Madrid, 28 October 1976), Paris, 1978
Foster, George. *Culture and Conquest: America's Spanish Heritage*, New York, 1960
Fraser, Valerie. 'Hierarchies and rôles of materials in building and representation' in Fraser, V. & Brotherston, G. *The Other America*, University of Essex, Colchester, 1982, pp. 41–55
    'The Architecture of Conquest: Building in the Viceroyalty of Peru, 1535–1635', unpublished PhD, University of Essex, Colchester, 1984
    'Architecture and imperialism in sixteenth-century Spanish America', *Art History*, vol. 9, no. 3, September 1986, pp. 325–35

Friede, Juan. *Los Chibchas bajo la dominación española*, Medellín, 1974
   *Descubrimiento del Nuevo Reino de Granada y fundación de Bogotá, 1536–39*, Bogotá, 1960
   *Los Quimbayas bajo la dominación española*, Bogotá, 1963
Gakenheimer, Ralph A. 'Decisions of Cabildo on urban physical structure: 16th century Peru' in Hardoy & Schaedel (eds.), *El proceso de la urbanización*, pp. 241–60
   'The Peruvian city of the 16th century' in G. Beyer (ed.), *The Urban Explosion*, pp. 33–56
Garnsey, Peter & Saller, Richard. *The Roman Empire. Economy, Society and Culture*, London, 1987
Gasparini, Graziano. *América, barroco y arquitectura*, Caracas, 1972
   'La ciudad colonial como centro de irradiación de las escuelas arquitectónicas y pictóricas', *BCIHE*, 14, 1972, pp. 9–24
   'Observaciones en Willka Waman (Vilcashuaman)', *BCIHE*, 18, 1974, pp. 93–116
   'Los techos armaduras de pares y nudillos en las construcciones coloniales Venesolanas', *BCIHE*, 1, 1964, pp. 97–112
Gasparini, Graziano & Margolies, Luise. *Inca Architecture*, London, 1980
Gento Sanz, Fr. Benjamin. *Historia de la obra constructiva de San Francisco de Quito*, Quito, 1942
Gibson, Charles. *The Aztecs under Spanish Rule: the History of the Indians of the Valley of Mexico, 1519–1810*, Stanford, California, 1964
   *Spain in America*, New York, 1966
   'Spanish-Indian institutions and colonial urbanism in New Spain' in Hardoy & Schaedel (eds.), *El proceso de la urbanización*, pp. 225–39
Gil Tovar, F. & Arbeláez Camacho, C. *El arte colonial en Colombia*, Bogotá, 1968
Gisbert, Teresa. *Iconografía y mitos indígenas en el arte*, La Paz, 1980
Góngora, Mario. *Studies in the Colonial History of Spanish America*, Cambridge, 1975
González Suárez, Federico. *Historia general de la República del Ecuador*, 6 vols., Quito, 1890–1903
González de Valcárcel, José M. *Architectural Conservation and Enhancement of Historic Towns in America*, Barcelona, 1977
Greenleaf, Richard E. (ed.), *The Roman Catholic Church in Latin America*, New York, 1971
Guarda, Gabriel. 'Tres reflexiones en torno a la fundación de la ciudad indiana' in Solano, *Estudios*, pp. 89–106
Guillén, Edmundo. *La versión Inca de la conquista*, Lima, 1974
Gutkind, Erwin A. *Urban Development in Southern Europe: Spain and Portugal*, New York, 1967
*Handbook of South American Indians*, vol. 2: 'The Andean civilizations', ed. J.H. Steward, Washington, DC, 1946
Hannestad, Niels. *Roman Art and Imperial Policy*, Aarhus, 1986
Hardoy, Jorge. *Precolumbian Cities*, Toronto, 1973

Hardoy, J. & Schaedel, R.P. (eds.). *El proceso de la urbanización en América desde sus orígenes hasta nuestros días*, Buenos Aires, 1969

Haring, Clarence H. *The Spanish Empire in America*, New York, 1947
   *Trade and Navigation between Spain and the Indies in the Time of the Habsburgs*, Cambridge, Mass., 1918

Harth-terré, Emilio. 'El asiento arqueológico de la ciudad de Lima', *El Comercio*, Lima, 18 January 1960
   'Hospitales mayores en Lima en el primer siglo de su fundación', *AIAA*, 16, 1963, pp. 34–47
   'El imafronte de la Catedral de Lima', *Arquitecto Peruano*, Year 5, 47, Lima, June 1941
   *Lima, Ensayos*, Lima, 1976
   'La obra de Francisco Becerra en las catedrales de Lima y Cuzco', *AIAA*, 14, 1962, pp. 7–28
   *Perú: Monumentos históricos y arqueológicos*, Mexico, 1975
   'Las tres fundaciones del catedral de Cuzco', *AIAA*, 2, 1949, pp. 29–69
   'Los últimos canteros incaios', *Actas del II congreso nacional de peruanistas*, vol. 2, Lima, 1958, pp. 1–10

Harth-terré, E. & Márquez Abanto, A. 'El artesano negro en la arquitectura virreinal limeña', *RAN*, 25, 1961, pp. 3–73
   'Las bellas artes en el Virreynato del Perú en el siglo XVII', *RAN*, 20, 1956, pp. 119–49
   'Historia de la casa urbana virreinal en Lima', *RAN*, 26, Pt 1, 1962, pp. 109–206
   'Perspectiva social y económica del artesano virreinal en Lima', *RAN*, 26, part 2, 1962, pp. 353–446
   'El puente de piedra de Lima', *RAN*, 24, 1960, pp. 99–176

Hemming, John. *The Conquest of the Incas*, London, 1970

Hyslop, John. 'El área Lupaca bajo el dominio incaico. Un reconocimiento arqueológico', *Histórica*, 3, no. 1, Lima, July 1979
   *The Inka Road System*, New York, 1984

Kauffmann Doig, Federico. *Influencias 'Inca' en la arquitectura peruana*, Lima, 1965

Kelemen, Pál. *Baroque and Rococco in Latin America*, New York, 1967

Kubler, George. *Building the Escorial*, Princeton, 1982
   Ciudades y cultura en el período colonial de América Latina', *BCIHE*, 1, 1964, pp. 81–8
   *Cuzco: Reconstruction of the Town* (UNESCO, Museums & Monuments, no. 3) Paris, 1952
   *Mexican Architecture of the 16th Century*, 2 vols., New Haven, 1948
   'The Quechua in the colonial world', *Handbook of South American Indians*, vol. 2, pp. 331–409
   *Studies in Ancient American and European Art. The Collected Essays of George Kubler*, ed. T.F. Reese, New Haven and London, 1985

Kubler, G. & Soria, M. *Art and Architecture of Spain and Portugal and their American Dominions 1500–1800*, Harmondsworth, 1959
Larco Herrera, Rafael & Valcárcel, L.E. *Cusco histórico*, Lima, 1934
Lee López, Alberto. 'La cofradía y la iglesia de la Santa Veracruz', *Boletín de historia y antigüedades*, 53, Bogotá, 1966, pp. 467–87
Leszek, M. Zawisza. 'Fundación de las ciudades hispanoamericanas', *BCIHE*, 13, 1972, pp. 8–128
Levillier, Roberto. *Don Francisco de Toledo, Virrey del Perú*, 2 vols., Madrid, 1935
   *Organización de la iglesia del Perú*, Buenos Aires, 1919
Locher, Gottfried W. *Transformation and Tradition*, The Hague, 1978
Lockhart, James. *Spanish Peru, 1532–1560*, London, 1968
López Martínez, Hector. *Rebeliones de mestizos y otros temas quinientistas*, Lima, 1972
McAlister, Lyle N. *Spain and Portugal in the New World, 1492–1700*, Minneapolis, 1984
MacAndrew, John. *The Open-Air Churches of Sixteenth-Century Mexico*, Cambridge, Mass., 1965
MacCormack, Sabine. 'From the Sun of the Incas to the Virgin of Copacabana', *Representations*, 8, 1984, pp. 30–60
Málaga Medina, Alejandro. 'Las reducciones en el Perú (1532–1600)', *Historia y Cultura*, 8, Lima, 1974, pp. 141–72
Marco Dorta, Enrique. 'Arquitectura colonial: Francisco Becerra', *Archivo Español de Arte*, 16, Madrid, 1943, pp. 7–15
   'La arquitectura del renacimiento en Tunja', *Revista de Indias*, Year 3, 9, Madrid, 1942, pp. 463–513
   *Cartagena de Indias. La ciudad y sus monumentos*, Seville, 1951
   'Iglesias renacentistas en las riberas del lago Titicaca', *Anuario de estudios americanos*, vol. 2, Seville, 1945, pp. 701–16
Mariátegui Oliva, Ricardo. *Techumbres y artesonados peruanos (Arte peruano de los siglos XVI y XVII)*, Lima, 1975
Martín, Luis. *Daughters of the Conquistadors. Women of the Viceroyalty of Peru*, Albuquerque, 1983
Martínez, Carlos. *Apuntes sobre el urbanismo en el Nuevo Reino de Granada* [Bogotá, 1967]
Mendiburu, Manuel de. *Diccionario histórico-biográfico del Perú*, 8 vols., Lima, 1874–90
   *Memoria de la Corporación de reconstrucción y fomento*, Cuzco, 1959
Mesa, José de & Gisbert, Teresa. 'Determinantes del llamado estilo mestizo', *BCIHE*, 10, 1968, pp. 93–119
   'Un diseño de Bramante realizado en Quito', *BCIHE*, 7, 1967, pp. 68–73
   *Iglesias con atrio y posas en Bolivia*, La Paz, 1961
   'El renacimiento en la Audiencia de Charcas: Hernández Galván y el Maestro de Ancoraimes', *AIAA*, 12, 1959, pp. 52–74
   'Renacimiento y manierismo en la arquitectura *mestiza*', *BCIHE*, 3, 1965, pp. 9–44
Millé, Andre. *Itinerario de la orden dominicana en la conquista del Perú, Chile y el Tucumán y su convento del antiguo Buenos Aires*, Buenos Aires, 1964

Moore, John P. *The Cabildo in Peru under the Habsburgs, 1530–1700*, Durham, North Carolina, 1954
Moore, Sally Falk. *Power and Property in Inca Peru*, New York, 1958
Morris, Anthony E.J. *A History of Urban Form*, New York, 1979
Morris, Craig & Thompson, Donald. *Huánuco Pampa. An Inca City and its Hinterland*, London, 1985
Morse, Richard M. 'Introducción a la historia urbana de hispanoamérica' in Solano, F. de, *Estudios*, pp. 9–53
    'Some characteristics of Latin American Urban History', *American Historical Review*, 67, New York, 1961–2, pp. 317–38
Murra, John. *The Economic Organisation of the Inka State*, Greenwich, Connecticut, 1980
    *Formaciones económicas y políticas del mundo andino*, Lima, 1965
    'Información etnológica e histórica adicional sobre el reino Lupaqa', *Historia y Cultura*, 4, Lima, 1977, pp. 49–61
Murra, John, *et al.*, *Anthropological History of Andean Polities*, Cambridge, 1986
Navarro, José Gabriel. *El arte en la Provincia de Quito*, Mexico, 1960
    *Contribuciones a la historia del arte en el Ecuador*, 2 vols., Quito, 1925
Neill, Stephen. *A History of Christian Missions*, Harmondsworth, 1977
Neumeyer, Alfred. 'The Indian contribution to architectural decoration in Spanish colonial America', *Art Bulletin*, 30, 1948, pp. 104–21
Noel, Martín S. *Arquitectura virreinal*, Buenos Aires, 1934
    *Contribución a la historia de la arquitectura hispanoamericana*, Buenos Aires, 1923
Nuttall, Zelia. 'Royal Ordinances concerning the laying out of new towns (1573)', *Hispanic American Historical Review*, Durham, North Carolina, 4, 1921, pp. 743–53 and 5, 1922, pp. 249–54
Pagden, Anthony. *The Fall of Natural Man*, Cambridge, 1982
Palm, Erwin W. 'Las capillas abiertas americanas y sus antecedentes en el occidente cristiano', *AIAA*, 6, 1953, pp. 47–64
    *Los orígenes del urbanismo imperial en América*, Mexico, DF, 1951
Palomero Páramo, Jesús M. *El retablo sevillano del renacimiento: análisis y evolución (1560–1629)*, Seville, 1983
Panofsky, Erwin. *Meaning in the Visual Arts*, Harmondsworth, 1955
Parry, John H. *The Audiencia of New Galicia in the 16th Century*, Cambridge, 1968
    *The Cities of the Conquistadores* (Canning House 8th Annual Lecture), London, 1961
Patrón, Pablo. *Lima Antigua*, Lima, 1935
Pérez Aquiles, R. *Las mitas en la Real Audiencia de Quito*, Quito, 1947
Porras Barrenechea, Raúl. 'Dos documentos esenciales sobre Francisco Pizarro y la conquista del Perú', *Revista Histórica*, 17, Lima, 1948, pp. 86–95, *see also* [Cuzco] under primary sources
    'La fundación de Trujillo' in [Trujillo], *Apuntes y estudios*, pp. 37–87
    'Jauja, capital mítica', *Revista Histórica*, 18, pt 2, Lima, 1950, pp. 117–48

*Las relaciones primitivas de la conquista del Perú*, Lima, 1967
Prescott, William H. *History of the Conquest of Peru*, 2 vols., New York, 1847
Quinn, David B. *The Elizabethans and the Irish*, New York, 1966
Quinn, David B. & Quinn, Alison M. *The English New England Voyages, 1602–1608*, London, 1983
Ricard, Robert. *The Spiritual Conquest of Mexico*, Berkeley and Los Angeles, 1966
Rosenthal, Earl E. *The Palace of Charles V in Granada*, Princeton, 1985
Rostworowsky de Diez Canseco, María. *Señoríos indígenas de Lima y Canta*, Lima, 1978
Ruiz Guiñazú, Enrique. *Garay, fundador de Buenos Aires*, Buenos Aires, 1915
Rykwert, Joseph. *The Idea of a Town*, London, 1976
Salamanca Aguilera, Rafael. *Guía histórica ilustrada de Tunja*, Bogotá, 1939
Schaedel, Richard P. 'On the definitions of Civilization, Urban, City and Town in Prehistoric America' in Hardoy & Schaedel (eds.), *El proceso de la urbanización*, pp. 5–13
Schenone, Hector, Mesa, J. de & Gisbert, T. 'El plateresco en el Perú: la iglesia de San Pedro de Andahuaylas', *AIAA*, 15, 1962, pp. 27–41
Sebastián, Santiago. *Album de arte colonial de Tunja*, Tunja, 1963
*Arquitectura del protorrenacimiento en el mundo hispánico*, Cali, 1969
'La decoración llamada plateresca en el mundo hispánico', *BCIHE*, 1966, 6, pp. 42–85
*Itinerarios artísticos de la Nueva Granada*, Cali, 1965
*La ornamentación arquitectónica en la Nueva Granada*, Tunja, 1966
'Notas sobre la arquitectura manierista en Quito', *BCIHE*, 1964, pp. 113–20
Sivirichi, Atilio. *La fundación de Lima*, Lima, 1935
Smith, Clifford T. 'Depopulation of the central Andes in the 16th century', *Current Anthropology*, 11, 4–5, Chicago, October–December 1970, pp. 453–64
Smith, Earl Baldwin. *Architectural Symbolism of Imperial Rome and the Middle Ages*, Princeton, New Jersey, 1956
Solano, Francisco de (ed.). *Estudios sobre la ciudad iberoamericana*, Madrid, 1975
Squier, George E. *Peru. Incidents of Travel and Exploration in the Land of the Incas*, London, 1877
Stanislawski, Dan. 'Early Spanish town planning in the New World', *Geographical Review*, 37, New York, 1947, pp. 96–105
'The origin and spread of the grid-plan town', *Geographical Review*, 36, New York, 1946, pp. 105–20
Stedman Jones, G. *Outcast London*, Harmondsworth, 1976
Summerson, John. *The Classical Language of Architecture*, London, 1963
Tibesar, Antonine. *Franciscan Beginnings in Colonial Peru*, Washington, DC, 1953
Tord Nicolini, Javier. 'El Corregidor de Indios del Perú: comercio y tributos', *Historia y Cultura*, 8, Lima, 1964, pp. 173–214
Torre Revello, José. 'Tratados de arquitectura utilizados en hispanoamérica, siglos

XVI y XVII', *Revista interamericana de bibliografía*, 6, 1956, pp. 3–23

Torres Lanzas, Pedro. *Relación descriptiva de los mapas y planos de Panamá, Santa Fé y Quito en el Archivo General de Indias*, Madrid, 1906

Toussaint, Antonio. *El plateresco en la Nueva España*, Mexico, DF, 1979

[Trujillo]. *Apuntes y estudios históricos sobre la fecha de la fundación de la ciudad de Trujillo*, Trujillo, 1935

Vargas, José María. *La cultura de Quito colonial*, Quito, 1941
  *Historia de la cultura ecuatoriana*, Quito, 1965
  *Patrimonio artístico ecuatoriano*, Quito, 1972

Vargas Ugarte, Rubén. *Ensayo de un diccionario de artífices coloniales de la América meridional*, 2 vols., Lima (?), 1947, 1955
  *Historia del culto de María en Iberoamérica*, Madrid, 1956
  *Historia de la iglesia en el Perú*, 5 vols., Lima, 1953–62
  *Itinerario por las iglesias del Perú*, Lima, 1972
  *Los Jesuitas del Perú y el arte*, Lima, 1963

Velarde, Hector, *Arquitectura Peruana*, Lima, 1978
  *Itinerarios de Lima*, Lima, n.d.

Vignale, Pedro J. & Noel, Martin S. *Documentos de arte colonial sudamericano*, Buenos Aires, 1943

Wachtel, Nathan. *Sociedad e ideología. Ensayos de historia y antropología*, Lima, 1973
  *Los vencidos: los indios del Perú frente a la conquista española, 1530–1570*, Madrid, 1976

Watkins, Alfred. *The Old Straight Track*, London, 1974

Wethey, Harold E. *Colonial Architecture and Sculpture in Peru*, Cambridge, Mass., 1971
  'Hispanic colonial architecture in Bolivia', *Gazette des Beaux-Arts*, 39, 1952, pp. 47–60
  'Retablos coloniales en Bolivia', *AIAA*, 3, 1950, pp. 7–14

Wilkinson, Catherine. *The Hospital of Cardinal Tavera in Toledo*, New York, 1977

# Index

Acora, 60
  San Juan, 166, plate 7
  San Pedro, 18, 124, 166, plates 5, 27
Acosta, José de,
  *De procuranda*, 114
  *Historia natural*, 29, 34
Actopan, 112
*adobe*, 14, 26, 32, 90–1
Alberti, Leon Battista, 38, 139
Andahuaylillas, 112, 124, 136, plate 20
Anserma (formerly Santa Ana de los Caballeros), 57
arch, as cultural signifier, 10, 34–5, 91–2, 123, 139–45, 156, *see also* vault
architect, 39–40, 106–7
architecture and conquest, 1, 20, 49–50, 82, 116–17, 158–60
architecture, classical style of, 6, 10, 14, 19, 21, 34–5, 47, 121, 123 *et seq*, 145–9, 156–9, 164–7
architecture, Inca, *see* Inca culture
architecture, Italian, 142, 145, 157–8
  Rome, Gesù, 139, 142
architecture, Spanish, 139–42, 145–6, 158–9
  Escorial, 136, 139, 146, 158
  Granada, Palace of Charles V, 146, 158–9
  Seville, 142
  Toledo, Santa Cruz, 146, 158; Tavera hospital, 146, 171 n24
Arequipa,
  cathedral, 111
  foundation, 55, 70–1
  houses, 91, 108
  Indian inhabitants, 75, 94
  lay-out, 73, 74
  Santo Domingo, 89, 149, plate 41
  site, 64
Aristotle, 24, 49
Arriaga, Pablo José de, *The Extirpation of Idolatry*, 79, 114
*arte*, 21, 24, 34–5, 48; *see also* architecture, classical style of
atrium, 10, 13, 15, 111–16, 144, 163–4, 166, plates 2, 3, 43, 44 & frontispiece
Ayacucho (formerly Guamanga), 57, 95, 109, plate 39
  Compañía, 123
  La Merced, 130
  lay-out, 55, 74
  San Francisco, 130, plate 31
  Santa Clara, 101
  Santo Domingo, 123
  secular architecture, 119, 144
  site, 64
Ayacucho Province, 79

Becerra, Francisco, 105–6, 139
Belalcázar, Sebastián de, 51
Betanzos, *see* Díez de Betanzos, Juan
Bogotá, 72, 96
  foundation, 52–3, 57
  lay-out, 39
  San Francisco, 101
  San Ignacio, 142, 153, plate 38
  site, 64
*bohío*, 26, 71–2
Borromeo, San Carlo, 'Instructiones fabricae', 139

brick, 19, 26, 90–1, 101, 164–6
Buenos Aires, foundation, 53, 57, 61

Cáceres (Honduras), 57
Cajamarca, 64
  cathedral 149
Cañete, Marqués de, Viceroy of Peru, 37, 42
Caracas, 72,
  San Francisco, 130
carpentry, 94–6, 100
*carpintería de lo blanco*, 100–1, 133, plate 18
Carrión, Bartolomé, 127
Cartagena, 99–100, 117
  cathedral, 100, 124, plate 23
  Santo Domingo, 124
Casas, Bartolomé de las, 1, 48
Cervantes de Salazar, Francisco, *Life in the Imperial and Loyal City*, 47, 113, 114
Chavín, 114
Chibcha, 10, 25–6, 63, 114
Chimu, 114
Chincheros, 67, frontispiece
Cholula, 67
  San Gabriel, 152
Chucuito, Province of, map 3
  architecture, 11–20, 88, 130, 160–7
  masons from, 90
Chucuito, town, 11–15, 116, 166
  La Asunción, 14–15, plate 3
  *picota*, 59, plate 13
  Santo Domingo, 11–15, 90, plate 2
  San Pedro, 15
Chuquisaca, *see* Sucre (formerly Chuquisaca)
Church, regular/secular rivalry in the, 15, 45, 86
Church and State, rivalry between, 15, 44–5, 162
Cieza de León, Pedro, 49
  *Primera parte de la Chrónica*, 29, 33, 93
  *Segunda parte*, 9
Cobo, Bernabé, 136
  *Historia del Nuevo Mundo*, 21, 32–3, 34–5, 50, 117
  *Historia de Lima*, 62, 63, 76
Collao, *see* Chucuito, Province of
Coluccini, Giovanni Baptista, 142

conquest, *see* architecture and conquest
Copacabana (Bolivia), 112
Coro, 85
Cortés, Hernan, 23, 37, 48
Covarrubias, Alonso, 146
Curaçao, 85, 86
Cuzco, 85, 96, 103, 109, 117, plate 8
  Amarucancha, 117
  cathedral, 65, 71, 111, 139
  foundation of, 53, 57, 59, 62–3
  Inca, 8, 24, 27–9, 33, 59, 62–3, 87, 89, 90, 114
  La Merced, 112–13
  Santo Domingo, 67, 68, 124, plate 16
  secular architecture, 119, 136, 144, 149, plates 21–3

Delgado, Gerónimo, 104–5
Díez de Betanzos, Juan, *Suma y narración*, 24, 87
Dominicans, 11–13, 15, 72, 73, 160, 162, 163
Doric, 127, 130, 133, 157, 158, 187 n5; *see also* orders of architecture

earthquakes and architecture, 110–11, 133
*encomienda*, 83–6, 88, 89, 97
Escorial, *see* architecture, Spanish
Española, *see* Santo Domingo (Española)

Fernández de Oviedo, Gonzalo, *Historia general*, 46
foundation of towns and cities, 51–7, 61–4, 107, 174 n5, 176 n34
Franciscans,
  architectural preferences, 101, 130
  schools for Indians, 96

Garay, Juan de, 53, 57
Garcilaso de la Vega, *Comentarios reales*, 95, 98
Gothic vaulting, 133, 136, 142, 145
Granada, *see* architecture, Spanish
Guamanga (or Huamanga), *see* Ayacucho (formerly Guamanga)
Guatemala, 111
Guayaquil, 89
guilds, 103, 104

Herrera, Juan de, 136, 142
Herrera Tordesillas, Antonio de, 92
Huancavelica, 74, 88
Huancayo, 78, 107
Huaro, 124, plate 25
Huayna Capac, 24, 64–5

Ilave, San Miguel, 15, 136, plates 4, 32
Inca culture, 8–9, 23–4, 27, 87, 91, 92, 114, 157
    architecture, 9, 27–35, 90, 92, 117–19, plates 1, 9, 10 & frontispiece
Indian craftsmanship, 89–103, 156, 166–7
Indian labour, 69, 72, 74, 83–92, 156, 160–2, 166–7
Indian styles and motifs, survival of in colonial architecture, 4, 114, 117–19, 121
Indian techniques and materials, in colonial architecture, 4, 72, 89–90, 109–11

Jauja, 62, 71, 92, plate 17
Jesuits, 11, 103, 114
Jiménez de Quesada, Gonzalo, 52, 57, 64
Juli, 11, 18, 162–6, plate 6
    La Asunción, 124, 163, plate 43
    San Juan, 149, 163, plates 40, 44, 45
    San Pedro, 163
    Santa Cruz, 163

La Paz, 19, 64, 74
    San Francisco, 149
Lima, 59, 62, 89, 96, 100, 105, 108–9, 114, 117, 147, plate 12
    cathedral, 55, 63, 65, 105–7, 110–11, 139, plate 12
    craftsmen, 100, 103, 104
    El Cercado, 76–7
    foundation of, 55, 63–4, 107
    houses, 71
    Indian inhabitants, 74, 76–7
    lay-out, 39, 73, 103
    San Agustín, 73
    San Andrés, hospital of, 47, 111
    San Francisco, 101
    Santo Domingo, 104
    secular architecture, 136, plate 138

site, 63–4
Lizárraga, Reginaldo de, 63
Lupaca, 18, 162

Machuca, Pedro, 146, 158
Mariquita, 72
Martínez de Arrona, Juan, 106
Materials, techniques, hierarchy of, 25–7, 35, 43, 72, 108–11
Matienzo, Juan de, 77, 78, 95
    *Gobierno del Perú*, 42–6, 98–9
Maya architecture, 114
Meco, Juan, 103
Meléndez, Juan, *Tesoros verdaderos*, 68
Mendieta, Gerónimo de, *Historia ecclesiástica indiana*, 84–5, 91, 93
Mendoza (Argentina), plate 14
Mexico, 11, 123
    Aztec, 10, 23, 48, 114
    Indian contribution to colonial architecture in, 91, 93, 116, 117, 121
Mexico City, 47,
    lay-out, 37, 39, 55
    Santo Domingo, 113
    site, 48, 62, 65
*mita*, 87–91, 161–2
Morúa, Martín de, *Historia general*, 24, 34, 93
*mudéjar*, 136, 146

Noguera, Pedro de, 106–7

Ollantaytambo, 117, plate 10
open chapel, 111–14
*Ordenanzas* of 1573, 37–9, 45–6, 49–50, 55–6, 61, 65, 116, 172 n38, 172 n39, 175 n16, 175 n17
orders of architecture, 133, 158, 187 n5; *see also* Doric
Oviedo, *see* Fernández de Oviedo, Gonzalo

Pachacamac, 32, 114
Pachacuti, 24, 87, 89
Pamplona (Colombia), 72
Panama, 36, 104, 109
Paucarcolla, La Inmaculada, 124
*picota*, 53, 55, 57–61, 155, 176 n34, plate 13
Pisac, plate 9

Pizarro, Francisco, 22, 23, 69–70
  authority to found towns, 51,
  foundation of Cuzco, 53, 57, 62–3
  foundation of Lima, 55, 59, 107
Pizarro, Hernando, 22, 64
Plato, 36, 59
*policía*, 23, 24–5, 29, 41, 42–5, 48, 77, 97
Polo de Ondegardo, Juan, 33, 90
Pomata, 166
Porres, Diego de, 82–3, 86, 88, 90
Portovelo (Panama), 104, plate 19
Potosí 19, 74
  silver mines, 88, 160, 162, 167
  San Agustín, 124, plate 26
  Santo Domingo, 130, plate 29
  San Francisco, 101
Puebla, 55

Quito, 70, 72, 109
  colonial architecture, 130, 136
  foundation, 62
  Guápulo, 130
  Inca, 65, 88
  Indian craftsmen, 94, 96, 97
  Indian inhabitants, 75, 77
  La Merced, 123, 149, plate 42
  San Francisco, 65, 96–7, 98, 101, 127–30, 133, 185 n27, plates 15, 18
  Santo Domingo, 130
  site, 64

*reconquista* of Moorish Spain, 5, 36, 158–9
*reducciones*, 24–5, 40–5, 49, 75–81, 107, 116, 173 n52
Riaño, Diego de, 142
Riobamba, 62, plate 11
Rome, see architecture, Italian

Sacsahuaman, 33, 119, plate 1
San Jerónimo (province of Cuzco), 112, 124
Sancho, Pedro, 22, 46
  Ramusio, *Navigationi*, 27–9, 32
Santo Domingo (Española), 46, 100
  cathedral, 152
Serlio, Sebastiano, 36, 139
Seville, see architecture, Spanish
Sillustani, 92
Simón, Pedro, 52, 57, 64, 83
  *Primera parte de las noticias historiales*, 26, 72

*solares*, 37, 43, 55, 171 n33
Suardo, Juan Antonio, 114
Sucre (formerly Chuquisaca), 19, 64, 74
  San Francisco, 101

Tiahuanaco, 114, 116
Tlamanalco, 112
Toledo, see architecture, Spanish
Toledo, Francisco de, Viceroy of Peru, 44, 76–9, 96, 107, 112
Toledo, Juan de, 136, 146
town plans, town planning, 6–7, 36–7, 155, 175 n16, 175 n17, 175 n18
  grid-plan, practice, 55–6, 72–4, 166
  grid-plan, theory, 36–47, 176 n31
  Inca, 24, 27–9
Trujillo (Peru), 55, 64
Tumbes, 64
Tunja, 55, 64, 133, 147
  cathedral, 127, 130, 133, 149, plate 28
  Cathedral, Estrada tomb monument, 136
  San Francisco, 101, 130, plate 30
  Santo Domingo, 47
  secular architecture, 136–9, plates 34, 36, 37

Urcos, 112, 124, plate 24
*usnu*, 59

Valverde, Vicente, Bishop of Cuzco, 71
Vandelvira, Andrés de, 139
Vargas, Luis de, 106–7
vault, 133
  as cultural signifier, 110–1
  see also arch
  see also Gothic vaulting
Velasco, Lázaro, 39–40
Velasco, Luis de, Viceroy of Peru, 89, 99, 160–2
Vilcabamba, 91
Vilcashuaman, 67
Vitruvius, 25, 36, 38–40, 46, 47, 49, 56, 59–61, 133, 139, 157, 172 n38

*yana, yanacona*, 93–5

Zamora, Alonso de, 64
Zárate, Agustín de, 24
Zepita, 166